Behind t

Agrarian society in ninete

Frances Fakes

Behind the Plough

Agrarian society in nineteenth-century Hertfordshire

Nigel E. Agar

UNIVERSITY OF HERTFORDSHIRE PRESS

First published in Great Britain in 2005 by
Hertfordshire Publications
an imprint of the University of Hertfordshire Press
Learning and Information Services
University of Hertfordshire
College Lane
Hatfield
Hertfordshire AL10 9AB

British Library Cataloguing in Publication Data
A catalogue record for this book is available from the British Library

ISBN 1-9542189-5-7

Design by Geoff Green, Cambridge, CB4 5RA
Cover design by John Robertshaw, Harpenden, AL5 2JB
Printed in Great Britain by Antony Rowe Ltd, Chippenham, SN14 6LH

Front cover photograph courtesy of The Children's Society

Contents

List of illustrations

OS map references Old or Imperial Series 1881. Six inches to the mile (reduced).

Preface

THIS BOOK IS ABOUT Hertfordshire at a time when farming was the main economic activity of the county. It is not, however, simply a history of farming in the county – it is the story of people who lived by farming. Most people in the modern county live by the commerce and light industry of a county on the fringes of London. Much of present day Hertfordshire is thickly populated town and suburb, but even today there is a surprising amount of farmland and woodland with the eastern third of the county still almost entirely rural up to, and even within, the ring of the M25. Nineteenth-century Hertfordshire was almost entirely a rural county dependent on the rich, arable agriculture of its fields and farms. This book is the story of its people.

I would like to thank my wife Ann for her help, advice and encouragement and for putting up with long preoccupied evenings in the writing of this book. My knowledge of the Hertfordshire countryside would be much less without many country walks – sometimes alone and sometimes in the company of at least one member of the family. In particular I shall always remember with affection many walks in the early eighties on Saturday afternoons with our daughter, Judith. In the years since, I have had the benefit of the academic experience of our son Jonathan and the computer expertise of our son Robert, for which I am most grateful.

This book would have been quite impossible without the always good-humoured help of the staff at the Hertfordshire Record Office and the Hertfordshire Local Studies Library (now Hertfordshire Archives and Library Services [HALS]). My then colleagues at North Hertfordshire College contributed more than they knew. Once again I must single out the Library staff for unstinting help finding books and periodicals that they must have suspected were way beyond my normal duties at the college.

It would be impossible to list the many Hertfordshire people who have, perhaps unwittingly, encouraged my interest in their county whether by their published work or their company.

N.E. Agar *August 2004*

CHAPTER ONE

Introduction

T HIS BOOK IS ABOUT the rural society of Hertfordshire in the nineteenth century. But much of its story applies to rural England as a whole. Where Hertfordshire did differ from other counties, it was not in a way that made the county seriously untypical.

The most important differentiating feature of the Hertfordshire economy, only shared by its northern neighbour, Bedfordshire, was the importance given to straw plaiting, which underpinned the important local industry of hat-making in Luton and St Albans. There was some variation within the county itself. Northern, eastern and central Hertfordshire specialised in arable farming while hay production for the London market prevailed in a number of parishes on the London clay in the south of the county.

Hertfordshire was little touched by the industrial revolution in the narrow sense that it was not an area where factories became the main source of employment. This does not mean that Hertfordshire was insulated from the spirit of the age, but of all the technological wonders of the nineteenth century, only the railway made much direct impression on the Hertfordshire scene. Nevertheless, this was no rural backwater. Agriculture too was undergoing great changes as profound in their way as the dramatic developments of industry. Those changes, which included the enclosure and drainage of the land and the use of artificial fertilisers and farm machinery in farming operations, were most marked in the prosperous arable counties of the south and east of England. Located between London and the burgeoning industrial activity of the Midlands and north of England, Hertfordshire was in no sense isolated from, still less indifferent to, the economic activity of the day.

Hertfordshire is a lowland county. The highest point of Hertfordshire is

153m above sea level at a point at Hastoe, near Tring in the far north-west on the boundary with Buckinghamshire. It is unremarked because the land continues to rise immediately to the west over the Buckinghamshire border to reach 250m above Halton at the highest point of the Chilterns. The lowest point in the county is a mere 19m above sea level on the marshes where the River Lea leaves the county near Waltham Cross.

The climate of Hertfordshire in the nineteenth century stood in much the same relationship as now with regard to the rest of England. Compared with other counties, Hertfordshire was always relatively dry and warm. The weather in the nineteenth century was on the whole cooler than at present and the process of warming has continued. Records taken at Greenwich and at Kew, both approximately twenty miles south of Hertfordshire, indicate that there were fourteen colder years between 1841 and 1892 than the coldest year in the first half of the twentieth century.

Hertfordshire's economic role, at least up to the twentieth century, has been as a small agricultural county near to, but not actually contiguous with, London. It lies astride the main routes between the capital and the rest of Britain to the north. Until the construction of the M11, which passes through Essex, it was impossible to go from London to the north of England by any reasonably direct route without passing through Hertfordshire. This was equally true of the Roman roads, the eighteenth-century turnpikes, the Victorian railways and the modern motorways.

England changed very considerably in the course of the nineteenth century. We all have a picture of the beginning and end of that century. We may think of England in 1800 as a society with an elegant aristocracy of polished wit and culture, hard drinking squires, a solid Georgian middle class and a desperately poor underclass. All in all, perhaps, rather a rumbustious, violent sort of society of drinkers and gamblers, hard swearing and quick tempered – a world of fairs and turnpikes, rough justice and public executions, ever on the edge of anarchy. England in 1900, by contrast, we may think of as a far more respectable place. By this time, a century of industrial discipline, civic worthiness and nonconformist morality had made its mark. England in 1900 had terraced housing for the working classes, villas for those in the middle and mansions for those at the top. There were railways in place of stagecoaches, elementary schools designed to keep the lower orders economically useful but firmly in their place, mass circulation newspapers, league football and organised party politics geared to a mass, if still totally male, electorate. Some things remained the same. There was still a powerful sense of national self-confidence, a genial contempt for foreigners, a respect for English law and justice and a pride in the British Constitution and Empire. Property was still a national obsession and the social hierarchy may, if anything, have been even more rigid at the end of the century that it had been at the beginning.

Compared with an earlier age, England in 1900 was a far more professional society. There were elementary school teachers instead of the dame schools and the county constabulary instead of the part-time parish constable. In this late Victorian world, vast, brick-built public institutions had been built to cope with every kind of social problem: workhouses, prisons, barracks, hospitals, schools and, something of a Hertfordshire speciality, lunatic asylums where the insane of Victorian London could be housed safely away from the public gaze.

Unlike many other counties by this date, Hertfordshire still had few factories. The paper works on the River Gade in the south-west between Croxley and Apsley and the silk mills of Tring were possible exceptions to this rule. The domestic industry of straw plaiting supplied the hat factories of Luton just over the Bedfordshire border. Luton, together with Watford, with its papermaking, printing and brewing, were rare examples in the Home Counties of nineteenth-century industrial towns. Hertfordshire industries such as brewing, malting and, of course, straw-hat making were all directly based upon the produce of the land.

Hertfordshire's communications

Communications had been vastly improved even before 1800 by the turnpike and the canal. As we might expect in a county that contained the main approach roads into London from the north, Hertfordshire's main roads had been put on to a toll basis quite early. Acts of Parliament had been passed to convert many of Hertfordshire's radial routes into London into roads maintained, not by the local parish, but by elected trusts with the power to collect tolls. These were the turnpikes named for the revolving posts that were used to control the traffic.

By 1700 there was already a pay-road from Cambridge to Ware where the distinctive mileposts with the brassard device of Trinity Hall can still be seen. By 1800 Hertfordshire possessed a good set of turnpike roads. By this time, virtually all the main arterial roads familiar to us today as trunk roads maintained directly by the government were then maintained by turnpike trusts. The highways mostly radiated from London and included the Sparrows Herne, the

2 WILL. IV.—Sess. 1831-2.

AN

A C T

For repairing, maintaining and improving the Road from *Stevenage*, in the County of *Hertford*, to *Biggleswade*, in the County of *Bedford*, and a Branch therefrom to *Arlsey*, in the said County of *Bedford*.

[ROYAL ASSENT, 1 *June* 1832.]

WHEREAS an Act was passed in the sixth year of the reign of King GEORGE the First, intituled, " An " Act for repairing the Roads from *Stevenage*, in the County of " *Hertford*, to *Biggleswade*, in the County of *Bedford :*" *Preamble :* 6 Geo. 1, c. 25.

And whereas another Act was passed in the twelfth year of the reign of King GEORGE the First, intituled, " An Act " for repairing the Roads from *Lemsford Mill*, in the County of " *Hertford*, to *Welwyn*, and from thence to *Cory's Mill*, and " from *Welwyn* (through *Codicot*) to *Hitchin*, in the said County ; " and for enlarging the term granted by an Act passed in the sixth " year of the reign of His present Majesty for repairing the " Roads from *Stevenage*, in the said County, to *Biggleswade*, in " the County of *Bedford :*" 12 Geo. 1, c. 10.

And whereas another Act was passed in the twenty-eighth year of the reign of King GEORGE the Second, intituled, " An Act " to continue and render more effectual two Acts of Parliament, " passed in the sixth and twelfth years of the reign of his late " Majesty King GEORGE, for repairing the Roads from *Stevenage*, " in the County of *Hertford*, to *Biggleswade*, in the County of " *Bedford* ; and for repairing the Roads from the North End of " the said Roads to the Tollgate at the North End of the said " Town of *Biggleswade :*" 28 Geo. 2, c. 30.

55.   A   And

1.1 The Stevenage and Biggleswade Turnpike: A local turnpike act.
Existing main roads were improved by converting them into turnpikes, taking their name from the barriers where officials collected the tolls. A local turnpike act would be passed by Parliament enabling a consortium of local notables to levy charges on travellers in order to maintain the main roads. This turnpike was administered by a group of businessmen and landowners usually meeting in the White Horse Inn, Baldock. During the mid-nineteenth century they shared a secretary in Samuel Veasey, a Baldock solicitor, with the trustees of the Ivel Navigation, which followed substantially the same route. The turnpike is now the route of the
A1 Great North Road

Wadesmill, the Welwyn and the Stevenage and Biggleswade Trusts. Only the Dunstable Turnpike ran from west to east though Hitchin and Royston along the route of the Icknield Way.

Once the turnpikes had been set up and had improved road surfaces Hertfordshire soon became served by stagecoaches. From the early eighteenth century until about 1840 they provided a fast and reliable service through the county, stopping at inns in the high streets of market towns. However efficient, they were expensive and had limited capacity. They vanished on the appearance of the railway.

Apart from the turnpikes, there was also a more informal system of green lanes, the 'drove roads' by which animals were driven to market. They wended their way through the county, mostly converging on London. They had no toll-gates and they avoided the towns – no one wanted to drive cattle or sheep down a busy high street. Apart from the Icknield Way running along the Chiltern crest, the drove roads crossed the Chilterns and headed for the great cattle and sheep fair at Barnet. Their usefulness for the cattle trade of the Midlands and even that of Scotland and Wales outlived the coming of the railways. Animals were still being sent by drove up to the 1860s after which a ban on cattle movements was imposed as a result of a plague of rinderpest which brought an end to the practice of overland droving. The drove roads still exist as green lanes and are delightful walking routes throughout the county.

River navigations and canals were also provided by local trusts set up by special acts of Parliament. Indeed, in some cases, the local turnpike trusts and the nearby river navigations were both administered by the same local worthies. The two trusts might even meet on the same day and in the same pub. For instance, the Biggleswade and Stevenage Turnpike Trust and the Board of the Ivel Navigation both met in the White Horse Inn in Baldock and shared a secretary in Samuel Veasey, a Baldock solicitor.

Canals, however, were much less important to the county as a whole than turnpikes. In the south-east of the county, the River Lea (or Lee) had been navigable up to Ware and possibly Hertford at least since Saxon times. The Lee Navigation Act of 1739 followed by the creation of the Lea Conservancy Board of 1868 brought the river under unified control and established a fully navigable canalised river from Hertford to the Thames at Limehouse. In 1766 its main tributary, the Stort, was also the subject of a navigation act. Both the Lea and the Stort were river navigations rather than true canals. Hertfordshire's only real, purpose-built canal, the Grand Junction Canal, (now the Grand Union Canal)

[1]

An ACT *for afcertaining, preferving and improving the Navigation of the River* Lee, *from the Town of* Hertford *to the Town of* Ware *in the County of* Hertford ; *and for preferving and improving the faid River from the faid Town of* Ware *to the New Cut or River made by the Mayor, Commonalty, and Citizens of* London ; *and for enabling the Governor and Company of the* New River *the better to fupply the Cities of* London *and* Weftminfter, *and the Liberties and Suburbs thereof, with good and wholfome Water.*

Whereas there hath been and ftill is an ancient and accuftomed Navigation on that Part of the River *Lee,* which runs from the Borough and Town of *Hertford* in the County of *Hertford,* to *Ware-Bridge* in the Town of *Ware* in the fame County; which Navigation hath formerly, at different Times, been carried on through different Branches of the faid River; but the fame, for many Years paft, hath been and now is carried from the faid Borough and Town of *Hertford* through a Channel running to *Ware Mills,* and from thence through a Ciftern or Lock near the faid Mills, and from thence to *Ware-Bridge* in the faid Town of *Ware,* and from thence to the River of *Thames:*

And whereas the Governor and Company of the *New River* brought from *Chadwell* and *Amwell* to *London,* have, for many Years paft, had and received into the faid *New River* a confiderable Quantity of Water, which iffued out of the faid River *Lee* at the Mouth or Opening of *Manifold Ditch,* which lies between the faid Town of *Hertford* and the faid Town of *Ware:*

And whereas feveral Difputes have arifen between the Corporation of the faid Borough and Town of *Hertford* and the Inhabitants of the faid

A   Town

1.2 A Lee (Lea) Navigation Act. This act authorising parts of both the Lee Navigation for boat traffic and the New River Water Conduit was one of several. The first legislation authorising these works was in the reign of Elizabeth I for the navigation and that of James I for the conduit carrying water from the upper Lea Valley near Ware right into Jacobean London – a remarkable engineering project for its day

was completed in 1799 in the west of the county along the Chess and Gade valleys from Rickmansworth through Watford, Hemel Hempstead and Berkhamsted to cross the Chiltern ridge at Tring on its way to the Midlands. There was no waterway within Hertfordshire to link the Grand Junction Canal in the west

ANNO NONO & DECIMO

VICTORIÆ REGINÆ.

****

Cap. clxx.

An Act for making a Railway from *Royston* to
Hitchin. [16th *July* 1846.]

WHEREAS the making of a Railway from or near the Town
of *Royston* in the County of *Cambridge* to *Hitchin* in
the County of *Hertford* would be of great public and
local Advantage, by opening an additional, certain, and expeditious
Means of Communication between the said Places, and also by facili-
tating Communication between more distant Towns and Places : And
whereas an Act was passed in the Eighth Year of the Reign of Her
Majesty Queen *Victoria*, intituled *An Act for consolidating in One* 8 & 9 Vict.
Act certain Provisions usually inserted in Acts with respect to the c. 16.
*Constitution of Companies incorporated for carrying on Undertakings
of a public Nature*, called " The Companies Clauses Consolidation
Act, 1845 : " And whereas another Act was passed in the said Eighth
Year of the Reign of Her said Majesty, intituled *An Act for con-* 8 & 9 Vict.
solidating in One Act certain Provisions usually inserted in Acts c. 18.
authorizing the taking of Lands for Undertakings of a public Nature,
called " The Lands Clauses Consolidation Act, 1845 :" And whereas
another Act was passed in the said Eighth Year of the Reign of
Her said Majesty, intituled *An Act for consolidating in One Act* 8 & 9 Vict.
[*Local.*] 34 Y *certain* c. 20.

1.3 The Royston and Hitchin Railway Act, 1846.
*Paragraph III of the act states: 'And be it enacted that the Right Honourable Lord Dacre,
Patrick Maxwell Stewart Esquire MP, William Wilshere Esquire MP, John George Fordham,
John Chevallier Cobbold, Samuel Vesey, and John Bailey Denton shall be united into a
company for the purpose of making and maintaining the said railway.'*
*Lord Dacre, Wilshere and Cobbold were Hertfordshire landowners. Fordham was a miller and
maltster in Ashwell and Royston, Vesey a Baldock solicitor who was also involved with both the
turnpike and the navigation, and Denton was a surveyor living in Stevenage. He acquired a
national reputation in his profession and was author of many reports. He was later to come
second to Joseph Bazelgette in a competitive contract to design and build the London
sewerage system*

with the Lee Navigation in the east. More ambitious plans to link Hertfordshire with either the rivers of East Anglia or those of the Fenland basin of the Great Ouse came to nothing. Legislation was passed in 1757 to canalise the Ivel and its tributary, the Hiz, up to Baldock and Hitchin respectively and so connect Hertfordshire with the Great Ouse. The project was completed no further upstream than Shefford in Bedfordshire, six miles north of Hitchin.

As with the turnpikes and the canals, Hertfordshire's railways had been built to serve the outside world rather than Hertfordshire itself. In 1838 Robert Stephenson built the London and Birmingham Railway along the line of the Grand Junction Canal through Watford and the Tring gap. In the railway boom of the 1840s the Northern and Eastern Railway, an associate of the Eastern Counties Railway, made tentative explorations up the Lea Valley eventually to reach Cambridge. In 1862 this became the Great Eastern Railway uniting almost all the railways of East Anglia. The pace quickened when the mainline of the Great Northern Railway was built in 1850 through Hatfield, Stevenage and Hitchin on its way to the north. A plan to connect Oxford and Cambridge by rail was revived to create a branch from Hitchin to Cambridge. This became the nominally independent Royston and Hitchin Railway, which had several local directors but always operated as a subsidiary of the GNR.

Seven years later, the Midland Railway embarked on an attempt to reach London by a line from Leicester to Hitchin to join the GNR. This was soon to be the victim of its own success and, by 1868, the Midland had built its own main line from Bedford to St Pancras via Luton and St Albans – the last Hertfordshire town to escape from dependency on the stagecoach. Finally, we ought to notice that England's last main line, the Great Central Railway of 1899 passed briefly through the county at Rickmansworth on a line borrowed from the Metropolitan Railway which otherwise served Buckinghamshire.

There was some effort during the nineteenth century to extend the system by building branch lines for the benefit of the county itself. These included a line from Little Amwell outside Ware to Hadham and Buntingford, the oddly named 'Nicky Line' from Harpenden to Hemel Hempstead and a wandering branch of the Great Northern from Hatfield to Dunstable. All are now closed with the exception of a secretive little line, known to its passengers as the 'Abbey Flier', from St Albans to Watford. Only the line from Royston to Hitchin still survives as part of the national network connecting the east coast mainline with Cambridge.

By 1900, the county was well served for transport and it was now much easier to get into London. The commuter, although not actually known as such, was already an additional resident in what were otherwise local market towns. Hertfordshire did not develop any purpose-built satellite towns in the course of the nineteenth century catering purely for a commuting population, unless Harpenden counted as one, although many more were to appear in the twentieth century. The traditional market towns such as Hitchin, Hertford and Hemel Hempstead quickly developed railway suburbs of middle-class villas and railwaymen's terraced cottages. These districts within towns sometimes included their own churches, chapels and shops distinct from those of the traditional town centres.

By the end of the century, the basic structure of Hertfordshire society was little changed. In 1900 it was still a county with about twenty-eight market towns, each dependent on its local farming district. The county town of Hertford was hardly more than *primus inter pares* – possibly not even that, as several other towns, such as Watford, Hemel Hempstead and St Albans were bigger. In 1888, the new county council found it more convenient to meet in London. In 1872, St Albans had at long last become the seat of an Anglican bishop and its abbey was now a cathedral. Hertfordshire, paired first with Essex and then Bedfordshire, was now part of the new diocese of St Albans.

How, then, was the agricultural landscape of Hertfordshire different from that of the present day? It is of course the case that large parts of the county are now covered with light industry and suburbs, but at least half the county is still basically agricultural even if a great number of non-agricultural people choose to live there. The first impression that the nineteenth-century landscape would have made on us would have been that it was very well wooded and there were far more hedges. The actual woodlands did not cover a much greater area than at the present day, but the impression of woodland would have been much enhanced by the sheer amount of hedgerow timber. The vast number of hedgerow elms that were present until the 1970s is now becoming a dim memory. In the nineteenth century, they were abundant. The landscape of the summer countryside would have been far lusher than at the present day with pasture fields resembling flowery meadows. The fields were mostly much smaller than is usual today, surrounded by bushy, hand-laid, hedges. In the absence of effective herbicides, nineteenth-century arable fields would have appeared very weedy.

The abundant wild flowers of the nineteenth-century fields may have fascinated Victorian naturalists but the farmers did not always appreciate their colourful profusion. One has only to read the works of a poet like John Clare to realise how, before the era of modern herbicides, weeds in the corn could spell failed harvests, hardship and famine.

A modern observer would probably think the nineteenth-century countryside was very crowded. Farms that nowadays hire one contract worker on a machine might then employ up to thirty full-time farm workers. Many more were hired for hay time and harvest. Even in the darkest days of winter, gangs of men were at work on the land digging ditches or laying hedges while the plough teams were at work more or less continually. Toiling groups of farmhands, sometimes accompanied by women and children, were to be seen everywhere. Even the woodlands, beset as they were with notices and mantraps, were patrolled regularly by groups of keepers, and gangs of woodmen were at work through the winter season cutting faggots and felling timber.

If one part of the county were noticeably different it would have been the high chalk of the Chilterns. Here, the vast wind-blown fields were less likely to be cultivated for arable crops than they are today. Much of the hill country was reserved for sheep that grazed on the short-cropped downland where shepherds lived a lonely life tending their flocks. There was more chalk grassland and more land covered with heather and bracken. Heath is now an almost forgotten feature of the Hertfordshire landscape. Even in the nineteenth century, heathland was considered the haunt of gypsies and highwaymen to be avoided by respectable folk and not to be crossed after dark, but tracts of it still existed as the names of Mardley Heath, Hertford Heath and Colney Heath testify.

The social structure of agriculture followed a fairly typical English pattern. Much of the county consisted of large agricultural estates, subdivided into tenanted farms. The farmers in their turn employed farm labourers, usually paid on a daily basis, although some work was paid by the piece and special arrangements were made for the harvest season. The vast majority of farm workers lived in their own households, usually in rented cottages, but farm servants living in at the farmhouse were still to be found. Most of the farm workers' cottages were in villages or small hamlets. Some cottages belonged to agricultural landowners but many were the property of people of modest status in the rural community such as tradesmen or publicans or indeed people with no resources beyond their cottage properties. Only a few of the workers lived in tied cottages owned by the employing farmer.

The field system of Hertfordshire was complex. Hertfordshire was just on the border between those southern counties, such as Kent or Essex, where enclosed fields had been usual for centuries, and the Midland plain which included Bedfordshire and the extreme north of Hertfordshire. Here, open-field agriculture with large fields subdivided into individually occupied strips was standard practice. In this area, formal enclosure by local act of Parliament had been going on through the latter part of the eighteenth century and much remained still to complete in the nineteenth century. Some northern Hertfordshire parishes, such as Bygrave, much of Clothall and the township of Hitchin, although not its outlying hamlets, remained unenclosed right into the twentieth century.

The central parishes of Hertfordshire had long practised a distinctive 'Chiltern' form of field arrangement by which several open fields each subdivided into strips were attached to different settlements within the parish. This arrangement was to prove just as inconvenient for modern farming practice as the classic three- or four-field systems of the Midlands and sometimes proved more difficult to modernise.

Farming had, of course, been transformed in ways other than the layout of its fields. The selective breeding of both animals and crops had made considerable progress. Much had been done to put in pipe drainage. Machinery, while not yet using the internal combustion engine, had made considerable progress with threshing machines and reaper binders. Even long-used implements like ploughs, harrows and cultivators were now scientifically made in a factory using standard interchangeable parts rather than built from scratch by village craftsmen. Finally, artificial fertilisers had become commonplace by the end of the century. As the basis of modern, intensive farming this must rank with steam power or electricity as one of the great step changes of technological development. Until the nineteenth century, all farming had been organic farming. With the development of super phosphates by John Bennet Lawes of Rothamsted, for better or worse, Hertfordshire could be said to have invented modern farming.

This is not to say farming was in a good state at the end of the century. Quite the contrary: back in 1800, it had been taken for granted that the British farmer fed the nation. Only a few tropical or semi-tropical products like sugar, tobacco and wine were imported. By 1900, Britannia ruled the waves and territories barely known at the start of the century were now producing massive quantities of food, much of which could be sent by refrigerated steamship to the mother country. Food was imported from Britain's colonies and ex-colonies. It was Canada, Australia and the US who now fed the British population with Britain's own farmers having to fight a desperate economic rearguard action. Prophets of doom such as Rudyard Kipling in his poem 'Big Steamers'[1] sternly warned that, in time of emergency, Britain must not lose control of the seas, not that Britain's own farmers should be enabled to feed the nation.

Farming was still seen as the mainstream activity of the countryside but, especially in the Home Counties, the countryside was seen also as a location for field sports and a desirable place for a man of means to live. As for the lower classes in the country, a generation of economic depression after the collapse of agriculture in the 1870s had left farm wages hopelessly trailing urban wages. Many villages had declined in size and were far less self-sufficient than had once been the case. The rural working class could almost be regarded as a remnant of those who were content to know their humble place and had no interest in taking advantage of a wider world. Apart from a few determinedly romantic idealists such as Jesse Collings MP, few were still attempting to achieve land reform. Perhaps it is significant that Hertfordshire's most successful builder of new communities, Ebenezer Howard (1850–1928), only carried out land reform as a byproduct of designing a new town. His garden cities at Letchworth and Welwyn were designed to be self-sufficient. Envisaged originally as a means of providing food for a self-sufficient community, the agricultural estate soon became little more than a land bank for urban expansion. The landed estate of Letchworth still exists but only as an appurtenance of Howard's primary objective to create an ideal urban community. In the event it was not even that, as the agricultural estate at Letchworth Garden City was to become little different from a set of ordinary farms, albeit farms with a social or educational orientation. The first Garden City never remotely succeeded in living on the produce of its own land. Welwyn Garden City, the second one, did not even try. Both towns developed into suburban, light industrial, commuter towns like most other Hertfordshire townships.

The Hertfordshire tradition of new settlements, which had begun with the Chartist Land Company's village at Heronsgate, near Rickmansworth, in the 1840s, continued with landowners' model villages such as Charles Hancock's reconstructed Willian in the 1860s. It included Ebenezer Howard's two Garden Cities and culminated with the post-war New Towns of Stevenage and Hemel Hempstead. By this stage the agricultural element of the new communities had dwindled to invisibility. Hertfordshire County Council retains a rural estate of smallholdings to this day, a commercial estate near Hitchin and Baldock and a green belt estate in the south but that concludes attempts at land reform in

Hertfordshire. Even the minor eccentricity of the Ovaltine farm at Kings Langley has now gone.

By no means all of the small and middle-sized towns that proliferated in twentieth-century Hertfordshire were planned new communities. The ordinary market towns of the county grew as a result of suburban expansion. We saw this trend beginning to appear in nineteenth-century Hertfordshire as 'railway suburbs' became established soon after the lines were built. Nonetheless, the society under consideration in nineteenth-century Hertfordshire was still very much a pre-urban rural society based on agriculture. The crucial invention that brought about the step change between the two centuries was the internal combustion engine. This effectively came into use at the end of the nineteenth century and it brought the benefits (and otherwise) of artificial motive power derived from fossil fuels directly into the countryside. Tractors made true mechanisation possible on the land. The internal combustion engine also helped to provide first local public transport and then automobility for individuals, altering the countryside for ever. For the first time it became possible to live in the country without having any real connection to the land.

That had not the case with nineteenth-century rural society. With very few exceptions, mainly people of independent means who might choose to live in a rural village, everyone living in the countryside, at that time, had some direct economic connection with the land. If they did not own or cultivate land themselves, they worked for those who did. All other members of the community, from the craftsmen to the clergy, were there because they provided a service that the farming community needed. Villages were essentially communities of farm workers. That is the world that this book attempts to explore.

References

1. Kipling, R., 'Big Steamers', (1914–18).

CHAPTER TWO

Population

THE POPULATION OF Hertfordshire increased in the course of the nineteenth century from 97,393 in 1801 to 250,080 in 1901, an increase of 157 per cent. Further research is needed to determine how much this was due to natural increase and how much to immigration.

In the same century, Hertfordshire also went through a process of urbanisation. In 1801 about fifty-seven per cent of the population of the county lived in the twenty-three towns with populations greater than 1,000 persons. In 1901, sixty-two per cent of Hertfordshire's population lived in the seventeen largest towns with populations greater than 5,000. No very large towns had grown up in this county but whereas in 1801, only Watford, with 10,777 had a population that was greater than 10,000, by 1901 there were five towns with populations greater than 10,000. These were Watford, St Albans, Hemel Hempstead, Cheshunt and Hitchin closely followed by Hertford itself with just under 10,000 if we include the suburb of Bengeo.

More significantly from the point of view of the evolution of rural society is the fact that, while the larger communities increased steadily throughout the century, the same cannot be said of the villages.

The growth of the villages was far more erratic. Only a minority of Hertfordshire village parishes recorded consistent growth throughout the century. Many of the villages reached a peak of population at or about mid-century and went into decline thereafter. It is believed that the growth of the villages was largely due to natural increase but the decline of so many of them was primarily due to emigration, sometimes to other villages, sometimes to neighbouring towns or to London. For some it meant leaving the country altogether to travel to America or the other colonies.

As this book is about rural society, it is beyond our scope to consider the fate or speculate on the prospects of those Hertfordshire people who chose to move away from their native villages. We do not know for certain whether the process is best described as being pushed off the land or if people were positively attracted to a life elsewhere. Most people's motives for moving were probably mixed.

Village populations in Hertfordshire

There was a general tendency for the smaller villages to go into decline first. The larger communities either went into decline at a point later in the century or retained their growth throughout the century. As noted, the largest single batch of villages that went into decline did so at or about mid-century.

We can draw some conclusions from this. If the incidence of social unrest is anything to go by, the worst years on the land were during the 1820s and the 1830s. Most Hertfordshire villages continued to grow through this period. Only Eastwick, Hexton, Little Gaddesden and Ayot St Lawrence reached a peak in 1821 and only Hunsdon, Sacombe and Rushden reached a peak in 1831. It should be noted that, not only are these all small in population, but most of them are parishes that are substantially under the control of sole landowners. They were what the nineteenth century knew as 'close parishes'.

At this time, the parish was entirely responsible for the sustenance of its poor and there was every incentive for landowners to restrict residence in their parishes to a minimum thereby reducing the need to pay poor rates. No landowner willingly allowed a parish under his direct control to maintain an unwelcome burden of partially employed, still less unemployed, residents. This was to some extent mitigated by the new Poor Law of 1834 after which the Poor Law was administered by groups of parishes organised in Poor Law Unions, but the problem was only finally settled by the Union Chargeability Act of 1863. Until that date, individual parishes were charged a rate commensurate with the number of paupers that the parish contained. Those landowners who exercised total control over a parish invariably tried to restrict residence to those clearly needed to work the land and maintain a close parish. They had every reason to keep numbers down. Nevertheless, such was the high birthrate in the nineteenth century that most villages continued to grow in population.

By 1841, however, it was very different. No fewer than fourteen parishes, mostly in the arable east of the county, went into population decline. They had an average population of 470. In 1851 as many as thirty parishes with an average population of 669 reached their nineteenth-century peak. This was followed by fourteen in 1861 and thirteen more in 1871. Something was causing the rural villages to lose population. As the birth rate remained high and the death rate only declined slowly, it follows that people were choosing to leave.

The parishes that lost population around mid-century were often substantial village communities with craftsmen, shops, pubs and chapels. By this date, they also had village schools, post offices and policemen. They were not desolate or lonely hamlets offering no social life or choice of company, shopping or employment. Also, at this period, agriculture was still prospering.

The fact remains that the flight from the land antedated the onset of agricultural recession in the 1870s by at least a generation. The reason probably lies in greater social awareness and the considerably greater economic prospects for the urban population. Even when farming was doing relatively well, not a great deal of the prosperity found its way down to the working population. Wages improved somewhat and some landowners provided other incentives such as better cottages, schools and allotments. For many of the mobile young this was not sufficient. Farm workers could not help but notice that virtually all other workers, even those who were unskilled or only semi-skilled, earned more than they did. This even applied to other occupational groups in the rural areas. Policemen, postmen, road menders and labourers on the railway (navvies), all earned more than the farm worker.

This is not to say that the prosperity of agriculture had no bearing on rural population trends. The onset of depression may well account for the tendency of larger agricultural communities to go into decline in the 1870s and 1880s. Not only villages but some small towns such as Royston, Baldock and some large villages that were nearly towns such as Ashwell also declined at this time. The first two of these are both of them market towns, and all three are on the railway. They were, however, on the corn-growing northern chalk and very dependent on the prosperity of the wheat trade. Some towns which appeared to stagnate generated population growth in villages on their outskirts. Indeed in those cases where middle-sized villages did maintain their growth, as at Ickleford or Bengeo, the village was on the edge of a town and was able to share in some suburban growth on the part of its urban neighbours, Hitchin and Hertford respectively. For Hertfordshire, therefore, the evidence confirms one of the important results of the industrial revolution, that although the population was rising, fewer agricultural workers were needed since manufactured exports could be exchanged for cheaper foreign food supplies and extra labour could be diverted into servicing the bourgeoisie.

The conclusion might be that, while agriculture was prosperous, the life of the Hertfordshire villager was never more than tolerable in the decades around mid-century. Farm work provided a reasonable life only for people of contented disposition and/or limited expectations. The life was less alluring for the mobile and the go-ahead young.

Farm workers were less trapped in their jobs and more readily employable in the outside world than might have been expected. It was not the case that farm workers had no saleable skills. In an urban world that still relied on horse-drawn transport, the ability to handle a horse with confidence was a saleable asset, even in a town. Farm workers could move if they wanted to. As a result the village community retained its middle-aged and elderly and there were still plenty of children. It was the younger generation of adults that tended to depart. Although as yet hardly noticed, the English village was beginning to rot from the centre.

CHAPTER THREE

Enclosure of the land

P ERHAPS THE MOST IMPORTANT structural change in English agricultural history was the enclosure of the land. Essentially this was the process by which land became sub-divided for the purposes of ownership, occupation and cultivation. Pastoral farming may be carried on at a rather low level of efficiency by allowing animals to wander and feed on land that is regarded as common property. Arable farming implies a degree of permanent occupation and the individual control of land.

In England, all land, although theoretically in the possession of the sovereign, has in fact been owned and occupied either by individuals, or by corporations treated for legal purposes as individuals. There were various forms of land tenure, the categories of which need not concern us here.

In practice, apart from some relatively small areas of common land over which more than one person has had some rights of cultivation or pasture, most land has been individually owned and either cultivated directly by the owner or let out to a tenant. It was the layout rather than the ownership of land that proved detrimental, or at least inconvenient, to efficient agriculture. Before the process of enclosure, much arable land was included in vast open fields sub-divided into strips. It was these strips that were owned by individuals who could either cultivate the strips of land themselves, or, as was the case with a large landowner who might own hundreds of strips situated in the fields of more than one parish, be let out to farming tenants. It was possible for an individual farm to consist of many strips of land, some directly owned, some rented from a landlord. Over the years, it had been the aim of many landowners to consolidate the strips that they possessed into compact blocks of land. The process by which the multiplicity of cultivated strips of land in the open fields were re-arranged into compact and convenient fields and farms under the control of individual farmers is known as the enclosure movement.

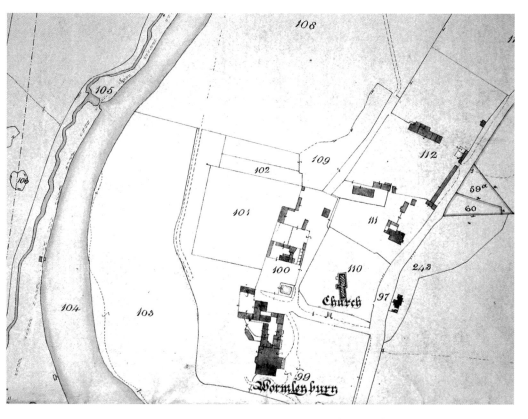

3.1 Wormley enclosure map, 1854. An example of a late enclosure after the tithe surveys whose numbers are included on the map

It was a process instigated by the landlords, sometimes by local agreement amongst themselves but sometimes involving the elaborate procedure of a local act of Parliament. The social effects of the enclosure movement, if any, were a by-product. The enclosure of the land was primarily concerned with the most efficient layout of fields and farms, whether they were rented by a tenant or owned outright by the person who cultivated the soil.

Looking at the modern landscape, it is difficult to remember that over much of England in the centuries before the eighteenth century, the land was organized for cultivation in way that has now all but disappeared. 'Fields' in this context were not patches of land surrounded by a hedge and normally cultivated as a unit but were large expanses of land commonly consisting of a hundred acres or more, sub-divided into multifarious strips of land of about one acre in size looking rather like elongated municipal allotments. These were separated by baulks that could be used as pathways. It was these strips of land, frequently called 'shotts' in Hertfordshire, that were individually owned or tenanted. The vast open fields contained the property of many individuals rich and poor. This was 'open-field' farming. It is extremely rare nowadays in Britain but still to be seen in parts of the European continent. Even England has some surviving open fields. The parish of Laxton in Nottinghamshire still works on an open-field basis and an isolated open field called the Stitches still exists between the church and the sea at Boscastle in Cornwall. There may be others. Even in this county there are unexpectedly elongated strips of land, now often the home of a pony, that is all that remains of a cultivated 'shott' or 'pightle' on the edge of a Hertfordshire village. The open-field system had been appropriate to the agricultural society of earlier centuries but by the eighteenth century it had come to be seen as outdated.

The open-field system of agriculture was extremely common at the height of its popularity but, in the early-modern centuries, much of the south-east of England had been enclosed. Extensive open-field farming still survived in the Midland counties until it was removed, often by local act of Parliament, in the course of the eighteenth and nineteenth centuries.

Hertfordshire appears to have been a transitional zone where much of the land had been enclosed at least since Tudor times but some open fields remained in most parts of the county. In the north of the county, along the chalk ridge and in the clay vale to the north of the chalk, the full open-field system prevailed until it was done away with either by act of Parliament or by landowners acting in concert. In a few northern parishes, such as Bygrave, Clothall and the township of Hitchin, the open fields persisted right into the twentieth century.

Some writers have suggested that the combination of enclosed land and a sometimes complex system of open fields attached to individual hamlets and settlements within parishes amounts to a distinctive 'Chiltern' field system.[1] The northern parishes such as Pirton, Hitchin and Ashwell possessed open-field systems involving the whole parish and centring on a nucleated settlement in the typical Midland mode. The parishes of central and west Hertfordshire often contained a complex system of open and enclosed fields that pertained to hamlets within the parishes rather than to any central settlement. At King's Walden, for example, open fields were attached to the hamlets of Flexmere, Wandon End and Breachwood Green. Three Houses, a hamlet of Knebworth; Cockernhoe and Tea Green, both in Offley, and Bendish in St Paul's Walden all possessed open-field 'commons' that were distinct from those of the nominate settlement of each parish. In some cases remnants of the open-field system

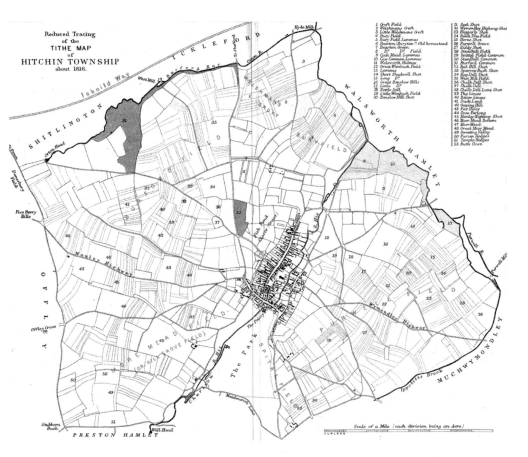

1 Croft Field
2 Welshmans Croft
3 Little Welshmans Croft
4 Bury Field
5 Bury Field Lammas
6 Bearton/Buryton ?/ Old homestead
7 Begyrton Green
8 D.º   D.º   Field
9 Cock Mead Lammas
10 Cow Common Lammas
11 Walsworth Holmes
12 Great Wimbush Field
13 Lammas
14 Short Shadwell Shot
15 Long   D.º
16 Great Benslow Hills
17 Little   D.º
18 Nettle Dell
19 Little Wimbush Field
20 Benslow Hill Shot

21 Rock Shot
22 Wymondley Highway Shot
23 Beggarly Shot
24 Rook Tree Field
25 Berne Shot
26 Purwell Grove
27 Oddy Shot
28 Standhill Field
29 Spital Field Common
30 Standhill Common
31 Burford Common
32 End Hill Shot
33 Sparrow Bush Shot
34 Rag Dell Shot
35 West Mill Field
36 Chalk Dell Shot
37 Chalk Dell
38 Chalk Dell Lane Shot
39 The Linces
40 Below Linces
41 Duck Land
42 Gaping Hill
43 Fox Holes
44 Crow Furlong
45 Manley Highway Shot
46 Moor Mead Bottom
47 Moor Mead
48 Great Moor Mead
49 Sweeting Valley
50 Purson Hedges
51 Temple Hedges
52 Butts Close

3.2 A map of Hitchin Township c.1816 from Frederick Seebohm's 'English Village Community'. The map, now believed lost but corresponding closely to the tithe maps of Hitchin, was used by Frederick Seebohm, a Hitchin banker, who made a study of the English village community. It shows the pattern of strip cultivation in the open fields of a small market town in north Hertfordshire. Hitchin used a six-field system and was never formally enclosed by act of Parliament in the manner of most of the surrounding villages, including its own dependent hamlet of Walsworth immediately to the east. As a result, some of the small strips used by cultivators remained and could be identified well into the twentieth-century

remained until recent times, often recognisable today as elongated building plots or pony paddocks.

Maps showing the enclosed and the open-field areas of England often indicate that Hertfordshire was largely an enclosed county apart from its northern fringe of chalk downlands. These tend to reflect the distribution of Parliamentary enclosure acts. Within a single county this may create a false impression.

Not all enclosure acts applied to whole parishes. Some were mere tidying up arrangements for parishes largely enclosed already.

Although 'whole parish' open-field arrangements were rare in the centre and south of the county, some open fields sub-divided into strips were to be found in most parts of the county in the earlier years of the century. Enclosure maps and awards for parts of a parish exist for Bengeo, Sacombe and Stapleford in 1851; for Benington, Aston and Little Munden in 1857 and Aspenden and Throcking in 1868 and 1869. Small patches of open-field strip-cultivation survived in a number of places in the county – at Langley near Knebworth until the 1890s, at Ninesprings near Hitchin until the 1970s and at Luffenhall Common north of Walkern to this day. The tithe map for Hatfield in 1838,[2] the largest parish in Hertfordshire and typical of the largely enclosed country of central Hertfordshire, reveals a clutch of strip-divided open-field commons just north of the main park. These were called Marsh, Rye and Lake Commons. Just to the west, however, another group called, Richel, Ham and Billet Commons were still unfenced but had been divided now, not into strips, but into rectangular blocks. This was presumably a preparation for outright enclosure. The Hatfield estate was the largest in Hertfordshire and its owner, the Marquess of Salisbury, was able to promote enclosures without recourse to Parliamentary operations. Elsewhere Parliamentary action was usually required.

Between 1766 and 1830 there were twenty-seven privately sponsored acts of Parliament applying to thirty-four parishes in the county. Seven more enclosures took place under the Public Act of 1836 involving arable land and about twenty more separate enclosures took place under the Act of 1845. About 40,000 acres were re-allocated under these acts, or about a tenth of the county. In seventeen parishes more than fifty per cent of the land was affected and in eight parishes, Hinxworth, the Wymondleys, St Ippolyts, Standon, Sandon and Ashwell nearly all the cultivated land was affected. The extent of enclosure by private arrangement is not known.[3]

It may be wondered why, with all its inconveniences, the open-field system sometimes lasted so long. The answer cannot surely have been that there were too many administrative or legal obstacles in the way of reform. The system must have had some positive merits in an earlier age to suit the society that made use of it. The evidence of will inventories in the sixteenth to the eighteenth centuries shows that many people possessed some land of their own. They were not necessarily subsistence peasant farmers. Many were craftsmen, small traders or innkeepers. For such people the possession of two or three acres of

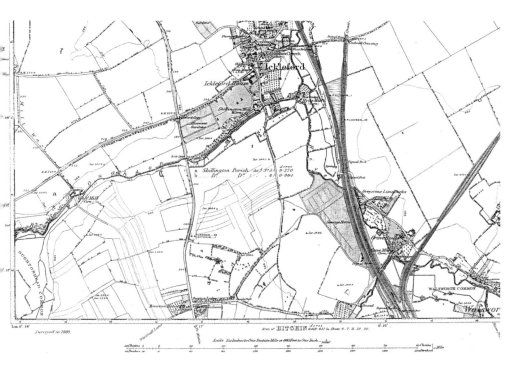

3.3 *Ickleford and north Hitchin. Note the contrast between enclosed fields of Ickleford and the open fields of Hitchin. The very square and geometrical fields of Walsworth over to the east were enclosed early in the eighteenth century. The two railways on the 1881 map are the main Great Northern Railway to the north built in 1851 and virtually eliminating the hamlet of Cadwell. Later the Midland Railway was built in 1857 from Leicester via Bedford to join the GNR at Hitchin. During the nineteenth century many little anomalies of county administration still survived. Note that Shillington Mill between Hitchin and Ickleford was in the parish of Shillington and therefore in Bedfordshire (OS map 1881 VII SW)*

wheat or barley whether in the form of an enclosed 'croft' or an unenclosed 'shott' or 'pightle' out in the open field was very important to them.[4]

In spite of the advantages of enclosed land over the open-field system the two systems ran in parallel for some time. Larger cultivators managed to operate the open-field arrangement without undue difficulty along with the enclosed holdings. In the 1720s the Radcliffes of Hitchin Priory kept a home farm at Hitchin of 220 acres 'in hand' operating both enclosed and unenclosed fields on a co-ordinated three course rotation which fitted in with the customary open-field practice of that township. The rotation was organised in three 'seasons' known as the Burfoot Season, the Moormead Season and the Purwell Season named after three of the six open fields of Hitchin. The Radcliffes also farmed land in the open fields of St Ippolyts, Pirton and Offley and what appears to have been a largely enclosed farm on the manor of Welbury which is also in the parish of Offley.[5]

On this land they produced wheat, barley, oats, peas, 'bullimon' (a combination of oats and vetches used for fodder), rye and hops. This would imply that they were not too closely tied into a three-field rotation to coincide with the three seasons.

The list of crops before and after enclosure indicates no additional crop, although on many farms root crops must have been an addition at this time. Two of the listed crops in the pre-enclosure period, rye and hops, do not seem to have been widely grown in the county later in the nineteenth century. Rye, it is true, is a grain associated with poor land, so possibly the greater care that could be taken of land after enclosure in the form of drainage and fertilising meant that rye ceased to be a profitable crop in the county as land was improved. Hops on the other hand are a specialist crop entirely cultivated for the brewing industry. This too seems to have dropped out of Hertfordshire farming during the nineteenth century in spite of the fact that barley growing and brewing remained major activities in the county. The decline in hop growing can hardly be due to any fall-off in demand. The reason therefore was probably climatic. Kent was able to produce sufficient hops for the whole of the London area while Hertfordshire concentrated on cereals. It is just possible that another factor might have been the production of hop poles. The traditional form of forestry in Kent was the coppicing of sweet chestnut for hop poles, a form of coppicing that is still commercially viable to this day. Hertfordshire forestry practice (see Chapter 9) concentrated on the coppicing of hornbeam which makes admirable firewood but rots too quickly to be of much use for hop poles.

It would seem then that open-field agriculture did not always prevent farmers from diversifying into the cultivation of minority crops like hops and rye, nor was enclosure always accompanied by more experimentation into new crops. The point about enclosure was that, by being able to carry out a more systematic rotation, farmers were able to produce their traditional crops more efficiently.

Hertfordshire farmers were able to compare the efficiency of open-field versus enclosed farming by accumulated experience acquired before the classic period of Parliamentary enclosure in the eighteenth century. Towards the end of the seventeenth century, there were some attempts to gain the benefits of enclosure before formal enclosure actually took place. One document from Offley in 1698[6] sets out a series of proposals to rationalise methods of cultivation in the open fields. It begins by stating that it must first be agreed how far each strip within the open fields may be cultivated separately. It goes on to consider within what time limits individual strips of land could be cultivated separately and how arrangements for ploughing, enclosing grazing animals on the open fields and carting crops might be organised if farmers cultivated different crops on various strips within the open-field system. In this parish at least, the open-field system was not allowed to impose an unwanted uniformity on farming practice. The possibility was explored of controlling the number of animals allowed to graze on a fallow by regulating the number of animals that a farmer was permitted to graze in proportion to the acreage of arable land that he possessed.

Most of these problems could not have been new. They must have existed in some degree for as long as open-field farming had been in existence. What was new was that there was now an awakened consciousness that open-field farming was becoming a hindrance to progress. It was no doubt the difficulty of making this type of agreement in the first place and then enforcing it afterwards that made some form of overall reorganisation and enclosure of the land so imperative.

Were the enclosures a success? In the long run, of course, they were. Although some agricultural improvements were possible before enclosure, in the sense that a certain amount of local flexibility was compatible with the open-field system, there can be no doubt that enclosure was an essential prerequisite for most long-term agricultural improvements. The case against enclosure has been largely derived from its social cost and in particular the supposed demise of the small landowner. Distress and poverty were of course endemic among the labouring population and a constant threat to hard-pressed farmers, but this had little to do with enclosure and more to do with inequalities of wealth, low productivity and over-population, conditions that existed whether the land was enclosed or not.

To ask whether enclosure was a success in the short run in the sense of bringing immediate benefits is less easy to answer. The leading commentator of the day, Arthur Young,[7] a man with Hertfordshire experience, was equivocal and to some extent changed his mind from being an enthusiastic advocate of enclosure to being fearful of its social consequences. His *General View of the Agriculture of Hertfordshire* is on the whole supportive of enclosure but not entirely so. He was aware of some of the adverse social consequences.

We have some local evidence that enclosure in Hertfordshire brought an immediate increase in the value of arable land. When an estate at Wymondley belonging to a Mrs Cracherode was valued in 1803, the value of land in the two enclosed farms, Wymondley Bury (320 acres) and Titmore Green (125 acres) was higher than that of a third, Delamere (247 acres), that consisted largely of land in the open fields of Great Wymondley. The comments of the valuer indicated that enclosed land commanded a higher price by that fact alone even when improvements had yet to be carried out. Enclosed land could be up to twenty per cent higher in value that comparable land in the open fields and it not surprising that Wymondley was in fact enclosed only eight years later by act of Parliament in 1811 taking advantage of the high corn prices of the Napoleonic Wars.[8]

Whatever the social consequences, there can be no doubt that enclosure was economically efficient. Arthur Young in 1804 writing at a time when the high corn prices of the Napoleonic Wars were stimulating a wave of Parliamentary enclosures in the northern chalkland parishes of Hertfordshire found that only Ickleford had not shown evident improvement in production and an increase in land values. Improvements had been noted at Norton, Offley, Lilley, Weston and Tring. Barkway and Reed were in the process of being enclosed and St Ippolyts and the Wymondleys were shortly to be enclosed in 1811.

Where enclosure had not taken place, as at Therfield, farmers complained of the sheep grazing on arable land and spoke of having to bribe the parish flock-master to keep sheep off the crops. At remaining open-field parishes like Hitchin, grazing was strictly controlled by a court leet[9] which met in the first two decades of the nineteenth century to determine grazing on the commons and on the meadows by the River Purwell that were grazed as Lammas Land. Here, the grass was cut for hay before Old Lammas Day (August 1st) after which animals were allowed to graze on the aftermath. Common grazing survived in several parts of the county from Patmore Heath at Albury near Bishops Stortford, where an area of acid land was left for common grazing, to the hilltop commons of the west of the county where Berkhamsted, Northchurch and Aldbury all possessed common land in significant quantities. On arable land there was no case at all for retaining communal rights of access, and rights of common to collect firewood or turves from the hedges and field edges were discontinued whenever possible.

Even before the onset of pipe drainage, it is probably significant that it was on the clays of mid and south Hertfordshire that piecemeal enclosure was first carried out. Open fields survived longest in the northern parishes where chalk lying immediately under the topsoil makes drainage of any kind unnecessary. On the ridge-top parishes like Clothall, Wallington and Sandon, the southern halves of the parishes lay on the clay that caps the chalk and were enclosed early

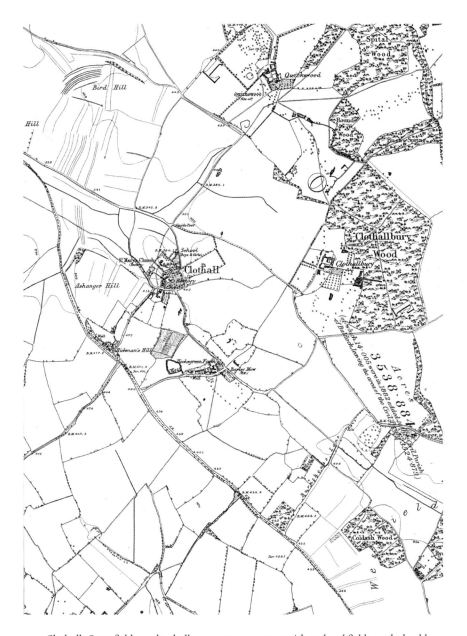

3.4 Clothall. Open fields on the chalk escarpment contrast with enclosed fields on the boulder-clay where drainage was needed (OS map 1881 VIII SW)

and farmed in severalty. The northern halves of each parish lying on the scarp slope, which is long and gentle east of the Hitchin gap, is virtually bare chalk, needing no drainage. They were left as open-field or 'champion' long into the nineteenth century.

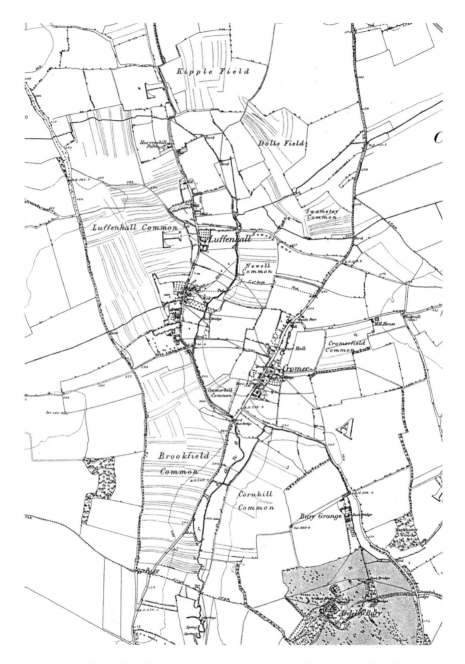

3.5 Open fields in the Luffenhall area. Amazingly the open fields of this small hamlet near Stevenage still survive to this day but, in these days of prairie farming, they do not stand out in the landscape (OS map 1881 XIII NE)

The actual process of enclosure did not necessarily either add to or detract from the number of land owners. Some small proprietors of land in the open fields, while not resisting enclosure wished to avoid the expenses of having to fence off their holdings and sold out to a larger neighbour taking advantages of increased land prices to obtain capital to set up a business or to provide the working capital for a tenanted farm.

The Pirton enclosure of 1818,[10] for example, contains about fifty names of proprietors. Some were absentee landowners but many of them were modestly endowed residents of the parish. They did not comprise anything like a majority of Pirton's population nor was their number seriously diminished by enclosure itself. In 1830 there were still forty-one payers of land tax and the number who considered that their main occupation was farming did not diminish. A number of those listed as proprietors can be positively identified as a blacksmith, a carpenter and several proprietors of cottages. Pirton was an open parish with no one, all-powerful owner of either farmland or houses. A number of small proprietors invested in cottage property which could be let at a premium to working-class families who found it difficult to find accommodation in more closely regulated parishes. One of the effects of enclosure in parishes like this might have been to create more graduations among the villagers themselves by establishing differences between a middle class of small proprietors, such as innkeepers and tradesmen, over a larger group of propertyless farm workers.

It may seem surprising that open-field agriculture, with all its disadvantages, persisted so long not in remote or backward parishes but in extensive areas of arable land near to the towns. The explanation must surely be not that the benefits of enclosure in terms of agricultural efficiency and rising land values were not realised but that the process of enclosure of some arable land near to the towns was more difficult.

Even after the extensive Parliamentary enclosure of farmland that took place during the Napoleonic wars along the north Hertfordshire chalklands, there were still considerable areas of open-field agriculture left. These included the open fields of Hitchin, large parts of Bygrave and Clothall abutting Baldock, Therfield Heath on the outskirts of Royston, those parts of Layston and Aspenden that encroach on Buntingford and, until mid-century, the parish of Ashwell. It should be noted that while Hitchin, an Anglo-Saxon foundation, had considerable lands within the township, Baldock and Royston were both post-Norman medieval foundations with virtually none while Buntingford did not have separate parochial status at all. In those towns the farmland around the

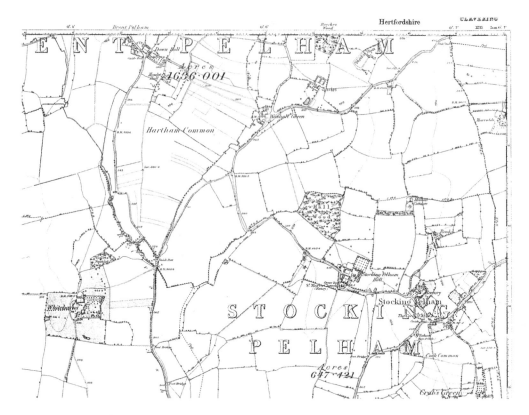

*3.6 Hartham Common, Brent Pelham. A late surviving open-field common in the Pelhams
(OS map 1881 XIV NE)*

township belonged to the adjacent village parishes. In each case however, town-dominated farmland showed a strong tendency to remain open-field country until a very late date. Even in more remote areas of Hertfordshire, considerable areas of open-field farming were still to be found when the first large-scale maps of the county were made in 1881. The remote village of Luffenhall, for example was still largely open field, as was Hartham Common. Brent Pelham, and even the neighbouring village of Stocking Pelham, which was mostly enclosed, showed a field pattern that indicated that the enclosure had taken the form of a modification of the open-field strip system, remnants of which could still be seen.

Nonetheless it is clear that much open-field agriculture remained around some towns. Possibly the explanation is that in a village parish it took no more than two or three landowners working in concert to bring about enclosure whether by private arrangement or by act of Parliament. Once they had decided to go ahead there was little that lesser landowners and even less that landless

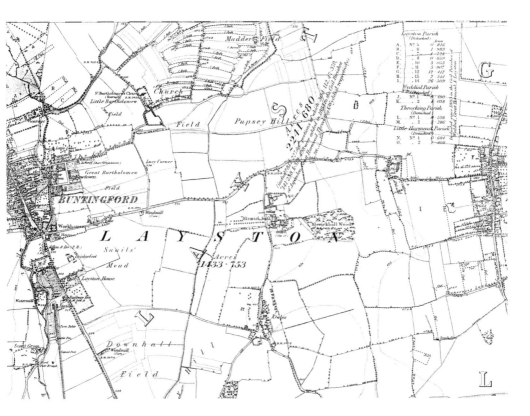

3.7 The Buntingford area. Open fields surviving near a small town. Buntingford itself was something of an anomaly. While not being a parish in its own right, Buntingford occupied the land of surrounding parishes. Landowners found it more difficult to enclose land where there was a multiplicity of small occupiers. This map illustrates the administrative nightmare that sometimes faced the enclosure commissioners of open fields when no less than four separate parishes were involved in a jumble of cultivation strips in the open fields: Layston, Wyddial, Throcking, and Little Hormead (OS map 1881 XIV NW)

villagers could do to stop the process, even if they wished to do so. The reaction of the lesser residents was more likely to be to try to collect their share rather than to mount an operation to stop the scheme itself. As the map of the Buntingford area in 1881 shows, the sheer complexity of boundaries where individual strips out in the fields could be in totally different parishes (in this case Layston, Wyddial, Throcking and Little Hormead), the process must have created an administrative nightmare that would have proved an obstacle to any would-be encloser.

Nearer to a town, the smooth and successful carrying out of an enclosure scheme might be more difficult. The tradesmen and craftsmen of a small town might be humble in status compared to a great landowner but were far less personally dependent than were the poor of a village. Not even a wealthy landowner could afford to outrage public opinion too far. The political roles of the two might indeed be reversed. The respectable shopkeepers of Ampthill, angry at the Duke of Bedford's enthusiasm for the French Revolution once put up posters saying 'Down with the Jacobin Duke!' Landowners with political aspirations did not wish to court unpopularity and risk some pet project becoming a humiliating fiasco. This could happen if the outraged locals happened to find a determined leader who might even be a rival landowner determined to put a spoke in the wheel of his neighbour. This happened at Berkhamsted in 1866 when a neighbouring landowner, Augustus Smith, went out of his way to wreck Lord Brownlow's plans to enclose Berkhamsted Common.[11]

Also, much of the debate about enclosure has emphasised the contrast between the two systems. The point is often lost that the two methods of land division co-existed for many years. Thanks to the Hertfordshire tradition by which the land of a parish was divided not merely into three but into six open fields as at Hitchin or nine (at least) at King's Walden it was fairly common for open-field to co-exist with limited enclosure within a single parish.[12]

Sometimes a parish would be divided into a largely open-field portion and an enclosed portion. As has been noted, when this was the case it was usually the open-field portion that abutted a built-up area. Aspenden in east Hertfordshire is a case in point. At the time of the 1843 Tithe Survey,[13] the parish was divided into a largely enclosed western area which comprised three large farms known as Buttermilk, Tannis and Barksdon Green. The eastern third of the parish was divided into at least ten open fields, known locally as 'commons', each in its turn sub-divided into cultivated strips.

At that date the largest landowner was Sir Henry Lushington, a retired judge of the Indian judiciary, who occupied 944 acres at Aspenden Hall. His estate was divided into four tenanted farms, two enclosed farms, Buttermilk, tenanted by Robert Clarke with 498 acres and Tannis, with John Overill with 209 acres. Two other farms, How Green (John Sibley with 41 acres) and the Home Farm (Matthew Woodward with 134 acres) were largely made up of accumulated strips in the 'commons' at the east end of the village. This land was enclosed in 1869 by one of the few enclosure acts to include a railway – the Ware, Hadham and Buntingford, which became part of of the Great Eastern Railway. The reference book compiled when the railway was planned in 1857[14] gives some indication of the type of person who occupied land in the open fields, each of whom had to be compensated when the line crossed his particular strip, within an open field called Windmill Field.

If the open-field system had been the last bastion of peasant agriculture one might have expected the tenanted occupation of the land, if not its outright ownership, to be widely dispersed among the community. Whatever had been the case in the past, this had ceased to be so in 1857. At that time fourteen of the thirty-eight strips in this open field were owned by Sir Henry Lushington, the largest landowner in the parish. Others belonged to the propertied families of the district such as the Sworders of Buntingford or William Butt of Corneybury or were part of the vicarial glebe. The tenancies of the rented strips are even more revealing. Twenty of the thirty-eight were rented by Sarah Woodward, who can be identified as the eighty-year-old mother of a farmer, Joseph Woodward. Others were rented by Joseph Woodward himself and by John Crouch, also a farmer. One strip was owned by George Micklem, a Buntingford tanner who rented it out as allotments to Aspenden and Buntingford residents. Only four strips can be identified as belonging to humbler locals such as John and William Body (millers) or Sarah Bunce (beerseller) who held the land in hand for personal cultivation. Small scale family cultivation still existed here but was very much a minority activity.

Nevertheless, open-field farming at least offered the possibility for the modest citizen to acquire a piece of arable land to cultivate on his own account in the manner of an allotment. Thus the open fields did survive, not only around Buntingford, but around most of the market towns in this part of the county. Unless there was a formal enclosure, the open-field system faded out gradually. It is not even clear when it finally disappeared. As late as 1919, the Corneybury estate, a large and well-equipped farm just north of Buntingford, was sold subject to the right of communal sheepwalk on Dowhall Field every third year after harvest.

The existence of an enclosure act affecting an extensive area of a parish has usually been taken to imply that the parish made an abrupt change from open-field to enclosed farming at that date. This may frequently have been the case but by no means always. At Offley for example, where an act of 1817 re-allocated 5,135 acres, the process of enclosure seems to have been already virtually complete. Mutual agreements to enclose land at the eastern end of the parish date from the seventeenth century while a survey of 1807 indicates that most of the land had been enclosed by that date.[15] The progress of the enclosure bill seems extraordinarily leisurely. The survey was produced in 1807 by a Thomas Brown.

A meeting to promote a bill was held in the church in April 1813 and the final apportionment, also by Thomas Brown, was made in 1819.[16]

It may be wondered, what was the purpose of lengthy and expensive legal proceedings if the actual enclosure had largely been carried out? The reason was, not so much to eliminate open fields and replace them with enclosed land, but to legitimise a highly complex arrangement of exchanges and sales and to get rid of outdated nuisances such as the tithe which was normally commuted into a substantial grant of land.

Typically, the Offley enclosure was the initiative of the major landowners and in this case it was supported by the larger tenant farmers. Much of the work was done by a Hitchin attorney, William Wilshere, himself a landowner whose main estates were away to the south at Welwyn. The initial notice of enclosure was signed on behalf of John Sowerby, a major land owner of Putteridge Bury, Lilley; along with John Bates, an Offley farmer who possessed only twelve acres of Offley freehold; Archdeacon Willes, also a landowner but representing the Bishop of Lincoln (then the local diocese) and William Wilshere representing Frederick Delme Radcliffe of Hitchin Priory, the most substantial landowner in the Hitchin area. It seems that the Reverend Lynch Burroughs, incumbent and tenant for life of the largest estate in Offley, was not directly involved at this stage. As a clerical incumbent, his status was that of the permanent vassal of the Bishop of Lincoln, whose interests were represented by Archdeacon Willes.

There were some twenty landowners in Offley. The largest, Lynch Burroughs, was vicar and tenant of a settled estate of 2,292 acres which amounted to forty-three per cent of the parish. The other substantial owners were Sowerby of Lilley with 939 acres, Radcliffe of Hitchin with 586 acres and Richard Sheppard of Little Offley with 495 acres. Four men therefore owned eighty per cent of the land of this parish.

It is hardly surprising that they got their way once they decided to co-operate. The difficulties were more in the way of patiently unravelling bureaucracy and legal red tape at Westminster than in overcoming opposition with the village itself, as the expenses incurred by William Wilshere testify. They amounted to £4,708, over sixty per cent of which went to 'ingrossing the bill' in both Houses of Parliament, in fees to surveyors, expenses of commissioners and printing costs, not to mention handouts to messengers, doorkeepers and other endemic hangers-on of the nineteenth-century legal process. The process of enclosure was not cheap.

The poor of the parish were not ignored in this process. The reason they come to notice, however, was not so much that they possessed rights which entitled them to a share of the land. Their value was rather that, in an age that put a high regard on local custom, the opinion of some of them was of value in applying local legal rights for their more fortunate neighbours.

The process of enclosure sheds some light on agricultural practice as it had been in the days of open fields. At Offley, depositions from elderly farm workers were taken to establish which tenant farmers had been accorded the right, by parish custom, of pasturing their animals on the commons and on the field baulks. In this connection, John Pipkin, resident at The Folly, Offley for thirty-five years, was prepared to affirm that farmers Cook and Dean had the right to pasture their cattle on Webber Field in the fallow season and their sheep on the common. John Joiner, a resident of forty-six years' standing was prepared to attest to a whole list of tenant farmers with the right to graze animals on the common. Richard Sheppard of Little Offley, a large freehold farm in the extreme north of the parish claimed the right, which others said had long lapsed, to graze animals on the Hoo, a common at the southern end of the main village, some two miles from his farmstead. Counsel's opinion was sought but the opinion, when obtained, merely threw the matter back upon local custom.

The respect accorded to humble witnesses such as Pipkin and Joiner, when they came to testify before the Commissioners at the Red Lion public house, goes some way to explain why enclosure went through with such little popular unrest. The testators were not without moral courage. They were quite prepared on occasion to attest that some local farmers had not got the right to pasture cattle on the common. Unlike the depositions of their social superiors who were entirely concerned with claiming their own legal rights, the humble witnesses were prepared to stand up for the rights of others and sometimes to boldly disavow the pretended claims of some of those more influential than themselves. Compared with the grand claimants whose whole concern was to secure broad acres in return for the surrender of prestigious but sometimes highly debatable privileges, such as the right to impropriate a greater or a lesser tithe, the claims of the poor were models of objective and disinterested public spirit. Indeed, there was, after all, very little in it for them. If humble residents of long standing were able to discriminate between the rights of neighbours more affluent and powerful than themselves and have their knowledge of local custom accepted by the enclosure commissioners, it implies that the whole procedure was rooted in long accepted rights, inequitable though those rights may have been.

The depositions of persons of higher social status like Radcliffe, Sowerby,

Lynch Burroughs or Hale rarely, if ever, refer to the rights of other people, and were invariably claims for property or for rights of grazing or tithe that could be turned into property. The depositions of the poor were seldom assertions of private privilege. They had few privileges to assert and their statements were of interest only insofar as they provided evidence of local custom. They gave statements of what they regarded as fair and hallowed by long tradition in an intensely deferential society where vast inequities were taken for granted. It may seem naïve to point to the greedy rich contrasted with the diligent and honest poor who were only anxious to be fair and claimed little for themselves – but that is the impression that prevails.

It would be unwise to make too much of the fact that a few elderly villagers were persuaded to vouch for customs that mainly benefited their social superiors. The witnesses who spoke out were not entirely altruistic. The mere fact that a villager was called to give evidence helped to establish the fact that he was a man entitled to some consideration. However poor he may have been, he was a man of the village not a vagrant. That was worth something, but it does not alter the fact that the rights of the rich and the rights of the poor were treated in quite different ways.

The final settlement here, as elsewhere, did not adequately reflect the petty rights of the poor to pasture their solitary cattle or to cultivate an allotment as of right. At best, they qualified only for some village charity by which a portion of the land was allocated for the benefit of the poor but was not directly available for their use. Such charity lands were usually administered by trustees, frequently local clergy, made over as rented land to a neighbouring farmer and the proceeds used to finance a modest village charity. As the beneficiaries of such a charity were normally nominated by the trustees, the system was easily transposed into yet another means of social control by the rich over the poor.

Here, as elsewhere, the claims of the poor were recognised, but interpreted with punctilious exactitude to make sure that no one got a yard more than he was entitled to. Expenses were costed to a penny, and no one was allowed to dodge his share. The claims of the rich, by contrast, were treated with a genial liberality. Lynch Burroughs gave up his possession of the tithe which was virtually a right to collect a private tax but one that could make him unpopular with his neighbours. He received not only broad acres of farmland but also all of Westbury Wood with some fifty acres of good timber with valuable rights to game and coppice wood to sell as firewood – a much more satisfactory arrangement.

The enclosure movement did not create new inequalities. The lack of socal unrest during the process would indicate that the inequalities were accepted. Enclosure may not have created inequality, but it may well have perpetuated it by setting the seal on a rigid hierachy that already existed.

References

1. Roden, D., 'Field Systems of the Chilterns' in Baker, A.R.H. and Butlin, R.A., *Field Systems of the British Isles*, 1973, pp. 325–74.
2. Hatfield Tithe Award. HALS DSA4/47, 1838, and D/ERy B292a.
3. Tate, W.E. and Turner, M.E., *Domesday of Enclosures* 'Hertfordshire', 1978, p. 137.
4. Hertfordshire Inventories. HRO *passim*.
5. Radcliffe papers. HALS DER E101.
6. HALS 51084.
7. Young, Arthur, *A General View of the Agriculture of Hertfordshire*, 1804, reprinted 1971.
8. HALS 60953A.
9. Hitchin Court Leet app. to Seebohm, F., *English Village Community*, London, 1884.
10. Pirton Enclosure Award, 1818, HALS 51346.
11. Froude, J.A., *Short Studies on Great Subjects* 'On the Uses of the Landed Gentry', 1877.
12. Roden, op. cit., pp. 329–33.
13. Aspenden Tithe Award, 1845, HALS DSA4/7.
14. HALS WHB Rly ref book and map. D/P8/28/1.
15. Offley Enclosure Map, 1807, QS/E 56.
16. Offley Enclosure Award, 1814, QS/E 55 and HALS 51225–51312.

CHAPTER FOUR

The development of agriculture up to the great depression

I N   S P I T E   O F   M A N Y natural advantages in terms of soil, climate and the proximity of London, Hertfordshire was not regarded as one of the pioneer counties of the first agricultural revolution in the eighteenth century. Only William Ellis of Little Gaddesden[1] made any impact as an agricultural improver of national repute and one foreign observer, Per Kalm from Sweden, was unimpressed with Ellis' abilities as a practical farmer.[2]

A better-known agricultural writer towards the end of the century was Arthur Young who, before he reached either the notoriety of the editorship of *The Annals of Agriculture* or the status of being secretary of the first Board of Agriculture, was tenant of a farm at South Mymms at an early, and not particularly successful, point of his career.

The Board of Agriculture sponsored a series of *General Views* of British agriculture in individual counties. These included an account of Hertfordshire agriculture by David Walker written in 1795[3] and a second, more widely known *General View of the Agriculture of Hertfordshire* written by Arthur Young himself in 1804.[4]

Later, William Marshall included Hertfordshire in his volume on the southeastern counties in 1820 which drew upon and criticised the work of Walker and Young.[5] William Cobbett wrote briefly on Hertfordshire in his *Rural Rides*.[6]

From then on there were no overall surveys until the *Journal of the Royal Agricultural Society of England* published one of their prize essays on the county's farming by Henry Evershed in 1864 with a smaller contribution by Richard Clutterbuck.[7] The best known early Victorian experts on agriculture, Philip Pusey, J.C. Morton and John Claudius Loudon said little about Hertfordshire and James Caird, who published a widely read survey of English agriculture in 1851, visited Hertfordshire but said very little about it apart from an account of the experimental work in fertilisers of John Bennet Lawes at Rothamsted and a brief mention of a

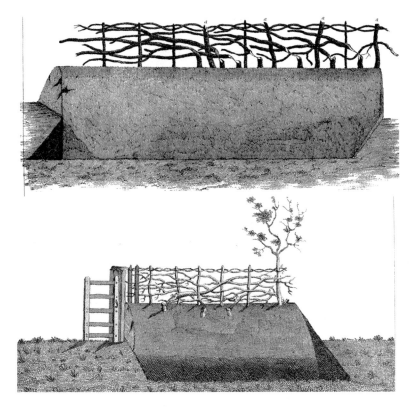

4.1 A Hertfordshire plashed hedge from Arthur Young's A General View of the Agriculture of Hertfordshire, *1804*

wealthy Hertfordshire farmer,[8] Richard Oakley of Lawrence End near Kimpton.

If we can pick out two main themes in the story of Hertfordshire agriculture in the course of the nineteenth century it is that, in common with the other arable counties, farming made increasing use of scientific method and also became increasingly market-orientated. The pictures of farming painted by Walker and Young in the early 1800s and Evershed and Clutterbuck in the middle of that century illustrate the progress of these two developments.

Some application of scientific method had occurred by the time Walker and Young were writing. Young describes extensive experimentation with crop rotation. In Hertfordshire this was loosely based on the classic 'Norfolk' four-course rotation of roots, barley, clover and wheat but included oats, other forage crops and bare fallows. Field drainage in the eighteenth century was a matter of trenches and stone-lined gulleys, and machinery had not developed beyond the great Hertfordshire wheel plough and the harrow. Only a few landowners, such as Lady Lamb at Brocket experimented with corn drills instead of sowing corn broadcast. Already horses were by far the most common draft animal in Hertfordshire, although oxen were still in use on some farms. Surprisingly, oxen survived not on small peasant holdings but on the extensive properties such as the Sebright estate at Beechwood near Flamstead, by Mr Cass-Major, a wealthy West Indian merchant who had set up an estate at North Mymms, and on the farm of Mr Doo at Bygrave which at 1,000 acres was the largest farm in the county. Presumably teams of oxen needed considerable capital outlay and were beyond the means of lesser farmers. Oxen were the caterpillar tractors of the pre-industrial age.

Walker makes the point that farming on the open fields was not significantly different in technique from farming on enclosed land, although the practice of pasturing animals on stubble must have made it difficult for a farmer to vary his crop rotations under the open-field system. The supposedly wasteful practice of 'bare-fallowing' outlasted the open fields and was still continued on some enclosed farms such as on the Hale estates at Kings Walden in the 1830s.[9] When Lane Farm was sold in 1831 valuers found that thirty-five acres out of 256 were under 'tillage' – repeated ploughings and harrowing of uncropped fields over the summer to eliminate deep-rooted perennial weeds. Bare fallows were often followed by turnips or swedes, root crops which could be repeatedly horse-hoed thus further discouraging weed growth. In an age without herbicides, there was no alternative to the occasional summer fallow to control perennial weeds, particularly on heavy lands.[10]

The mainstay of arable farming in the county was the cultivation of cereal crops, particularly wheat and barley. Wheat was normally sown in the autumn and barley in the spring. Early in the century, a bearded wheat called 'Rivetts' was popular. By mid-century it had been replaced by 'Red Lammas', a wheat introduced from Cambridgeshire partly because its straw was highly suitable for straw plaiting. Barley, grown mainly for the malt trade, was the second most profitable crop. Maltings were to be found in most Hertfordshire towns with the biggest concentration in the south-east around Bishops Stortford, Sawbridgeworth and Ware. Oats were far less important. Some farmers, like Abel Sharpe at Maidencroft near Hitchin, giving evidence to a parliamentary committee in 1837, said he grew hardly any.[11] John Church at Woodside Farm, Hatfield[12] grew only enough to feed his own horses. The Hoo Farm at Kimpton[13] produced wheat, barley, clover, beans and turnips in the harvest of 1869 but not oats. It is possible that the production of oats was influenced by the railways. The acreage

4.2 A barn at Tring.
Apart from purpose-built farmsteads on the larger estates, it is probable that most
Hertfordshire farmers went through the century with a mixed set of farm buildings. The
valuation of Mrs Cracherode's estate at Wymondley in 1803[14] describes the Bury Farm as
having timber stables and cowhouses, both tiles and thatch, a brick and tile dovecote and a
timber and tiled granary. The farmhouse was partly brick and partly timber frame. There was
also a corn barn of timber with an oak threshing floor between two double doors. This was so
that the threshers with their flails could work between the unthreshed corn stack at one end of
the barn and the thrashed straw at the other while the wind blew the chaff away through the
double doors as they worked. Another farm on the estate, Delamere, at Great Wymondley
had similar buildings. Some farms had barns for each crop. In 1864 a farm at Westmill
was described as having separate barns for wheat, barley, oats and pease

of oats at Berkhamsted in 1837 was about equal to that of barley. As this was the
first part of the county to have a direct rail connection with London, it is possible that farmers were growing oats to sell to the London market as well as for the
needs of local horses. The slightly wetter climate of western Hertfordshire may
have had some bearing on the choice of cereal crop by farmers in this area. Peas,
the most important of the legumes, were more extensively grown than oats.
Other legumes were beans, clover, tares and, for a time, sainfoin which had a
period of intense popularity on the Knebworth estates in the 1890s. Turnips

were grown mainly for sheep feed and were an important component in the four-course rotation.[15]

Hertfordshire does not seem to have had any particularly distinctive style of farm buildings. Although there were many adequate and sound buildings in the county, particularly on the larger estates, there is little evidence that any of them were outstanding. When John Bailey Denton, a well known surveyor and engineer resident at Graveley near Stevenage, wrote what would now be called a coffee table book, the *Farm Homesteads of England*, in 1864[16] none of the examples in this lavishly illustrated book were taken from Hertfordshire apart from a brief reference mentioned in the appendix to sheep houses put up by Richard Oakley at Lawrence End.

Farm buildings were usually made of local materials at this date although the importation of materials was increasing. A specification for Hoo Farm at Whitwell on the Brand estates in 1800 mentions slates and timber, presumably imported, as coming from London as well as lime from Maidencroft and bricks from Rabley Heath near Codicote. Imported timber was frequently used for farm buildings even when house building had largely abandoned the tradition of the timber frame. The specification in 1873 for a new barn at Great Hallingbury, just over the Essex border, calls for the best Memel pine imported from the Baltic.[17]

Farm buildings at the end of the century were essentially developments of the earlier pattern. The two farms on the Stagenhoe estate which changed hands in 1893 also possessed stables, five bay cow houses, and barns but also shelter accommodation for carts and farm implements and machinery. Neither Stagenhoe Bottom Farm nor Stagenhoe Park Farm was adapted for milk production so there was no special dairy.[18]

The Tithe Survey

A series of parish reports on agriculture were made following the Tithe Commutation Act of 1836. In Hertfordshire 138 districts were investigated and seventy-nine reports completed between 1837 and 1845.[19] They do not completely cover the county. The northern chalklands are under-represented because it was here that most Enclosure Acts were carried out and the tithe issue was frequently done away with under these Acts. The written reports vary greatly in completeness and insight. There is an element of randomness arising from casual comment. Wheat for example, although known to be the most important crop in the

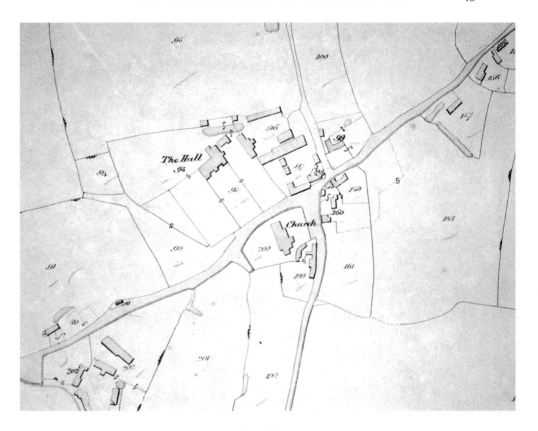

4.3 Extract from Brent Pelham tithe map, 1839.
Tithe maps were made as a result of the Tithe Commutation Act 1836 which converted the right of collecting tithes in kind into a monetary levy. They were only made in those parishes that had not dealt with the tithe issue by means of an Enclosure Act, in most cases because the parish concerned had already been enclosed in times immemorial. Where they exist, and they are available for about half of Hertfordshire's parishes, they provide an accurate survey of the parish and information for each parcel of land regarding ownership, the name of the occupier (usually a tenant), and the nature of land use – primarily arable, pasture or woodland. They sometimes provide useful data regarding public highways and rights of way

county, is mentioned only twice, while turnips, which were seen as evidence of a progressive attitude to crop rotations, are mentioned sixty-one times. Again, when forestry plantations are mentioned it is not always clear from the text whether it means extensive woodland planting as a major economic activity as at Hexton or merely a few shelter belts as at Willian.

Nevertheless the tithe reports present a more comprehensive parish by parish account than anything else we possess in the course of Hertfordshire agriculture and furthermore they were made just as the agricultural revolution was entering the decades of mid-century prosperity.

The basic pattern is familiar. It confirms the impression of the corn-growing north and the hay-producing south of the county. It mentions hay being sent into London from as far north as Ardeley while conversely it is surprising that one place that complained of difficulties in importing London manures was the important river port of Ware on the Lea. This may of course have meant that the volume of trade was putting a strain on port facilities rather than that the supply was deficient in the first place.

Only three parishes were singled out as places of marked improvement in productivity. These were Throcking, Standon and Wyddial – all three recently enclosed parishes on east Hertfordshire boulder clay. 'Chalking', a much older form of improvement, is only mentioned in the case of Bovingdon in the far west.

The practice of 'high farming', i.e. a high ratio of capital to acreage, is only mentioned in the cases of Hatfield, Radwell, Shenley and Wallington. It is difficult to know what to make of this particular set of parishes. Hatfield, the largest in area of any parish in the county, had both arable and grassland areas and was dominated by the mighty Cecil estates. Tiny Radwell on the clay vale in the north is virtually an extension of the larger Bedfordshire village of Stotfold, while Wallington, high on the chalk was a two-farm, corn-growing parish entirely owned by one small estate. Finally, Shenley, on the Middlesex border to the south, was a hay-growing parish typical of the London clay. High farming was often cited by agricultural pundits like James Caird as a way in which the more affluent farmer could prosper in the free trade years after the abolition of the Corn Laws in 1846. It was not of course open to the farmer without access to working capital.

'Low farming', implying a more laid-back attitude that failed to invest sufficient funds, was identified at St Albans, Ayot St Peter, Wyddial, Brent Pelham and Shenley again. It is not easy to make much of this assortment either except to note that Ayot St Peter was also criticised for adopting a wasteful five-course rotation.

The three-course rotation was also held up for criticism as it was redolent of the old open-field system which dispensed with root crops and legumes. There were twelve of these: Aspenden, Bovingdon, Bushey, Buckland, Clothall, Measden, Sawbridgeworth, Stocking Pelham, Standon, Therfield, Thundridge and Widdial. All of these either possessed residual open fields or were hay-growing parishes.

4.4 Mowing

4.5 Haymaking

The tithe records do shed some light on the general productivity of agriculture at this period. Wheat accounted for about twenty three per cent of the acreage and barley about twenty per cent. Wheat commanded a higher price but yields for barley were often higher which meant that the profitabilty of the two main cereals was about the same. Oats, in some districts, rivalled the acreage of barley but was far less profitable. It was necessary as a forage crop for horses. Rye barely gets a mention at this date.

Apart from the production of hay on the London clay of the southern parishes specialist cropping was rare in Hertfordshire. Young mentions cherry growing around Sarratt and Kings Langley in 1804[20] but Clutterbuck[21] remarked in 1864 that the acreage of orchards had not increased in the railway age. The railways had brought much more suitable areas in reach of the capital. He put down the lack of interest to Hertfordshire's propensity to sudden winter frosts.

Even on the hay-belt of the south, some farms produced cereal crops as well as grass. Kendall Pound Farm at Aldenham in 1805 was almost equally divided between twenty-four acres of hay grass and twenty-seven acres of arable land growing eleven acres of wheat, ten acres of oats and three acres each of barley and pease. Water cress was something of a Hertfordshire speciality and greater awareness of public health had encouraged the development of cultivated cress beds sited on springs as opposed to collecting the cress from often polluted stream beds. According to Clutterbuck[22] the first cress beds in Hertfordshire were established at West Hyde near Rickmansworth on the River Colne in the 1850s. A specialist cress grower is also recorded in the 1851 census of Whitwell on the river Mimram in St Paul's Walden parish. Cress beds appeared along most of the many chalk streams of the county including the Lea at Lemsford and the northward flowing Purwell at Walsworth.

Market gardening did not develop in Hertfordshire to the extent that it did in some neighbouring counties with the possible exception of the lower Lea Valley. Even so this was largely a development of the later decades of the century and will be discussed in connection with the agricultural depression of that period.

After the uncertainties of the 1830s and 40s, the picture of Hertfordshire agriculture in the 1860s painted by Evershed and Clutterbuck in the Royal Agricultural Society's prize essays of 1864 was one of confident prosperity. Evershed drew a distinction between the light lands – the river gravels and the London Clay of the south and the heavy boulder clays and clays with flints that capped the underlying chalk in the bulk of the county.[23]

On the light lands, the common rotation was roots, clover, wheat, possibly oats and a root crop which by this date could be swedes, mangles or white turnips. Horse hoes made by such firms as Garretts of Leiston were used to

4.6 Thatching a hayrick

eliminate weeds between the rows of root crops so that the practice of bare fallowing was no longer necessary to get rid of perennial weeds. Heavy dressings of
London manures, guano from Peru and the new artificial fertiliser superphosphate developed by Lawes of Rothamsted in the 1840s were spread on the root
crops.

After sheep had been folded on the land to feed directly on the root crops,
barley was sown in the spring. Two varieties. 'Chevalier' and 'Long-eared Nottingham' were popular. Legumes such as clover were often sown with the cereal
and left after harvest until the following summer when the land was ploughed
and drilled with wheat in the autumn. This also was dressed with guano which
with the nitrate that leguminous crops help to build up in the soil provided a fertile tilth for the wheat.

On the heavier lands, rotations of fallow, barley, clover, wheat, oats or roots
were common. Heavy land had to be ploughed frequently to keep down trouble-
some annual weeds like charlock which meant that bare fallowing was never
entirely dispensed with even at this date.

Even in 1864, it was coming to be felt that fields were often too small for efficient agriculture, and hedgerow timber was preventing the uniform ripening of
the crops. The arguments in favour of prairie farming were already beginning to
be heard.

4.7 Finance and fertiliser: an advertisement from the Herts Mercury *of 19 April 1873*

On the chalk of northern Hertfordshire the fields were already large and the transition from open fields to enclosures together with the retention of open fields in some parishes meant that farmers were not hampered by excessive hedges. This region between Hitchin and Royston was cultivated with a combination of wheat growing and sheep farming and once the enclosure question had been sorted out there was no longer a conflict between the two. The use of London manures brought by the Royston and Hitchin Railway of 1851 increased productivity on the thin chalk soils.

It would seem from Evershed's account that the changes that had brought about prosperity – the use of artificial or imported fertilisers, field drainage and the spread of railways had served mainly to accentuate trends that were already there. He does briefly mention the embryonic milk trade into London by rail but implies that this was more or less confined to the Hatfield area. In some counties this was to prove a lifeline for farmers in the great depression but, as we shall see, this did not happen in Hertfordshire on a large scale.

Evershed mentions one Hertfordshire example of the mid-Victorian sanitarian's dream of harnessing the efficient disposal of town sewage to the productivity of the land. Reformers such as Edwin Chadwick had long considered that it should be possible to solve the problem of sanitation in the towns by establishing extensive sewerage systems to remove effluent. The problem was to remove the effluent without fouling the rivers and the obvious solution was to spread the sewage on the land.

He describes an experiment whereby the Earl of Essex had set up a system at Cassiobury Park by which sewage from nearby Watford was spread on the farmland by the action of a stationary steam engine in order to produce heavy crops of grass and hay.

Steam power was used on the other side of the county by an incoming entrepreneur, John Prout, who used steam-driven mole-ploughs to drain and plough land at Sawbridgeworth to produce heavy crops of wheat. He seems to have been an example of a well-known figure in Victorian agriculture – the wealthy businessman who came on to the land bent on showing the stick-in-the-mud farmers how to prosper by the dynamic use of industrial methods. J.J. Mechi, a maker of patent razors, who set up in farming at Tiptree in Essex and then published his experiences together with his accounts,[24] was a well-known example. Mechi eventually failed in his farming enterprise but Prout survived to have his achievements cited by a Royal Commission on the 1870s depression in agriculture as a shining example to his fellows.

The reality of the agricultural depression of the 1870s is not to be doubted. The decline in wheat production is evidence of that. Not many farmers actually went bankrupt but profits diminished and, in parts of the county, landlords had to remit part of the rents.

It was not however a technical problem. The Corn Law crisis of the 1840s had been to an extent an economic problem curable by more efficient methods. Corn prices had gone down after the repeal of the Corn Laws in 1846 but not catastrophically. By the 1850s farmers had made use of new fertilisers and drainage techniques which had combined with the steadily growing market of British cities to create an unheralded prosperity in the 1850s and 60s that was never to be repeated in an agriculture unsuppported by state protection. All went well as long as there was no stockpile of surplus foodstuffs overseas. With the coming of low American wheat prices and the onset of freezing and chilling techniques for meat this was no longer the case.

No amount of superior technology or investment could enable the Hertfordshire farmer to withstand the really formidable overseas competition presented by the prairie farmers of North America. The problem of how to deal with that was not so much a technical problem as a social one. Was the Hertfordshire farmer so entrenched in a rigid system of agriculture and so burdened by having to support an affluent landowner class (whose attitudes the farmer largely shared or, at any rate, did not publicly challenge) as to be incapable of adapting to conditions of free trade in a cheap-food economy when depression finally struck? That question will be discussed later in Chapter Fourteen.

References

1. Ellis, William, *Chiltern and Vale Farming Explained*, 1733, and *The Modern Husbandman*, 1750.
2. Kalm, Per, *An Account of Unusual Things in England* trans. Joseph Lucas, 1748.
3. Walker, David, *Report on Hertfordshire*, Board of Agriculture, 1795.
4. Young, Arthur, *A General View of the Agriculture of Hertfordshire*, 1804, reprinted 1971.
5. Marshall, David, *Rural economy of the South-eastern Counties*, 1820.
6. Cobbett, William, *Rural Rides*, 1912 ed.
7. Evershed, Henry, 'Agriculture of Hertfordshire' and Clutterbuck, J., 'Notes on Hertfordshire', County Prize Essays in *JRASE*, 1864, pp. 269 and 302.
8. Caird, James, *English Agriculture*, 1851.
9. HALS Hale papers 58884: Wilshere to Hale, 2 Aug 1832.
10. HALS Wilshere papers 55885.
11. SC on the State of Agriculture 1836. BPP 1837 V. Evidence of Abel Sharpe, p. 224.
12. Coppock, J.T., 'Agricultural Change in the Chilterns' in Perry, P.J., *British Agriculture 1875–1914*, London, 1973.
13. HALS Brand Dacre papers 40682.
14. HALS Wilshere papers 60953A.
15. HALS Knebworth papers 57440 also 22929, 33139–46, 57392.
16. Denton, John Bailey, *Farm Homesteads of England*, 1864.
17. HALS D/E P10 P15.
18. Stagenhoe papers, 1893.
19. PRO IR 3250.
20. Young, op. cit.
21. Clutterbuck, op. cit.
22. ibid.
23. Evershed and Clutterbuck, op. cit.
24. Mechi, J.J., *How to Farm Profitably*, 1860.

CHAPTER FIVE

Farm machinery in Hertfordshire

W HEN CONSIDERING THE development of agriculture it is important to recognise not only what implements were in existence at any given time but also to appreciate to what extent they were available for sale to the farmer and how widely the implements were in fact actually used. The advancing technology of agriculture can be ascertained from farming textbooks and the technical literature of engineers. An impression of the range of implements on sale in a farming region can be deduced from the advertisements in the local press. The stock of machinery actually in use can be judged partly by commentators but a more rounded picture can be arrived at only by indirect methods such as the occasional farm valuation and the inventories of farm sales where 'dead stock' is sometimes listed. Even here, we do not necessarily know how long before the sale the farmer actually bought the items of equipment listed. In the sixteenth and seventeenth centuries there is a fair amount of data about farm equipment to be gleaned from probate inventories but these are sparse for the eighteenth century onwards. Fortunately, with the spread of local newspapers in the nineteenth century, we can make use of advertisement material of farm sales. These are less detailed than the will inventories, but lists of equipment in advertisements are probably a fair guide to the more prestigious items of farm equipment bought from factories and in use at the time. It is unlikely that an important item would be left out of an advertisement or a flysheet. Mention of a Ransome's harvester or a Howard's plough would serve to attract customers to a farm sale.

Another important difference between seventeenth-century material and nineteenth-century data is that the nineteenth-century farms were usually much bigger. The seventeenth-century probate material often refers to small peasant holdings of less than ten acres possessing a plough, a harrow and hand implements. Holdings of this size were untypical in the nineteenth century.

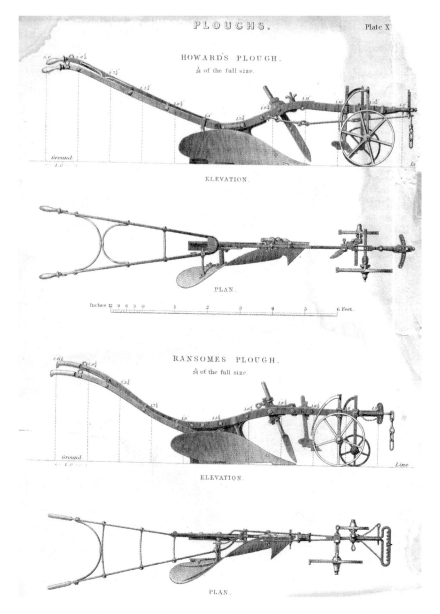

*5.1, 5.2 and 5.3. Some nineteenth-century state-of-the-art farm implements. Howard's of Bed-
ford and Ransome's of Ipswich were leading manufacturers of ploughs. Both exhibited at the
Great Exhibition of 1851. Other machines such as Crosskill's clod crusher from Beverley in the
East Riding of Yorkshire were spreading throughout Britain. More contentious was the new
generation of farm machinery coming in from the USA such as McCormick's and Hussey's
Reapers. British farmers were impressed but, not sharing either the vast acreages or the nor-
mally expensive labour costs of their American counter-parts, were slow to make use of them*
(Morton's Cyclopaedia of Agriculture, *1846[1]*)

REAPING MACHINES.

Plate XXXV

Mc CORMICK'S AMERICAN REAPER.

1/16 of the full size.

Henry Stone del.

HUSSEY'S AMERICAN REAPER.

J.W. Lowry fc.

1/16 of the full size.

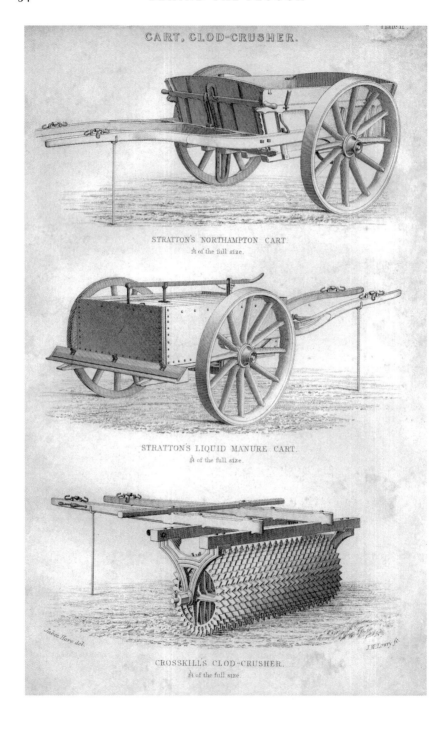

CART, CLOD-CRUSHER.

STRATTON'S NORTHAMPTON CART.
¼ of the full size.

STRATTON'S LIQUID MANURE CART.
¼ of the full size.

CROSSKILL'S CLOD-CRUSHER.
¼ of the full size.

WALLINGTON BURY NEAR BALDOCK,
On the Hitchin, Royston & Cambridge Railway.

IMPORTANT SALE
OF VALUABLE

AGRICULTURAL IMPLEMENTS,
INCLUDING

HORNSBY'S PROGRESS REAPING MACHINE,
HORNSBY'S SWATHE-DELIVERY REAPING
MACHINE,
SAMUELSON'S Self-Acting REAPING MACHINE
BURGESS & KEY'S Screw-Delivery REAPING
MACHINE,
HUNT & PICKERING'S MOWING MACHINE,
BARFORD & PERKINS' STACKING MACHINE,
with horse work under,
BURRELL'S THRESHING MACHINE,
GARRATT'S Combined THRESHING MACHINE,
Nicholson's and *Smith* and *Ashby's* haymaking
machine, *Nicholson's* and *Couch's* dressing machine,
8 narrow-wheel iron armed carts, lamb cart, strong
spring luggage cart, light spring cart, 2 iron-armed
waggons, iron-armed spring van, iron water tank (on
carriage and wheels), *Garratt's (Chambers'* patent)
broad cast manure distributor, and bean and seed drill
with steerage, *Holmes'* clover and seed drill (30 row),
and *Guest's* corn drill, 3 *Howard's* double iron ploughs,
6 iron ploughs, 6 sets of iron harrows, 2 sets of seed
harrows, Norwegian harrow, patent iron harrow (on
wheels), potato washer, 2 *Nunn's* horse hoes for corn
and turnips, *Bentall* and *Hill's* cultivator, 3-share iron
scuffler, *Cambridge's* iron roll, *Croskill's* clod crusher,
iron cylinder land rolls, wood roll, *Perkins'* drag,
hand drags, 2 iron horse rakes, *Nunn's* adjusting rotary
screen, hand barley-hummeler, barn tackle, weighing-
machine and weights, iron and wood pig troughs, cow
cribs, 150 sacks, turnip cutters, pulper, oil-cake breaker,
rick-cloth (20 yards by 18 yards) with poles, &c.,
fagots and hardwood ;
IRON LATHE AND DRILLING MACHINE,
3 MILCH COWS,
17 Well-bred HEIFERS, AND A YOUNG BULL,
TWO WELL-BRED HACKNEYS,
2 STACKS OF CLOVER AND MIXED HAY,
Excellent Double-Seated SOCIAL LANDAU, either
opened or closed; INVALID CHAIR with shafts,
suitable for hand or pony; chaise harness, saddles,
bridles, horse-clothing, *Kase's* FIRE ENGINE, and
numerous effects ;
To be Sold by Auction, by
Mr. GEORGE JACKSON,
ON THE PREMISES, WALLINGTON BURY FARM,
On THURSDAY, May 22nd, 1873, at Ten for Eleven
o'clock, on account of the number and value of the
Lots, by direction of James Smyth, Esq., who is
giving up the farm.

5.4 Machinery sale at Wallington Bury. An advertisement from the Herts Mercury *of 17 May 1873 showing the range of factory-made machines in use on a large farm on the north Hertfordshire arable chalk-lands*

The developments in the eighteenth century had been less well documented than before or after. Ellis speaks of 'Horse Hoeing Husbandry'[2] which implies the existence of the horse hoe but usually seems to have meant little more than the habit of planting crops in rows for easier management. Young[3] in 1804 took a very disparaging view of the great Hertfordshire wheel plough, a massive implement with a wooden beam that could cope with Hertfordshire's heavy, flint-strewn clays. In his day, the lighter swing ploughs were used only along the Essex border. Apart from harrows which were often little more than spiked hurdles there were few other implements. Lady Melbourne at Brocket Park was experimenting with seed drills and Robert Salmon, the land agent of the Woburn estates in Bedfordshire had designed a haymaking machine, which was in use in this county. A few early threshing machines were in use at this time but only a few wealthy farmers like Mr Doo at Bygrave and Mr Greg at Westmill actually possessed one. Neither was probably typical of the county. It may be significant that Mr Doo possessed the largest farm in the county while Mr Greg belonged to a family of industrialists and had close connections with Lancashire cotton industry and all its technical know-how. He had both money and an interest in technology.

Perhaps it is slightly surprising that none of the major nineteenth-century manufacturers of agricultural machinery was based in the county. The best-known firms were not, after all, confined to the major centres of heavy engineering in Britain but were often situated in country towns or even villages. Noted firms during the century included Ransome's of Ipswich, Smith's of Peasenhall and Garrett's of Leiston, (all in Suffolk) Howard's of Bedford and Crosskill's of Beverley. Hertfordshire firms seem to have been content to act as agents of out-county suppliers, although Gatward's of Hitchin advertised locally that they constructed as well as repaired farm machines.[4]

Both the seed drill and the threshing machine were beginning to make headway in the county by the 1830s. The seed drill, which was not seen as a threat to employment, is recorded at Winches Farm, St Albans in 1833, Hill End, Hatfield in 1844 and Lannock Farm, Weston in 1855. In addition a 'seed machine' is reported at Flamstead in 1844 but this could have been a portable seed 'fiddle' rather than a seed drill mounted on wheels.

More controversially, use of the threshing machine was also spreading in the 1820s and 1830s. These were widely seen as direct threats to employment particularly in the winter. The seed drill, needed only in spring and autumn, did not undermine employment at times when jobs were hard to come by. The threshing

5.5 A mechanical reaper. These machines, first developed in the USA, were shown at the Great Exhibition of 1851 at the Crystal Palace in Hyde Park and became widely used on the larger farms of Hertfordshire about that time

machine, on the other hand, threatened the very survival of the worker during the winter months of the year. In some parts of the country threshing machines were frequent targets of the labourers' wrath during the Swing Riots of 1830.

Nevertheless, threshing machines are recorded from Hemel Hempstead in 1836, Ardeley Bury in 1838, Sandridge, Corney Bury near Buntingford in 1844 and Breachwood Green, Sandon and Hertford in 1852. Machine owners began offering their services with travelling machines in the 1840s.

Perhaps it is not surprising, in view of Young's comments on the traditional wooden Hertfordshire wheel plough, that it was the factory-made plough that was most often imported into the county as soon as they became available. Hampshire ploughs were listed at Benington Park and ploughs from Ransome's of Ipswich were listed for a farm at Willian in the 1830s. The Plenty Plough, patented in 1800 and also made in Hampshire was in use at Cassio Bridge, Watford in 1835, and Dell's Turnpoint Wheel Plough was recorded at Kings Langley in 1837.

In the course of the 1840s and 1850s factory-made ploughs spread rapidly. Ransome's ploughs are recorded for Shenley, Widdial, Barley, Sawbridgeworth and Pirton in the 1830s. Davis' wheel plough was used in Hemel Hempstead in 1837 and the Plenty plough was still in use at Charlton in 1850.

Ransome's of Ipswich was evidently the market leader. Their great rival, Howard's of Bedford, was publicised by their appearance at the Great Exhibition of 1851 and their machines are recorded at Three Houses Farm, Knebworth in 1852 and Dog Kennel Farm, Charlton in 1855. A smaller Bedfordshire firm, Hensman of Woburn, was also represented with a plough at Charlton in 1855.

Although these scientifically designed factory ploughs came into common use by mid-century, wooden ploughs of local manufacture still appear in farm inventories right through the century. Mr Kidman of Ramerick near Ickleford was advertising cheap traditional wooden ploughs made by a local craftsman, E.H. Roberts, for as little as £3 in the local press, as late as 1888.

By the 1850s, the most obvious gap in the market was the lack of an effective mechanical reaper. Robert Salmon, the ingenious land agent of Woburn, had invented one early in the nineteenth century but there is little to suggest many local farmers actually invested in one. During the 1840s a Scottish farmer, Patrick Bell, brought out a reaper, but it does not seem to have caught on in the south. At the Great Exhibition of 1851, however, two American models by Cyrus McCormick and Hussey were exhibited and aroused considerable interest among British farmers.

Samuelson, along with Burgess and Key, both of London, manufactured the McCormick reaper under licence in Britain in the 1850s while Crosskill's of Beverley in the East Riding produced the Hussey reaper. Crosskill's clod crusher was already widely used by Hertfordshire farmers.[5]

Burgess and Key reapers were listed in farm inventories at Ludwick Hall, Hatfield Hyde in 1855, Great Hadham and Munden Lordships in 1860, Aston Park in 1865, Darnell's Hall, Weston in 1869, and Wymondley, New Park and Coldharbour farms, Hatfield in 1870. Miss Jane Smith of Bygrave Manor possessed six reapers by Samuelson and Burgess and Key in 1873.

Howard's of Bedford brought out a reaper of their own in 1870 and this was recorded for Breakwater Farm, Stevenage in 1870, by which time George Innes of Royston was offering Samuelson machines for sale. Gatward of Hitchin was selling Burgess and Key machines in 1873 although Perkins, also of Hitchin, claimed to be the sole Hertfordshire agents for Burgess and Key.[6] R.H. Hatton of Aston Park referred to a 4 HP reaper/thresher, also in 1873, which sounds like an early version of a combine harvester, but no details are given.

How widely these sophisticated, factory-made machines were used is difficult to assess. It seems reasonable to conclude that where farm inventories simply state the 'usual machinery' and quote no maker's name for the ploughs,

5.6 Steam on the land. The nineteenth-century steam engine, so invaluable on railways and in factories and mines, was too heavy to be much use on the land. However, both stationary engines and, as in this case, mobile engines in a static position were widely used, particularly towards the end of the century, to power threshing machines or to haul the type of plough shown in the foreground by means of a steel cable. This type of machine would usually belong to an itinerant contractor who visited the larger and more affluent farmers

harrows, scarifiers, etc., the machines were of local manufacture and unremarkable design. Thus there was nothing thought specifically worthy of mention when Edward Hawke gave up Austage End at King's Walden in 1870, or when Westbury Farm was given up at Offley in the same year. There may well have been some advantage to be gained by using machines that were both cheap and could be repaired locally by village craftsmen.

Whatever the immediate motives, it seems clear that the change to mechanisation was gradual. Traditional implements made by local craftsmen co-existed with the sophisticated products of factories in Bedfordshire and Suffolk. Abundant cheap labour meant that the impulse towards mechanisation was leisurely to say the least. It is also difficult to point to any striking development in agriculture that new machinery made possible.

Frequent references to new machinery in farm sales throughout the second half of the century should not blind us to the fact that, in the Victorian age, mechanisation of agriculture was far from complete. The problem of motive power by anything other than the horse was never cracked. Until the development of the internal combustion engine no true field tractor was available to the farmer. Steam traction, with its need for a heavy water-filled boiler, plus a portable reservoir of water readily available and a supply of fuel, made the steam engine impracticable in the field-traversing role. Steam engines could only be used as static engines to draw machines across the land with the aid of cables. The locomotive was too easily bogged down and, even in dry weather, its use caused unwelcome compaction of the soil. It could be used for tillage purposes only by employing a cumbersome cable system. A survey carried out by the Royal Agricultural Society in 1867 revealed just three sets of steam tackle in use in Hertfordshire. True mechanisation had to wait for the internal combustion engine and, as it happened, one of the first field tractors in Britain, if not the very first, was developed just outside the county by Dan Albone of Biggleswade, Bedfordshire, who developed the 'Ivel' tractor in 1904. It was to be many years before the tractor became universal on British farms.

It is possible that technical ingenuity might have produced a light and mobile steam locomotive suitable for use on the land but perhaps the motive was not there. The continued availability of cheap labour during the years of prosperity followed by the economic uncertainties of the depression had meant that the Hertfordshire farmer, unlike his American counterpart, had seen no particular need to economise on labour. Until the twentieth century, farm mechanisation was an optional extra not a necessity.

References

1. *Morton's Cyclopaedia of Agriculture*, Blackie and Son, London, 1846.
2. Ellis, William, *Chiltern and Vale Farming Explained*, 1733, and *The Modern Husbandman*, 1750.
3. Young, Arthur, *A General View of the Agriculture of Hertfordshire*, 1804, reprinted 1971.
4. Examples of farm machinery possessed by Hertfordshire's farmers throughout this chapter are taken from inventories included in advertisements in the leading local newspapers, notably the *Hertford Mercury* and the *Hitchin Gazette*.
5. Fussell, G.E., *The Farmer's Tools*, 1952, p. 88 and p. 162.
6. ibid.

CHAPTER SIX

Rural pauperism

THE PICTURE PAINTED so far of Hertfordshire's agricultural society has been on the whole one of progress. Enclosure, whatever its social
consequences, and it is by no means certain that these were all nega-
tive, did at least promote agricultural efficiency. Almost any enclosed farm could
be run more efficiently than one that consisted mainly of scattered strips of land
in the open fields. Techniques of field drainage, crop rotation and animal breeding could all be employed more effectively under enclosure and this was bound
to increase the prosperity of the land in the long run.

The question must be asked how far this undoubted technical improvement
brought material benefits to the rural community as a whole. In the period we
are considering, only a small minority of the rural population had any control
over any land. It is entirely possible that Hertfordshire had never been a true
peasant society where the majority of the population enjoyed any access to land
to cultivate on their own account. Certainly Hertfordshire had long since ceased
to be a frontier society where land to cultivate could be carved out of the forest
or the waste. If an English countryman wanted that kind of opportunity in the
nineteenth century he had to emigrate. The vast majority had to work for a
living by obtaining employment on land belonging to someone else.

Looking back from the twenty-first century, the lives of rural working people
in the nineteenth century seem harsh, monotonous and poverty stricken. Poverty there certainly was and at best their lives would seem intolerably limited by
the standards of almost any modern society. The existence of a hierarchy of
wealth and status reinforced by attitudes of, by modern standards, extreme deference is also undeniable. (It may well the case that the degree of modern egali-
tarianism that exists today is easily over-estimated by members of a professional
middle class who are no longer the class that is deferred to.) Conversely, much of
the spirit of deference that comes across in the written record may give a

misleading impression. Much of the respect bestowed by the Victorian lower orders on their social betters may well have been more tongue in cheek than we nowadays always appreciate. The Victorian literary classes may well have taken the automatic deference of the workers far too much at face value. Suffice to say that there were intense economic differences between individuals in Victorian rural society and these differences, far from being seriously challenged, were indeed hotly defended at practically every level as legitimate differentials normal and necessary for the well-being of society.

Village society in the past might have had its examples of rugged individualism expressed by those few persons who could afford to maintain an air of independence but, in general, neither the existence of a strong social hierarchy nor its inevitability were seriously challenged. What is more, for practical purposes it was very difficult for individuals to propel themselves out of the class in which they were born and bred. The self-made man certainly existed but was highly exceptional and when he did appear he was not necessarily either emulated by his fellows nor was he accepted socially by members of the upper echelons who were prone to regard the nouveau riche with suspicion.

Whether the lives of the working classes were tolerably happy or not is very difficult to judge at this date. Too many commentators have projected their own political views or social attitudes on to the past. On the one hand radicals have imagined a society seething with social discontent. It is, of course, the case that no revolutionary movement in fact emerged in rural England as it did in France, and really there was very little overt hostility to the ruling classes. This may well be countered by saying that the rural working classes were merely ground into apathy by malnutrition, overwork and drink and adopted a sullen acceptance of their lot. The towns and the colonies provided an opportunity for those who thought otherwise.

On the other hand, there are the neo-conservatives, who, while not denying the poverty, point to the burgeoning opportunities in the industrial districts or the colonies. Their stance implies that those who stayed behind were the naturally deferential or the ultra-conformist who were reconciled to their station in life and saw no prospect of changing it.

(Those same present-day century neo-conservatives, being believers in individual effort and enterprise, would have been considered 'men of advanced views' in nineteenth-century Hertfordshire. They would have been more at home in the radical camp, opposing the Corn Laws and game laws and calling for tenant rights and the reform of the land laws. Conservatives in the nineteenth-century sense of being prepared to defend hereditary status on principle in the mode of Disraeli or Lord Salisbury would have difficulty in being taken seriously today.)

There is a certain amount of credibility in both points of view but, as the literature of the day was almost entirely written by the socially superior, it is unlikely that we shall ever learn the truth. It is common ground to both viewpoints to assert that there was no concerted effort to change society either by violence or otherwise and that the truly discontented nearly always took the opportunity to leave. With America and the other colonies available and the expanding cities of England readily to hand, rural England had no shortage of safety valves in the form of escape routes for the young and determined. The question is rather whether rural society provided a tolerable life for the ordinarily endowed and the normally well-adjusted members of society.

We may not be able to say with certainty whether people were happy with their lot in Hertfordshire but we can try to work out how society managed to carry on and how things compared with life in other parts of the country at that time. One measure of social content in any society is the incidence of actual unrest in terms of crime, sedition or outright revolutionary activity. It cannot be denied that the first part of the nineteenth century was a period of distress and unrest. The riots of 1830 that occurred at Stotfold and Flitwick, both just outside the county but near enough to have a bearing on our story, were not repeated later in the century.

A consideration of Hertfordshire society in the nineteenth century must first take into account the fact that the years 1792 to 1815 were years of war and the period immediately after was one of economic recession. Furthermore, the long war with France was a peculiar war in the sense that it was a war against a country where revolution had occurred partly in consequence of social distress and frustration. The British establishment had seen the Napoleonic War as not only a conflict with a rival nation but also a war against Jacobinism. British opinion even in rural Hertfordshire could not but be aware of this.

English rural society was not revolutionary but it was often lawless. England was regarded, at the personal level at least, as a land where violence was not far below the surface. Unlike France, either before or after the revolution, England possessed no armed gendarmerie, indeed virtually no organised police at all and only a small and none too popular regular army. Honorary magistrates supported only by voluntary constables recruited from the local population maintained law and order. All classes, even in a rural society, were well aware that distress could become riot and an angry crowd could become a rampaging mob.

Nor was violence confined to the towns. Riots occurred in the villages and small towns from Kent to Wiltshire and from East Anglia to the Midlands. Hertfordshire, then as later, was relatively peaceful. Was this because Hertfordshire was better off or merely better controlled? Was there indeed some third factor like the presence of London as a safety valve for the discontented? Was straw plaiting already acting as an amelioration of the worst discontent? Was the system of poor relief carried out more effectively or with greater justice than in comparable counties? Was anything different about the poor of Hertfordshire? To answer these questions it is necessary to take a closer look at the social structure.

The Hertfordshire farm worker

During the eighteenth and nineteenth centuries the vast majority of Hertfordshire country people worked on the land – as farm workers in the case of the men and as straw plaiters in the case of the women – from about 1800 onwards. There had been considerable social change over the years. The inventories that survive from the sixteenth and seventeenth centuries indicate that a substantial proportion of country people had access to land to cultivate or to keep animals on in their own right. This had very largely gone into abeyance by the time we are considering. From the mid-eighteenth century onwards, the vast proportion of countrymen earned their living by working on land belonging to someone else as labourers earning a wage. Even here there had been a significant change. William Ellis of Little Gaddesden writing in 1742[1] describes a system by which farm servants were hired by the year at Statutory Fairs held, in his instance, at Hemel Hempstead, St Albans and Kimpton. He differentiates between 'ploughmen', 'horse keepers', 'taskers' and 'shepherds'. According to Ellis, a man hired as a ploughman might be asked to drive a wagon in times of inclement weather but, in no case, could be asked to dress a hedge still less to clear out a ditch. These were the jobs of a common tasker.

The farm servants of Ellis's day lived as members of their employer's households almost, but perhaps not quite, as members of the family. They ate at the kitchen table and they were expected to take part in family prayers. Ellis quotes with approval a farm servant who asked to be able to attend the parish church as well as family devotions. Presumably they had to accept the religious inclinations of the household and it is possible that the tendency to move out to independent cottage life may have had something to do with the rise of the chapel in village life.

Arthur Young, in his account of 1804[2] states that the bulk of the work on Hertfordshire farms was done by domestic servants hired by the year. However he also pays great attention to the employment of day labourers. These he describes as earning eight shillings in the summer and six in the winter. Piece-work was also available and day wages were greater in some parts of the county – up to fourteen shillings around Watford but sums of ten to twelve shillings were paid in places as far apart as Barkway, Berkhamsted and Ware.

By the middle of the nineteenth century, the living-in farm servant had become very much an exception. They were still recorded in some areas – particularly in the St Albans area – but, apart from a few old retainers, they were usually young unmarried men employed to look after horses or cattle. Three young men hired at Kimpton Park in 1844, William Ashby, William Crew and Thomas Walsh, were contracted at between two shillings and sixpence and three shillings and sixpence per week plus keep to look after animals for a year. It was a kind of apprenticeship for young farmers.[3]

In the period we are considering, the bulk of the work on Hertfordshire farms was being done by labourers hired by the week or even by the day and who lived in cottages that they rented. A few were regarded as specialists – shepherds retained this separate status. Most farms had a senior man employed as a foreman who was paid slightly more than the others but, in general, the farm workers were employed in a general capacity and expected to turn their hands to any work that was necessary. Employers and workmates acknowledged any special skills that workers might possess only informally alike. Farm work, with the possible exception of shepherding, did not have rigid demarcations.

Part of the problem of rural society was that the demand for labour in arable farming varied very considerably in the course of the farming year. Farm workers might expect to earn up to a quarter of their annual wages in the harvest period of about five weeks in August and September. In this period they were either paid a higher day rate or were contracted at a fixed sum from first to last. Traditionally the five pounds or so paid the rent of the cottage and bought any large item such as new boots. Other periods of high labour demand were haymaking and the period of maximum weed growth in late spring. There were some jobs that could only be done in the winter such as ditch and hedge maintenance and most woodland work, but in general winter was a thin time. Even after the introduction of the threshing machine threshing by flail was continued to provide much needed winter employment. The routine work of caring for animals was needed all the year round and indeed lambing time provided work for a few trusted specialists early in the year.

There were, however, times in the year when by no means all the available labour could be adequately employed and as the wages even in times of full employment were the minimum needed for subsistence, intense hardship was inevitable. In a totally agricultural and inland county like Hertfordshire there was no alternative employment in most areas of the county.

The Poor Law

During the first three decades of the nineteenth century, the income of working class families on the land was bound up with the system of poor relief. The reason for this was the effect of war-inflation early in the century. The system of poor relief that applied in early nineteenth century England had been first set up in the last years of the reign of Elizabeth I. The Elizabethan Poor Law allowed the parish vestries to collect a modest rate from occupiers of property. The parishes employed a clerk to use the funds to provide relief for those unfortunates who needed sustenance from the public purse. These might include the sick, the handicapped, the old or the merely unlucky. Surviving accounts of parish clerks refer to allowances for bread and blankets for the poor of the parish. There were whispers of favouritism and incompetence but, in a small closed community, it was unlikely that any major malpractice was normally the case. For most of its history the only recipients of the Poor Law allowances were the minority of the unfortunate that any community possessed. The wars against the French Revolution and Napoleon changed all that. Far more expensive and fought bloodily to a finish, they were far more of an economic burden than the commercial wars earlier in the century. Prices of basic foodstuffs increased out of all expectation and working-class families faced mounting hardship. The government, long used to ignoring poverty, could not afford to ignore the possibility of serious unrest. Revolution in France could spread to England. The system of parish relief was extended semi-officially to subsidise wages or at least to augment basic food supplies in many places throughout depressed rural areas. The system of bread scales that applied in some corn-growing counties became known as the Speenhamland Bread Scale from its onset in rural Berkshire at or about 1795. A considerable proportion of the working-class families in the south of England became dependent at least at times on parish relief. When the wars came to an end with the final defeat of the French at Waterloo in 1815, the economic problem did not. Economic recession combined with low wages and the lack of alternative employment meant that the incomes of very many rural working class families were bound up with the Poor Law and the parish. Pauperism, defined as dependence on the public purse, had become a part of life.

The rationale of the old Poor Law[4] was not unlike the supplements and rebates that are available to the poor today with not dissimilar results. Allowances served to ameliorate the worst effects of poverty without doing a lot to either get rid of poverty altogether or to enable individuals to escape from it. In practice the parish clerks had a considerable amount of latitude about the way the Poor Law was administered locally. Parish clerks were supervised by locally elected vestries and by the magistrates but even they exhibited wide variation in the interpretation of their duties. A series of Parliamentary enquiries tried to establish how the Poor Law was being administered locally and evidence from Hertfordshire parishes is available from the Select Committees of 1824, 1828 and 1831[5] and the Royal Commission on the Poor Laws of 1834.[6]

Witnesses described how the Poor Law was being administered locally. They often took the opportunity of describing what they considered the origins of poverty to be and they outlined their views on the course of action that the government might take.

It seems that the classical Speenhamland Bread Scale was not widely in use in Hertfordshire. The returns for the 1824 enquiry have survived for the parishes in the half hundred of Hitchin.[7] The parishes of Pirton, Offley and Lilley along the Bedfordshire border admitted to using the 'roundsman' system. This was a practice that was fairly common in some counties including Bedfordshire. By this system farm workers without regular jobs were sent round the parish to get what work they could from the farmers. At the end of the week, the parish clerk examined a chit signed by the employers and made up the wages to an accepted minimum. In this set of parishes only Pirton described a system by which the wages of all workers were regularly made up in this way. In the other parishes the roundsmen were a minority. In one of the parishes of the half hundred, King's Walden, the disbursement book kept by the overseers has survived giving a complete run of records from 1804 to the end of the old Poor Law in 1834.[8] In this parish there were two overseers of the poor, both local farmers chosen annually at the Easter vestry. About ten men held the office on and off over the thirty year period. They kept careful records and divided the payments between regular pensions of two to six shillings per week made to about twenty widows over the whole year and the varied 'one off' payments made to the ill and the unfortunate. Payments were often made in kind – boots, blankets or occasionally the expenses of a funeral. There are also payments made to unemployed villagers and small sums to families, which vary without any mention of illness or accident that were presumably paid to families whose breadwinner was on short time. This humane practice was not admitted to in the return that the overseer (Mr John Gootheridge judging by the handwriting) sent to William Wilshere's enquiry. Nor was the frequent allegation that 'the poor rates' were eating up the substance of the nation born out by the facts in this parish at least. The total spent in 1832 (£300) was the same as in 1804 while the 1828 total of £367 was never exceeded – hardly a sum to beggar a prosperous village community.

In the rest of the county, only parishes in the Hundred of Dacorum and part of the Hundred of Hertford admitted to the enquiry of 1824 that they were in the habit of making up wages out of the poor rates. In view of what we know about the north Hertfordshire evidence it may well have been that the hard-pressed overseers took advantage of an ambiguity in the questions put to the parish officials. The first question was 'Do the labourers receive the whole or any part of their wages out of the poor rates?' The answer was invariably 'No'. The second question was 'Is it usual for married labourers having children to receive assistance from the poor rates?' The answer was frequently 'yes'. This failure to distinguish clearly between wages and income made the inquiry less useful than it might have been.

Nevertheless the interviews with knowledgeable locals provided much information about the actual working of the Poor Law in the Hertfordshire villages. It was even more revealing about the attitudes to poverty to be found among some of the gentry and the farmers. In 1828, Nathan Driver, a farmer of Furneaux Pelham, explained how the farmers balloted among themselves to employ workers who could not find employment in the ordinary way.[9] In 1831 the Rev. Joseph Faithful explained how the very large parish of Hatfield had attempted to ensure that unemployed workers could only obtain sustenance in the workhouse and were encouraged to seek employment in such industries as the district possessed. This included a silk mill in St Albans and a paper mill in Hemel Hempstead. The Marquess of Salisbury on the Hatfield estates provided some extra employment.[10] This was very much a foretaste of things to come in the new Poor Law of 1834 and Faithful was indeed in favour of abolishing the Poor Law altogether in the belief that the poor could fend for themselves.

Some parishes experimented with a system that was known as 'labour rate'. This was in effect a formalisation of the practice described by Nathan Driver at

THE POOR LAW QUESTIONNAIRE OF 1824

Hitchin
22nd April 1824

GENTLEMEN

You are by order of a Committee of the House of Commons required to deliver forthwith to the Justices of the District of Hitchin answers to the following queries to be transmitted to the clerk of the House of Commons.

– Do any labourers in your parish employed by the farmers receive the whole or any part of their wages out of the poor rates?
Not any.

– Is it usual for your married labourers having children to receive assistance from the rates – if so at what number of children does the allowance begin?
It is not usual.

– Are any of your labourers who cannot find work sent as Roundsmen and if so, what do they receive and from whom?
We have no labourers sent as Roundsmen. If any want work they are employed by the Surveyor on the roads in digging gravel from whom married men receive eight shillings and single men six shillings a week.

– Has the number of unemployed labourers in your parish increased within the last few years?
From 1819 to 1822 the number of unemployed labourers considerably increased, since that time it has again decreased.

– What is the lowest rate of wages paid to an unmarried labourer?
The lowest rate of wages is from 5/- to 6/- a week.

C.W. Gibbon
Clerk to the Justices.

(HALS doc 61346)

SELECT COMMITTEE OF THE HOUSE OF LORDS ON THE POOR LAW 1831

Evidence of the Rev. Francis Joseph Faithful, Vicar of Hatfield 15th March 1831

– Will you state the principal regulations under which the law is administered?

The principal one was that no pension or permanent allowance shall be granted to any person, except in the case of sickness. It was previously the custom to allow weekly relief to widows and aged persons outside of the (work) house.

– Was it also the practice to give relief to persons on account of the number of their families?

Yes, it was.

– Has this since been forbidden?

Yes, it has.

– Under what conditions can persons now receive relief for the number of their family?

The parish will receive one or two of their children into the house as an assistance to them.

– Will you now have the goodness to read the regulations relating to the administration of relief to the poor?

'All relief shall be given as provisions or necessaries. A sum not exceeding 5 shillings in provisions or necessaries may be given to women in confinement; ... the expenses of funerals may be defrayed by the parish ... widows or families may receive relief out of the workhouse for up to one month after the death of the master of the family. ... A list shall be made of all persons who have received parish relief, stating their residence and the amount they have received; and copies shall be fixed to the church doors, in large and legible characters on the Sunday after the passing of the annual accounts. The family of a person sent to gaol for any crime or misdemeanour or under suspicion of the same shall not be relieved except by admission into the workhouse.'

Furneaux Pelham in 1828.[11] Employers could have the choice of employing labour or paying an extra poor rate. At Weston a parish meeting was held on 29 November 1832 at which a select vestry consisting of three-quarters of the rate payers decided that all occupiers of arable land were to employ one labourer at full wages for every £30 of rental.[12] Any labourers left over would be considered 'surplus' and farmers could then choose between employing such men or paying a rate into parish funds. The object was to maintain a high level of employment and, as far as possible, ensure that the only payments from the parish poor fund would be those made to the sick, the old and the infirm. Plans to control employment were criticised on two counts. One was that it put pressure on the employers to take on more labour than they really required and encouraged over-manning. Secondly there was the problem of those ratepayers who did not ordinarily employ labour at all – or those tradesmen who only employed men with specialist skills. The category of non-employing ratepayers could include the labourers themselves. Indeed one Poor Law riot not far away at Eaton Bray in Bedfordshire took place in protest at the demands of the poor rate not the paucity of the allowances paid to the needy.

Obviously more work needs to be done on the working of the old Poor Law in Hertfordshire. It is certainly not evident at first sight that the expense of pauperism was in any way out of hand or that the poor were not being looked after with reasonable compassion and humanity by the standards of the day. What did save the situation in this county, both in the sense of enabling the working-class families to survive and in maintaining a degree of public order, was not so much the provisions of the Poor Law but the presence of a domestic industry. It was straw plaiting that enabled women and children to augment the family incomes of the labouring class.

Straw plaiting[13] seems to have become a well-established domestic industry at or about 1800 when fashion changes from the cotton mob-cap for women to ubiquitous straw bonnets for summer wear. Another form of straw hat had become fashionable for men as summer wear during the nineteenth century, although it was not until the very end of the century when the British plait industry was actually into decline that the straw boater become de rigueur for both sexes as summer leisure wear. In theory, straw plaiting could have become a viable industry in any cereal-growing region. In fact the mid-century censuses indicate that virtually all the straw plait industry supplying the hat trade in England was concentrated on an area of central and north Hertfordshire and in Bedfordshire south of the Ouse. It existed to supply a hat trade based in Luton in

Bedfordshire and, to an extent, hat factories in St Albans and other Hertford-shire towns. There was another minor straw plaiting district around Braintree and Bocking in Essex. Apart from that the only other concentration of straw plaiters in Britain was the Orkneys. Apart from the accident of local tradition there is little to suggest why the industry should have such a bizarre distribution pattern. It has been suggested elsewhere in this book that the availability of London manures may have made farmers in the Home Counties more willing to make straw available for sale as raw material for the straw plaiters.

Straw plaiting remained a popular occupation for women and children and even to some extent for men in north Hertfordshire and parts of Bedfordshire until it succumbed to oriental competition in the late nineteenth century. According to Young in 1804, nimble fingered young women could earn as much as a pound a week at straw plaiting – far in excess of a labourer's wages. Such high earnings were in fact rare but the rewards were good enough to ensure that almost every working-class woman could claim to be a straw plaiter in an area from St Albans to Bedford. Straw plait was sold, either on the markets of St Albans, Luton, Dunstable or Hitchin or to itinerant plait dealers who toured the villages.[14]

The Swing Riots and Hertfordshire

The presence of a viable domestic industry in the area helps to explain the other-wise unaccountable immunity of Hertfordshire from the wave of riots known as the Swing Riots that swept through the agricultural counties of southern Eng-land in 1830.[15]

Although rural unrest was far from unknown, even in Hertfordshire in the early years of the nineteenth century, the year 1830 saw a climax of unrest in southern England. Beginning in Kent in the summer, the troubles spread west-wards along the south coast like a brush fire and then doubled back eastwards along the chalk ridge north of the Thames into Buckinghamshire and East Anglia. There were two serious outbreaks in Bedfordshire. There was a riot on the 6 December 1830 at Stotfold, less than a mile from the Hertfordshire border and a few days later there was a series of riots in the villages near the Bedford estates at Woburn, notably at Flitwick. The main trend of the disturbances then moved eastwards again with more riots at Bassingbourn and Fowlmere in south Cambridgeshire and then into Norfolk, Suffolk and Essex where there were local insurrections on a level that rivalled the original outburst in Kent.

Hertfordshire, almost alone of the southern counties had been largely exempt. Apprehension there certainly was. The Lucas Diaries record the anxiety in Hitchin during the rioting a few miles to the north.[16] The vicar of Hinxworth, the Rev. John Lafont, rode through the night to warn the authorities of the Stotfold outbreak and was then somewhat annoyed to be left out of the official congratulations. A letter from the 'respectable citizens of Puckeridge' was sent to the Home Secretary asking for the assistance of the newly formed Metropolitan Police.

Help from outside was not normally forthcoming and, as things turned out, not necessary. The Hertfordshire authorities proved well able to cope with such troubles as there were in 1830. On 3 December 1830, Lord Verulam, the Lord Lieutenant of Hertfordshire issued a proclamation to rally the forces of law and order and to appeal for calm. It was decided to divide the county into districts each with a force of special constables to be sworn in and paid two shillings and sixpence per day with a shilling extra for night duty. This was highly significant, as at times the force of special constables must have included nearly all the able-bodied men in the village willing to serve. The Pirton Poor Law assessment for example includes an entry for the 5 March 1831 for forty-seven special constables to be paid a shilling each by Mr Charles Kingsley, a local farmer, who presumably commanded the force as its sergeant. In a sense, the special constable system gave the lower classes an element of control over the situation as it implied that law and order could only be preserved with their consent and co-operation. There were instances when local men refused to carry out the wishes of the leaders. Hertfordshire men refused to cross the border into Cambridgeshire to deal with the riot at Fowlmere. On the other hand, the magistrates could successfully appeal to men of neighbouring villages to help suppress a riot. Lord Grantham, the Lord Lieutenant of Bedfordshire, brought in men from Henlow and Arlesey to suppress the Stotfold riot and, where there was no recorded trouble, as at Pirton, the practice of paying generous allowances to constables may well have had the effect of buying off trouble.

The village of Standon seems to have witnessed the only known instance of actual criminal unrest that came to court when a group of men were arrested for arson and one condemned. A troop of the Hertfordshire Yeomanry was assembled at Royston to deal with the Cambridgeshire troubles and a force of 200 special constables was assembled to protect John Dickinson's paper mill at Hemel Hempstead. In Buckinghamshire some paper mills had already been attacked.[17]

In some parts of the country, the trouble had been triggered by the newly introduced steam threshing machines that were as yet rare in Hertfordshire. In East Anglia the problem of the tithe helped to exacerbate the situation and sometimes led to unrest that was, to an extent, condoned by the farming community who were often highly resentful of the tithe burden. Tithes had been largely dealt with in arable north Hertfordshire by the enclosure acts where tithe proprietors had been allocated grants of land in lieu and the tithe was no longer an issue.

In Stotfold, the rioters had demanded a guaranteed wage of two shillings per day together with the dismissal of an unpopular Poor Law overseer. At both Stotfold and Flitwick local conditions had helped to trigger off the riots and it should be remembered that nearly all other parishes in Bedfordshire remained peaceful, which would indicate that riot was the exception rather than the rule. They occurred where a combination of circumstances produced an unusually inflamed state of opinion.[18]

The wave of rioting died away as mysteriously as it had arisen. The rural riots of southern England do not appear to have been political in any but the most primitive sense, nor did any national leader emerge. The legendary 'Captain Swing' after whom the riots were named was never identified although there was a suggestion that a Hertfordshire plait dealer might have been involved. At times like these any stranger was suspect. The authorities in a normally peaceful rural society always have difficulty in believing that unrest can be as spontaneous as it appears and are very ready to believe in agitators coming from outside.

The Poor Law after 1834

The most direct effect of the riots of 1830 was that they brought the whole issue of rural pauperism to a head. As soon as the constitutional issue of parliamentary reform was settled a Royal Commission was set up to look into the Poor Law question yet again in 1834, and this time it came up with a concrete suggestion for radical reform. This was the Poor Law (Amendment) Act, 1834 by which parishes were to be federated together into district Poor Law Unions each of which was to build a workhouse. A number of Hertfordshire parishes were investigated in the 1834 enquiry without adding a great deal to what had been already established in the previous enquiries of 1824, 1828 and 1831, except perhaps insofar as the presence of migratory Scots and Irish farm workers was noted in some parishes.

The new Poor Law unions were to be administered by elected boards of guardians and they were strictly controlled by central government. An assistant commissioner, Daniel Goodson Adey, moved into the county in order to set up Poor Law unions in Hertfordshire and Bedfordshire. He took a house at Marky-ate Cell on the border of the two counties. In Hertfordshire, Poor Law unions were set up with workhouses at Berkhamsted, Hemel Hempstead, Watford, St Albans, Hatfield, Welwyn, Hitchin, Hertford, Buntingford, Royston, Bishops Stortford, Barnet and Ware. The parish of Cheshunt was attached to Enfield in Middlesex and in several cases parishes in neighbouring counties found themselves attached to Hertfordshire unions. The Act was deliberately no respecter of county boundaries, much to the irritation of the county magistrates. The break with previous administration was to be as sharp as possible.

The industrial areas of the country were bitterly hostile and an anti-Poor Law movement quickly came into being which in some areas had some degree of support from the gentry who felt bypassed by the new elected boards of guardians. Working-class opinion was suspicious. Some rural areas were antagonistic at first. There were serious riots at Ampthill in Bedfordshire[19] and at Saffron Walden in Essex. Even in Hertfordshire there was some unrest as the new workhouse at Bishops Stortford was set on fire and a demonstration occurred on Therfield Heath in protest at the Royston workhouse.

The administrators of the new Poor Law set their faces strongly against any form of relief by cash handouts or subsidised wages, although what was known as 'outdoor relief' never entirely disappeared. The last resort for the destitute was to be the strictly administered workhouse, an institution that was hated and feared from the start.

After the Ampthill troubles of May 1835, the organised anti-Poor Law movement of the north of England sent two investigators, James Turner and Mark Crabtree, to assess the situation of the poor in the south of Bedfordshire. Much of what they found would apply to the villages on the Hertfordshire side of the border and they were allowed to give evidence to a Commission on the working of the Poor Law along with local figures more representative of the establishment.[20]

One possible reason for the acceptance of the new Poor Law among rural people after the initial hostility was that the new railways provided employment opportunities. This was said as early as 1836 by Thomas Bennett, agent to the Russell estate, in evidence to a commission on agricultural distress.[21] Turner and Crabtree insisted that the benefit was not as great as might be assumed because the opportunities were only available for the young and the fit and the work of construction was likely to be both local and temporary. Robert Stephenson's new London and Birmingham railway was under construction at this time through Berkhamsted, Tring and Leighton Buzzard.

To an extent, the Hertfordshire Poor Law unions carried on some of the practices of the parish under the old system. The workhouses acted as hostels and labour exchanges for the younger workers although they were further apart than the old parish poor houses had been. Farmers in east Hertfordshire, for example, grumbled at having to go into Bishops Stortford to recruit extra labourers. The workhouses at Royston and Hitchin operated a ticket system that was reminiscent of the old roundsman system. Paupers were issued with printed tickets to take round the farms getting employers to sign either that they had provided a job or that no work was available.[22] The ticket system seems to have been first used at the workhouse of the borough of Saffron Walden in 1829 and become fairly widespread in the eastern counties even after the change in the law. Even as perceptive an observer as James Caird remarked that there was little difference in the distribution of surplus labour by the parish or by the ticket system after the reform.[23]

What the reform of the Poor Law did achieve was to take the pauper question out of politics as far as the rural areas were concerned. Agricultural workers were now totally dependent on their wages and on the earnings of their families at domestic industries – in our case this meant straw plait. The workers were no longer a charge on the rates and from now on their problems were largely their own.

In theory, wages should have risen to reach an economic rate and the surplus population should have left the land to seek better prospects elsewhere. To an extent that is what happened but the process was a very slow one. The younger and more mobile members of the rural working class certainly did depart from the land in large numbers – sufficient to cause apprehension among the employers in the mid-century decades. Farm wages did rise slowly from around nine shillings per week in the 1830s to about eleven or twelve shillings per week in the 1860s which still compared badly with the eighteen shillings or so that an unskilled worker in a town could earn. Even a labourer on the railway could expect more. There was no comparison at all with the wage of a skilled carpenter or bricklayer who could double a farm worker's wages.

Even by using the market forces argument, it is not easy to see why farm workers in a county like Hertfordshire should have been quite so badly paid. They were after all indispensable skilled workers in an essential and, until the

1870s, an expanding and prosperous industry. They lived in a rich area with plenty of alternative employment to offer at the price of a move even if there was little in the immediate vicinity. Why were highly skilled farm workers paid worse than unskilled labourers in their own localities?

The answer is that farm workers started from a very low base. The seven or eight shillings a week earned by a Hertfordshire farm worker in the first decade of the nineteenth century was a reflection of overpopulation and the use of the Poor Law to bail out wages on the land. Gradually wages did improve after 1834 partly because workers were now wholly dependent on them. At Great Gaddesden, for example, wages rose from nine shillings a week in 1839 to twelve shillings in 1842. At Woodside Farm, Hatfield [24] and at Beechwood Park, Flamstead,[25] wages rose from eleven or twelve shillings per week in 1852 to thirteen or fourteen in the 1860s. By the end of the 1860s the Royal Commission on Children, Young Persons and Women in Agriculture of 1867 was quoting wages of thirteen to fifteen shillings in many parts of the county.[26] This of course was still low by almost any other standard and considering the interest on the part of landowners in providing cottages, schools and allotments with the express purpose of inducing working families to remain on the land it is difficult to argue that Hertfordshire villages were overpopulated at that date.

The labourers' problem was that their skills were too widely diffused. A skilled and reliable man might be more regularly employed but could not command much higher wages. His only opportunity to increase his income was by means of intensive piecework and even that was not highly rated. Skills were to little avail unless there was some means of controlling their deployment. Farm workers did not have to serve any kind of formal apprenticeship and had no means of rationing the amount of skilled labour on offer. Apart from informal group bargaining between gang leaders and farmers at times when special tasks were required, there was no form of restricting skilled manpower or of carrying out any form of collective bargaining.

Hertfordshire farm workers had no tradition of trade unionism until the coming of the National Agricultural Labourers Union in the early 1870s, so few workers of any trade in Hertfordshire possessed any form of collective bargaining. It is possible that in Hertfordshire smallish numbers of skilled engineers, stonemasons or printers may have belonged to one or other of the famous 'new model unions' of the 1850s but their activities seem to have made little impact on employment practice in this county.

For the moment however, with the passing of the new Poor Law of 1834, the condition of the working class in Hertfordshire ceased to be an issue for anyone but members of the working class itself. The cost of pauperism diminished and there was no longer any suspicion that crafty employers were passing on their wages bill to the ratepayers via a complaisant parish clerk – even supposing that practice had ever been widespread in the first place. Outdoor relief did not actually cease but far fewer members of the working class found themselves as inmates of a workhouse than had managed to get some kind of parish relief from a benevolent parish before the 1834 act.

Conditions gradually began to improve for the working man and his family. Railways and increased farming prosperity provided more employment while cheaper imported foodstuffs began to bring down the cost of living. As far as public order was concerned, the combination of slightly better conditions plus a widespread desire for respectability served to induce a new mood of public tranquillity. In addition the forces of law and order were becoming more efficient as the new county police instilled more respect. Hertfordshire had been one of the first counties to implement the, then optional, County Police Act of 1839 by setting up the Hertfordshire Constabulary in 1841. Although sporadic and surreptitious violence and arson still went on, open insurrection was no longer on the cards. The rural labourer was still patronised, exploited, only perfunctorily educated and only well housed if he was lucky – but he was no longer feared.

References

1. Ellis, William, *The Modern Husbandman*, 1742.
2. Young, Arthur, *A General View of the Agriculture of Hertfordshire*, 1804, reprinted 1971.
3. HALS 40673, 18 Sept 1844.
4. Blaug, M., 'The Myth of the Old Poor Law and the Making of the New' in Flinn, M.W. and Smout, T.C., *Essays in Social History*, Clarendon Press, Oxford, 1974.
5. SC 1824 in BPP 1825 XIX, pp. 382–5; SC 1828 in BPP 1828 IV, pp. 29–32; SC 1831 in BPP 1831 VIII, pp. 267–281.
6. The Poor Law Commissioners' Report of 1834.
7. HALS Wilshere papers 61354 A- G.
8. HALS King's Walden overseer's accounts, D/P 112/12/1.
9. BPP 1828 IV. SC on the Poor Laws, pp. 29–32 (printed) and p. 165 (written) evidence of Nathan Driver.
10. BPP 1831 VIII.
11. BPP 1828 IV.
12. HALS D/P 121/8/1, Weston Vestry Book.
13. Dony, J., *History of the Straw Plait Industry*, 1940.
14. ibid.

15. Hobsbawm, E.J. and Rude, G., *Captain Swing*, 1969.

16. Lucas Diaries, Hitchin Museum. M534.

17. PRO HO 52/7.

18. *The Times*, 6 Dec 1830.

19. Agar, N.E., *The Bedfordshire Farm Worker*, 1981.

20. BPP 1837–8 XVIII pt 2. SC on the Poor Law Amendment Act (1834) 1838. Evidence of H.H. Musgrave, D.G. Adey and J. Turner, p. 65 and ff.

21. BPP 1836 VIII pt 1. SC State of Agriculture. Evidence of Thomas Bennett, pp. 213–22.

22. Digby, A., 'The Labour Market and the Continuation of Social Policy after 1834' in *Economic History Review* 2nd ser. xxviii, Feb 1975.

23. Caird, James, *English Agriculture*, 1851.

24. HALS Salisbury estate papers D/Ex 55 E2.

25. HALS Sebright papers 18780.

26. BPP 1868–9 XIII. RC on Children, Young Persons and Women in Agriculture. Evidence of George Culley, pp. 185–98. Returns on Hertfordshire, pp. 734–60 (pp. 660–8 written).

CHAPTER SEVEN

Landlord, tenant and labourer in the era of high farming

T HE PASSING OF THE Poor Law (Amendment) Act of 1834 effectively took the labourer out of politics for a generation. The cost of pauperism was no longer seen as a problem and the labourers themselves
did not call attention to themselves by any concerted attempt to demand their
rights or redress their grievances. The centre of controversy passed to the decision-
making classes – the landlords and the farmers.

Together, the landlord and the tenant made up the 'agricultural interest'.
Most of the farmland in Hertfordshire was rented from middle-sized estates.
There were some large estates, such as the Cecil estates at Hatfield or the Cowper
estates at Panshanger, but the average estate in this county was smaller than in
many other counties.

Some working farmers of course owned their land and paid no rent but, on
the whole, tenanted farms rented from agricultural landowners were the norm
in this county. The actual terms by which this was done became a source of controversy in the course of the century. Some tenant farmers, but by no means all,
claimed that insecure tenancies discouraged the farmer from investing in his
business.

The law and custom of land tenure varied from county to county in nineteenth-
century England. The custom of Hertfordshire was described in the evidence
presented to parliament by Charles Lattimore, a Wheathampstead farmer and
maltster and a keen advocate of tenant rights, to the Select Committee on Agricultural Customs in 1848[1] and later in an article by Clement Cadle in the *Journal
of the Royal Agricultural Society of England* in 1868.[2] The point at issue was
whether or not a tenant could claim as of right financial compensation from the
landlord for any investment that the tenant might have made to the holding.

In Hertfordshire, an incoming tenant entered possession of a farm at
Michaelmas but had the right to take over the fallows for pasture at the previous

Lady Day. This custom was dying out in 1860s as the practice of fallowing was becoming less common. Hay and straw could only be sold off the farm if an equivalent amount of manure was brought on to the farm. It was this provision that enabled farmers to take advantage of the ready supply of London manure to make straw available for the straw plait industry.

Not all farming tenancies were governed by a formal lease – many Hertfordshire farmers were tenants at will – but progressive agriculturalists usually advocated leases and the lease system did at least give the landlord the opportunity to lay down the ground rules of farm management while giving the farmer a degree of security for a period of years. When Edward Garner, who came from Essex, leased 379 acres at Great Wymondley and Willian from William Wilshere of the Frythe, Welwyn in 1845 for twelve years[3] he had to agree to farm according to the best traditions of the parish: to lay down two-fifths of the land to either turnips or fallow every year, not to grow wheat on more than two-fifths of the land for two consecutive years and to provide two cart loads or one wagon load of manure for every ton of straw sold off the farm.

Leases gave a measure of security to the tenant in return for a degree of control on the part of the landlord. They could also delineate the degree of responsibility over the permanent installations of the farm. When the tenant, Ellis Wilkerson, took over a farm at Barley belonging to Lord Dacre of Kimpton Hoo[4] he agreed to a rent of £762 per year for 578 acres with the landlord retaining rights to timber, minerals, game and hunting, and the tenant had to maintain land and buildings. The tenant undertook not to plough pasture without permission and not to sell hay, straw or 'stover' (wood for domestic use) off the farm without permission. Hedges had to be coppiced (cut for regrowth) at intervals not less than five years and not more than thirteen and must not be grubbed up without permission.

The lease system, apparently so sensible and flexible, was to lead to controversy in the county but, in general, the tenantry of the county could look to the landlords to use their political and social influence to protect the interests of agriculture as a whole. Where the nineteenth century differed from all previous centuries was that, for the first time ever, Britain was becoming an industrial country. This meant that the towns, which had hitherto been little more than market centres for the surrounding countryside, now possessed burgeoning populations of industrial workers needing to be fed but caring little where their food came from. The urban manufacturers, conscious of their world monopoly of factory produce, believed in free trade and saw no reason why the farming community should need to protect its interests by an import tariff on its main product. The stage was set for confrontation. This happened with the Corn Law crisis of the 1840s.

Hertfordshire and the Corn Law crisis of 1839–46

The prosperity of the Hertfordshire farmer at the start of the nineteenth century had been underpinned by the high price of corn due in large part to the war with France. When the wars came to an end in 1815, trade was resumed, grain being mainly imported from the Baltic ports such as Danzig and Riga. A parliament of landlords decided to continue to protect the agricultural interest by imposing a tariff on imported grain. These were the famous 'Corn Laws' and, although modified by succeeding governments in the 1820s, remained the lynchpin of government agricultural policy until 1846 when a combination of increasing pressures from growing urban interests mobilised by a powerful pressure group, the Anti-Corn-Law League led by Richard Cobden and John Bright, combined with the effects of the Irish famine of 1845, induced the Government of Robert Peel to abolish them.

The Anti-Corn-Law League had been founded in Manchester in 1839 and it rapidly established itself in the manufacturing areas to campaign for free trade in corn. The case was skilfully presented and soon gained widespread support in the manufacturing districts. Not only did it appeal to the self-interest of the urban population but it accorded well with the prevailing mood towards free trade and the absence of state intervention in all forms of business. It was some time before a countervailing movement arose among the farming community to protect their interests. This tardiness might be surprising but farmers were not used to banding together to defend their interests which they thought would be well protected by their landlords assembled in Parliament. An Agricultural Protection Society had come briefly into being in 1836 led by Lord Chandos, son of the Duke of Buckingham, who was anxious to set himself up politically as the farmers' friend. He had been instrumental in ensuring that tenant farmers had been enfranchised under the 1832 reform of Parliament by inserting the 'Chandos' clause into the reform bill. The new society was mentioned by the *Hertfordshire County Press*[5] but does not seem to have had a local branch. A meeting at Aylesbury in 1836 attracted no Hertfordshire delegation.

Faced with a direct threat, however, in the form of the Anti-Corn-Law League, a group of farmers in Essex led by a Robert Baker of Writtle formed a local protection association and the case was taken up nationally by a new Central Agricultural Protection Association formed at a meeting held after the Smithfield Show in December 1845 at the Duke of Richmond's town house.[6]

Interest in the new movement spread rapidly among farmers, landowners and backbench Tory MPs. A meeting of the new association was held on 2 February 1844 at St Albans and addressed by Lords Salisbury, Verulam and Essex with a letter of support from Lord Dacre. It was attended by many Hertfordshire landowners and farmers and passed a resolution asserting that the repeal of the Corn Laws would destroy investment in agriculture, bring desolation to the agricultural labourers and prove destructive to the landed interest.[7]

A Hertfordshire Protection Association was set up. It was led, not by members of the landowning gentry, as might have been expected, but by working farmers. Two of them, George Passingham of Lilley and Thomas Oakley of St Albans were elected chairman and secretary respectively. A committee was established composed of two farmers from every parish. At that time it was the practice to set up a massive 'committee' for political purposes largely with the purpose of enrolling as many committed names as possible. Usually, only an inner circle actually met.[8]

The agricultural movement of 1844 was very much a farmers' movement to which the landowners, or some of them, lent their names, rather than a landowners' movement that the farmers had perforce to support as the free traders tended to assert. Even among the farmers there was some dissent. At the inaugural meeting, two farmers, a Mr Welford of Northaw and Charles Lattimore of Wheathampstead tried to propose a counter-motion calling for security of tenure rather than tariff protection. They were howled down but the *Hertfordshire Mercury*, traditionally a pro-free trade and liberal paper, later published the text of their proposition.[9]

The *Hertfordshire Mercury*, being opposed to the Corn Laws, pointed out that, although as impressive galaxy of Hertfordshire grandees had either been present or had expressed support, quite a number of eminent county figures of Whig leanings had been conspicuous by their absence. They included Lords Cowper, Cavendish, Melbourne and Clarendon. Nevertheless, the list of farming subscribers published in the same paper on 2 March indicates what must have been almost total support among the farming community in parishes as far apart as Weston, King's Walden and Hertingfordbury.

Judging by the Hertfordshire evidence, it would appear that the farming community with the exception of a few dissidents like Lattimore were united on the issue of protection while the great landowners were less certain. Opinion among the latter was more evenly divided along party lines. Historians have sometimes debated whether the campaign to preserve the Corn Laws was instigated by the landlords trying to protect their rents and dragooning the tenantry into support but, from the Hertfordshire evidence, it would seem that the initiative came largely from the farmers themselves. Free-traders among the farmers existed but were the exception rather than the rule. When a meeting was held in St Albans to promote free trade in general, not merely in agriculture, it was Charles Lattimore who was chosen to take the chair.

The landowners, for their part, went along with the farmers' cause at this stage but were quick to recognise a lost cause when the Corn Laws were finally abolished. In a highly significant speech to the Watford Farmers Club after abolition, the Earl of Essex virtually apologised to the farmers for raising expectations about retaining the Corn Laws and advised them to come to terms with free trade and concentrate on becoming more efficient.

Hertfordshire as a corn growing county must have seemed unpromising territory for the anti-Corn Law protagonists but even so the League made a sterling effort to win over opinion in the county and did not lack for local support. In January 1846, the League held public meetings in Hertford, St Albans and Royston chaired by Henry Cowper, Liberal MP for Hertfordshire, while Samuel Lucas, a Hitchin banker and a well-known Quaker, chaired a meeting in that town. The meetings were addressed both by a Mr Falway who was one of the League's professional lecturers and by Charles Lattimore by now a well-known local supporter of the free trade cause. The Hitchin meeting was interrupted by a group of local farmers led by a Mr Titchmarsh.

In the spring of 1846, the Peel Government grasped the nettle and abolished the Corn Laws with the support of a considerable portion of the Whig-Liberal opposition and in the teeth of its own back benchers. The protectionists rallied their forces in Parliament under the leadership of hitherto little known figures, Lord George Bentinck and Benjamin Disraeli. In the general election of 1847 two Tory protectionists, Sir Henry Meux and Thomas Plumer Halsey were returned for Hertfordshire while the successful Liberal was Thomas Brand, now known as Thomas Trevor, and a man who had at least attended the inaugural meeting of the Protection Association. Later in 1852 three Tory protectionists, Halsey, Meux and Sir Edward Bulwer Lytton fought and won the county election in 1852 against three Liberal free-traders. Nevertheless, rigid protectionism gradually expired in Hertfordshire as it did in most counties in the face of the orthodoxy of free trade. The attitude of the Earl of Essex was more typical of the Hertfordshire landowning community. Agricultural protectionism became as much a lost cause in rural Hertfordshire as it already was in more industrial counties and the issue was not to be raised again until the agricultural depression at the end of the century. The prospect of a tax on food remained an election loser for many years after.

The game laws and tenant right

The anti-Corn Law movement, having chalked up a success, made efforts to consolidate their position by winning over the farming community. The new generation of farming publicists such as James Caird took the line that free trade was now a fact of life and that prosperity for the farmers lay in more efficiency. This meant a high ratio of capital to land to make full use of the latest technology of drainage, fertilisers and farm buildings – a policy known as 'high farming'. Some but not all of the advocates of high farming saw the laws of tenancy as an obstruction. They argued that without an agreed custom by which the landlord paid for 'unexhausted improvements' made by the tenant at the end of his lease, or when he gave up the tenancy if he was a tenant at will, there was not enough security to provide any real degree of incentive to invest in the farm. The custom of 'tenant right' existed in some counties such as Lincolnshire and a movement grew up among farmers to campaign for tenant right to become more general. Closely associated with the campaign for tenant right was an allied campaign against the game laws which allowed the game species such as pheasants, partridges and hares to eat the farmers' crops without hindrance. This was all the more of a nuisance to the tenant farmer if the landlord took steps to artificially raise the numbers of such species by active preservation carried out by gamekeepers. It was customary for landlords to retain game rights over land which was let out to a farming tenancy and in any case, the woodlands of the estate were normally retained in hand by most owners of agricultural estates. Landlords retained the exclusive right to shoot not only pheasants and partridges but also 'ground game', including rabbits and hares, which were both serious agricultural pests.

The Liberal position now was that, while fiscal protection was as unnecessary for the British farmer as it was for the manufacturer, it was nevertheless the case that the farmer, unlike the manufacturer, suffered from unfair disadvantages brought about by the landlord by imposing restrictions on farming for the sake of game and by denying any right of compensation for any improvements carried out by the tenant.

The lines of battle were being drawn even before the Corn Laws were abolished. In 1845 there was a by-election for one of Hertfordshire's three county seats. Thomas Plumer Halsey fought the seat unadopted nominally as an independent but making his support for the protectionist cause clear. He claimed to be a man of conservative principles but of no party. In the nineteenth century formal party allegiance in the modern sense was not expected of candidates.

Halsey made a tour of the county and at Bishops Stortford on 6 December he held a public debate with Lattimore on the subject of free trade in corn. When pressed Halsey, who was a landowner from Little Gaddesden, asserted that he would vote against the Peel Government if the Corn Laws were threatened. Lattimore opened the question of security of tenure and the game laws. On both Halsey adopted a trenchant Tory position stating that farmers were already well protected by their leases and, if any suffered under the game laws, it was their own fault for taking a tenancy on an estate where game was strictly preserved. He went on to deny that tenants were under any sort of duress to vote as the landowner commanded. This last provoked an expostulation from Lattimore and a subsequent letter to the *Hertfordshire Mercury* from a farmer named John Forster claimed that he had been evicted by a landowner, Elizabeth Darton of Temple Dinsley, from his farm near Preston, Hertfordshire, for voting against her expectations. (The ballot was not secret at this time.)

Also in 1845, a dinner was held in March by Charles Lattimore and Mr Welford, leaders of the free trade movement among Hertfordshire farmers to honour one of their number, a farmer named John Horncastle, a tenant of the Earl of Essex at Cassiobury who had managed to claim seventy-one pounds and ten shillings in compensation for damage done by the landowner's strictly preserved game on forty acres of corn and clover. John Bright MP, one of the two national leaders of the anti-Corn Law movement, attended the occasion and made an address arguing that the alliance of landlord and tenant in defence of the Corn Laws was one of coercion and deference not true economic interest.

After the abolition of the Corn Laws, John Bright turned his attention in Parliament to the game laws as a means of splitting the alliance between landlord and tenant. A Select Committee was set up at his instigation to examine the issue. A Hertfordshire farmer, William Bates, gave evidence before it.[10] Bates's story was that he had taken up a farm on the estate of the Marquess of Bute of Luton Hoo. Bates, who had been a tenant of a farm at Lilley

SELECT COMMITTEE ON THE GAME LAWS 1845

Evidence of William Bates 16th April 1845
(Questions asked by John Bright MP)

– Will you state to the committee where you come from and what is your occupation?
I am a farmer living in the County of Hertfordshire. I farm two farms, Stagenhoe Bottom Farm and Little Offley Farm, a few miles from Hitchin.

– Have you observed the workings of the game laws and game preserving generally?
Yes I have.

– Where?
Where I was a sufferer in the county of Bedfordshire at Luton Park Farm, that is just adjoining Hertfordshire.

– Do you consider the rigid preservation of game a hindrance to agriculture and to high farming?
Very great. … the fact is that if you are keeping stock where hares are kept, they are not only very injurious to the turnips but you cannot grow tares. When the tares are bitten once they seldom come to perfection.

– Do farmers generally receive compensation for the damage done by game?
Never, I never knew an instance.

– Do you think there are cases in which game temptations allure men from a state of labour and make them idle and dissipated?
There are many men who go out at night after the game and spend the whole of the next day on the sale of the game and they are fit for nothing.

Hoo in Hertfordshire, had taken a tenancy on the Marquess' estate. For a time
all went well but then, after a visit from the Duke of Wellington, the Marquess
had been convinced that his estate should adopt the measures of game preservation that Wellington had found successful at his estate at Stratfield Saye in
Hampshire. The result, according to Bates, had been continual friction between
the tenantry and the keepers employed by the Marquess. Damage to Bates' farm
had amounted to £200 per year. As a result, Bates had given up the tenancy and
at the time of the hearing was a tenant on a farm belonging to the Stagenhoe
estate owned by an incoming landlord, a Mr Rogers of Boston, Lincs who was
presumably not a shooting man. In spite of the testimony of Mr Bates and his
fellows, the farming tenants had to wait until 1881 before Parliament passed the
Ground Game Act (1881) enabling tenants to shoot hares on their land.

Tenant Right was a more serious matter. If the protagonists of statutory
tenant right were correct, the farming prosperity of the country was being put
under restriction by the heavy hand of the landlord. In 1848, another Select
Committee on Agricultural Customs examined the question of tenant right.
Charles Lattimore, not surprisingly, gave evidence regarding the situation in
Hertfordshire. He told the committee that in this county farmers were inhibited
from investing in their land and farming as efficiently as they might because of
the anxiety that they would lose their investment if evicted or have their rents
progressively increased to take account of the increased value of their farms. In
his own district (presumably around Wheathampstead) he said, there were
twenty-seven farms. Six were farmed by their owners and three worked on leases
which made provision for the control of game and compensation for unexhausted improvement. These he said were the best farmed holdings in the district.
Given the security of full compensation for unexhausted improvement, he
claimed that most Hertfordshire farmers would be willing to invest in chalking,
drainage and in fertilising the land. One important consequence would be an
increase in employment.[11]

Whatever the problems of the tenantry, it was possible for the landlords to
invest and to obtain public loans for investment. The repeal of the Corn Laws
was part of a package deal by which loans were made available for the landlords
for the purposes of land improvement. At least three large Hertfordshire
landowners – Essex, Cowper and Bulwer Lytton, obtained loans for this purpose
between 1846 and 1850.

In a sense, both sides of the Corn Law controversy were wrong. Hertfordshire farmers did survive the abolition of the Corn Laws. The expanding urban

SELECT COMMITTEE ON AGRICULTURAL CUSTOMS 1848

Evidence of Charles Higby Lattimore

Chairman: You are a practical farmer in Hertfordshire?
I reside at Wheathampstead Place near St Albans.

– What is the prevalent term in Hertfordshire?
Yearly tenures are the rule – leases are the exception.

– What is the custom as to the entry and quitting of farms as regards acts of husbandry?
The custom of entry is usually upon entering the fallows at Lady Day commencing entry at the Michaelmas following.

– What are the landlord's claims for dilapidations?
The landlord has a claim for dilapidations, which are generally and indeed frequently enforced. These include dilapidations of premises, waste on the soil, injury by cross cropping and neglect of tillage. The landlord has legal power and frequently recovers compensations on these grounds.

– Do you mean where the ground is fouled by weeds?
When there is grass, weeds and rubbish.

– What are the tenant's grounds for compensation?
I never knew an instance when the tenant could enforce a claim against a landlord for any improvement.

markets for food plus the fact that there was, at this date, no great stockpile of foreign grain, ensured that farmers remained in business. On the other hand, those farmers also managed to survive without the tenant right or even the right to destroy game that the Bright-Lattimore lobby held was so vital.

The *Hertfordshire Mercury* quoted at length an article by John Villiers Shelley of Lewes who argued that the farmer in the southern counties including Hertfordshire was already better off even though the price of grain had fallen from fifty-six shillings per quarter in the 1830s to forty-two shillings in 1850. The hypothetical farm accounts that Shelley quoted were not unrealistic but the contention he makes that mechanisation had increased and that the wage bill had gone down is more questionable.[12] Mechanisation was still at a very early stage in 1850 and wages would appear to have gone up. It was part of the case of the anti-Corn Law lobby that wages would go down in money terms because farm wages were said to be linked to the price of bread. This was one reason why the Corn Law lobby was opposed by some working-class elements such as the Chartists.

Labourers' wages were not lavish but did not fall in the 1850s – in fact they rose from about nine or ten to eleven shillings a week. It is far from certain that the farmers' costs were falling at all at this date. It does appear to be true that those farmers who could afford it, took to heart the advice about high farming and that improvements were put into effect even if there was not the dramatic revolution in technique that improvers had foreseen.

The labourer under high farming

At the labourer level, there is considerable evidence that life was improving in the villages. Wages were increasing, most villages were provided with schools, allotments were becoming more readily available, there was a considerable improvement in rural housing and women no longer had to work on the land except by choice at times such as the harvest.

It was almost certainly straw plaiting that enabled women to leave the land possibly combined with the demise of the live-in farm servant. Farm records indicate that women were only employed on the land intermittently in nineteenth-century Hertfordshire and the 1867 Commission on Children, Young Persons and Women in Agriculture found little to report about either women or young children working regularly on the land in this county although it had much to say about social conditions in general.

There was no farm in the county that could be described as entirely typical, but in 1853 at Woodside Farm, Hatfield owned by John Church, six men, two youths and two younger boys were employed throughout the year. Weekly wages were a pound for the foreman, twelve or thirteen shillings for the adult labourers and nine, four and three shillings for the boys. Five women and girls were taken on for the harvest period at between three shillings and sixpence and four shillings and sixpence per week.[13]

Women were more regularly employed on the hay farms in the south of the county for the hay season but the regular organised gangs of women and child

VILLAGE LIFE IN THE 1860s

Willian* – population 281, acreage 1,854. Information of Charles Sworder, occupier and (Poor Law) guardian

'Boys are employed from 10 years of age. Girls are not employed. About six or eight women are employed for two or three months weeding and haymaking working from 8 a.m. to 5 p.m. I do not think it is desirable to restrict the age at which boys are permitted to work on the land. There is a village school which is fairly attended. Some of the cottages are very good and others very bad. They are sufficient in number and some take in lodgers. Some are well supplied with water others are deficient. Most have gardens or allotments. Ploughmen and horsekeepers earn from 14 to 15 shillings per week. Shepherds and stockmen earn from 15 to 16 shillings. Machinists earn from 16 to 18 shillings and ordinary labourers 13 to 14 shillings sometimes plus beer.'

(Royal Commission on Children, Young Persons and Women in Agriculture, 1867 BPP 1868–9 XIII)

*Willian was bought in its entirety by a wealthy incomer, Charles Hancock, a Bond Street goldsmith, in 1868 and almost totally rebuilt.

workers that were a feature of East Anglian farming had no counterpart in Hertfordshire. Small children taken on during the long hours of the harvest could be at risk. In 1869 the Hertfordshire coroner called attention to the dangers of employing small boys in charge of heavy wagons and horse teams after an accident near Royston when an eleven-year-old was killed falling from the driving seat of a harvest wagon.[14]

For the male workers, Hertfordshire was still very much a low-wage county in spite of the general improvement in wages. Farm workers' wages compared badly not only with urban wages but also with other forms of rural employment. Railwaymen, policemen, brick workers and builders' men were all paid considerably more. A Hertfordshire police constable for example was paid nineteen shillings a week when the force was established in 1841. A railway porter could get about eighteen shillings a week and a skilled carpenter about thirty shillings. Nationally, farm workers were paid most where there was alternative employment in industry or coal mining. The north of England was on the whole a better paid region even for the farm workers. One reflection of this was shown by the practice of the Great Northern Railway[15] whose wage scales for unskilled workers were higher from King's Cross to Barnet but then fell off only to rise again north of Grantham. Wages continued to vary somewhat within the county, being highest in the extreme south particularly the lower Lea valley below Ware and around Watford in the south-west. Wages in villages near to towns were slightly higher than in the depths of the country. In the more remote areas of East Hertfordshire, around Buntingford and Royston, wages were of an East Anglian bleakness throughout the century.[16]

One result of this was a steady flight from the land even when farming was prosperous. From being concerned that the land was over-populated and carrying a population of paupers that were a drain on the rates, the landowners and employers became concerned about the supply of labour and started to consider ways of inducing farm workers to remain on the land.

References

1. Select Committee on Agricultural Customs BPP 1848 VII.
2. Cadle, C., 'Farming Covenants', in *JRASE*, 1868, p. 154.
3. HALS Wilshere papers 59896.
4. HALS Dacre papers MISC VI 40669.
5. *Hertfordshire County Press*, 12 Apr 1838.
6. Lawson-Tancred, Mary, 'The Anti-League in the Corn Law Crisis', *Historical Journal* iii.2, 1960.
7. *Hertfordshire Mercury*, 10 Feb 1844, 2 May 1844.
8. *Hertfordshire County Press*, 10 Feb 1846.
9. *Hertfordshire Mercury*, 18 Apr 1846.
10. SC on Game Laws. BPP 1846 IX, p. 8.
11. SC on Agricultural Customs. ibid. BPP 1848 VII.
12. *Hertfordshire Mercury*, 27 Apr 1850.
13. HALS D/Ex 55 E2.
14. RC on Children, Young Persons and Women in Agriculture 1867. BPP 1868–9 XII.
15. PRO BTHR files GNR 1 and RHR 1.
16. Hunt, E.H., *National Wage Variations in Britain 1850–1914*, 1975.

CHAPTER EIGHT

Landed society

O NLY TWO COMPREHENSIVE surveys have ever been carried out
to find out who owns the land of England. One was the Domesday
Book of 1086 and the other was a survey carried out in the late nineteenth century on the instructions of Lord Derby in 1873. For present purposes
then we have only the 1873 survey which was published both in the government
Blue Books of the day[1] and in a summary by a Victorian landowner, John Bateman in his *Great Landowners of Great Britain and Ireland* of 1876.[2] There is, of
course, more information available mostly pertaining to individual parishes
available in tithe returns, enclosure awards, poor rates records and the like but
no other complete survey, although the records of land valuation under the
Finance Bill of 1910 attained a high level of coverage.

The first point to note about the Hertfordshire landed gentlemen with their
country seats is that there were rather a lot of them. Hertfordshire ranks third in
a list of English counties with regard to the number of country seats per square
mile. Only Rutland and Staffordshire had a higher density. Why were they so
thick on the ground in Hertfordshire? A cursory glance at the map reveals that
many Hertfordshire parishes still possess more than one house at the centre of a
landed estate. In many instances there is not only a traditional great house
belonging to some ancestral family but also a number of substantial properties
built by people who wished to consider themselves as country gentlemen and
adopt their lifestyle. Offley, for example, had a traditional great house, Offley
Place, seat of the Salusburys; Clouds Hill was built by a landowning vicar; Welbury was constructed by Francis Gosling, a London banker in or about 1870 and
Little Offley was home of a substantial owner-occupier farmer.

Further south, at St Paul's Walden, were three houses belonging to agricultural landowners: St Paul's Waldenbury owned by a 'traditional' landed family, the Bowes-Lyons; The Hoo, (demolished in 1948) belonging to the Trevor-Brand family (Lord Dacre); and Stagenhoe, a house that changed hands several times but was the centre of a small estate of farms and woodlands. In addition, the parish contained four substantial owner occupiers among the farmers. In a number of parishes, the great houses of Hertfordshire seem to go in pairs. At Puckeridge, there is Hamels, a traditional family house, and Coles Park which had a series of owners. Some parishes had only one major house. At Rushden there was only Julians, seat of the Meetkerks, Dutch in origin but well established by the nineteenth century.

Other parishes, hitherto without a great house, acquired one in the course of the nineteenth century. At Willian, an incomer named Charles Hancock, a prosperous Bond Street jeweller and goldsmith, who had already bought Hendon Hall, Middlesex, bought the close parish from Baron Dimsdale, who was himself a descendant of a medical pioneer. The title of 'baron' is unusual in England but the first Baron Dimsdale was a pioneering eighteenth-century doctor whose work introducing vaccination to Russia had resulted in the title of Baron of the Russian Empire in 1769 and a fortune to buy an estate in Hertfordshire. The Dimsdales had been absentees at Willian, but Hancock not only rebuilt the village but also built a new mansion, Roxley Court, where there was none before.

Hertfordshire was a popular county with those who had made enough money to set up as a country gentleman but still wished to keep in touch with the metropolis. The excellent communications with London may not be the whole story. Surrey, so popular with the upper-middle classes does not seem to have been so attractive for the really great estates although it was popular enough for the lesser landed gentry. It came only eighteenth in terms of country seats. Berkshire, a county very comparable with Hertfordshire in size, scenery and distance from London came only sixteenth in this particular league table; while Essex was a distinctly ungentrified county at thirtieth. If the often underrated countryside of Essex is cited as an explanation for its neglect by the wealthy, there is the even lower position of Buckinghamshire to be considered – a county with attractive hills in the south and hunting country in the north but only rating at thirty-third in the order of nineteenth-century gentrification. A house in Hertfordshire was certainly a prime choice for those members of the upper classes who wanted a place in the Home Counties.

Presumably the reason for the large number of landed seats in Hertfordshire was the convenience of the county for monied families either originating in

London as bankers, merchants or professional men, or families with northern or Scottish connections who wanted a place near London but on the route north. Whatever the reason, the proliferation had meant that the average acreage of country estates was often rather low compared with other counties. At the time of the 1873 survey, the largest estate in the county, the Marquess of Salisbury's estate at Hatfield with 13,389 acres, only amounted to about three per cent of the county. In neighbouring Bedfordshire, the mighty Russell estate at Woburn had over 30,000 acres and amounted to eleven per cent of that county.

Only two other landowners owned estates in Hertfordshire of over 10,000 acres. They were Abel-Smith of Woodhall near Watton at Stone with 10,212 acres and Lord Cowper of Panshanger near Hertford with 10,122 acres. There were twenty-seven landowners in the county with estates within the county of more than 3,000 acres.

It was the number of smaller estates of 1,000 to 3,000 acres, about forty in all, that made Hertfordshire somewhat different from most other counties. Nationally about twelve per cent of England was owned by property owners on this scale but about seventeen per cent of Hertfordshire was owned by estates in this category. Only two other English counties had a higher percentage of their land owned by estate owners of this amount of property – Surrey and Dorset.[3]

It was this type of small estate that was most varied. Some were owned by old families settled in the county since Tudor times or earlier and whose interests were entirely agricultural and were dependent on farm rents. In most cases their banking or mercantile origins had been long left behind but in some cases merchant or professional interests had been continued. The Radcliffes of Hitchin Priory retained their connection with the Levant Company throughout the eighteenth century. Others were quite clearly monied incomers like Charles Hancock of Roxley Court or Francis Gosling of Welbury.

An open elite?

The degree to which the landed gentry of England were either an open or a closed society has been a matter of debate. There has been a persistent belief that, unlike other European countries, England possessed a relatively open elite that, while consisting of a core of hereditary landed families, was nevertheless open to entry by newcomers who had gained their wealth from industry, trade or the professions. Work by Lawrence Stone and Jeanne Fawtier Stone has accumulated evidence to the contrary.[4] Their work examined three English counties,

Northumberland, Northamptonshire and Hertfordshire, and concluded that, although family descent was often interrupted by infertility or accident, on the whole landed families were people of landed origin themselves. Although there were successful professional men who acquired landed estates, by far the most usual way to gain control of landed estates was by inheritance or by marriage.

The Stones found that this conclusion was less true of Hertfordshire than the other two counties but nevertheless, non-landed incomers did not amount to more than about twenty per cent of the landed families at any one time. Even some undoubted incomers were aristocratic landed gentry with estates else-where. The Countess of Caledon acquired Tyttenhanger Park and the Earl of Strathmore, St Paul's Waldenbury in order to have property closer to London than their main territorial bases in Ireland and Scotland respectively.

Actual industrialists were certainly uncommon, although the Greggs of Styal Mill near Manchester bought Hamels at Puckeridge. Brewers, bankers, lawyers were more common as were soldiers, sailors and courtiers. New purchasers were not necessarily practising their professions at the time they became Hertford-shire landowners nor did they always continue to practise the family business or profession once they had obtained their landed estates in the county.

Hertfordshire was a county of small estates. Many of them were not really large enough to sustain a great house or a gentlemanly lifestyle without income from elsewhere. Although the Stones' point about a non-open elite may on the whole be true of the larger and long established estates, it was less true of the numerous gentlemen's houses with estates of 1,000 acres or less. The county has many examples of country houses built or re-built in the nineteenth century with a small estate of perhaps 800 to 1,000 acres sub-divided into two or three farms together with some woodland kept in hand.

To build a house in the first place and keep it up with a complement of ser-vants would need a substantial income, yet Hertfordshire has many examples in almost every parish. Unlike the traditional estates such as Hatfield, Panshanger or Cassiobury, the small gentry estates are not well documented. They are often ignored by traditional county historians such as Chauncy or Cussons[5] who go no further than discuss the manor on which such an estate may be based. The Vic-torian directories list the owners of these houses but are not usually so indelicate as to enlarge upon the origins of their wealth if it happens to be in trade. The early career of Sir Henry Lushington of Aspenden Hall of the Indian Judiciary might get a mention but a veil was often drawn over the commercial origins of a Bond Street shopkeeper such as Charles Hancock of Roxley Court. Furthermore, unlike the traditional gentry the newcomers tended to be less conspicuous in the life of the county as magistrates or as lords lieutenant although some made a point of more discreet public service such as subscribing to local charities or village schools.

The landlord as entrepreneur

However much the landed gentry were replenished by successful incomers from trade, industry or the professions, it must also not be forgotten that landowners as such were economically active themselves as entrepreneurs. The continued survival of a confident and capable ruling class in an industrial society would not have been possible otherwise.

It is true that most members of the aristocracy were not particularly technically minded although an exception might be made of the Marquess of Salisbury, a keen amateur scientist who supervised one of the earliest installations of electric light into a country house. The best known technical figure to be associated with Hertfordshire, Henry Bessemer, although undoubtedly successful did not set up as a landed proprietor in his native county. Generally the role of the landowners in industrial development was to provide capital and add social prestige to large projects. An early example was Francis Egerton, Duke of Bridgewater with the construction of the Grand Junction Canal. The most notable figure among Hertfordshire landowners as both a technical innovator and a commercial entrepreneur was John Bennet Lawes of Rothamsted, a self-taught agricultural chemist and successful developer of superphosphates. He was, of course, very much an exceptional figure and nearly impoverished himself before achieving final success and acclaim.

Landed gentry could not only supply money and status but also land itself. Apart from their initiative in agricultural enclosure and improvement they were able to make economic initiatives in areas where the possession of land was a prerequisite. In other counties, the development of mining and building projects were obvious outlets but, in Hertfordshire, there was no prospect of mining and no landlord-inspired new towns appeared in this county. Hertfordshire's best known experiments in community development, the Chartist 'O'Connorville' at Heronsgate and Ebenezer Howard's Garden Cities at Letchworth and Welwyn owed little to the support of local country landowners.

The gentry did show sustained interest in railways once the early misgivings were overcome and the economic advantages of railways became accepted. It has already been said that the main Hertfordshire railways were the result of initiatives from outside the county seeking to create links between London and the north. Hertfordshire men, whether landowners or not, only played a very ancillary role in these schemes. The first main line, the London and Birmingham, was very much the creation of Robert Stephenson and his northern colleagues; the Great Northern of 1850 likewise was a northern initiative but here the local notables did play a part. Although the Leeds businessman Edmund Denison was the prime mover, the company produced a galaxy of nobility representative of the counties that the line was to pass through. Once again Lord Dacre of the Hoo was the Hertfordshire representative. Otherwise however, the Hertfordshire gentry were conspicuous by their absence. In the list of prominent scrip holders were included William Hale of King's Walden and Baron Dimsdale, both Hertfordshire landowners, together with Richard Oakley, a farmer of Offley, Joseph Sharples, a Hitchin banker, John Curling of Gosmore and William Lucas, maltster of Hitchin – all solid Hertfordshire figures but hardly the landowning elite of the county.

The London and York Railway was assisted in its early days to fend off a rival project called the Direct Northern Railway by a campaign of meetings and petitions led by north Hertfordshire business figures, but with landowners Frederick Delme Radcliffe and G. Dudley Ryder chairing both the committee and the public meetings that followed. The role of the county gentry was to use its prestige to grace public occasions and give a project of sufficiently impressive scale, such as the London and York Railway company, a helping hand.

The third main line, resulting from the decision by the Midland Railway to establish a new main line to bypass its connection with the GNR at Hitchin with a direct line from Bedford to St Pancras, was taken entirely by its senior directors who were exclusively midlanders – James Allport of Birmingham, John and Henry Ellis of Leicester and Samuel Beale of Derby. They did enlist the support of a local landowner William Henry Whitbread in their initial effort to penetrate Bedfordshire to get as far as Hitchin from Leicester in 1856 but seemingly had no local ally in their final move through Hertfordshire to London in 1865.[6]

The shorter, lateral railways were more likely to be the objects of local initiatives. One early, and largely Hertfordshire example, was the abortive Cambridge and Oxford Railway of 1845. Chaired by Lord Dacre of Kimpton Hoo, the line was planned from Cambridge to Oxford via Royston, Hitchin and Luton. Apart from Dacre himself, most of the Hertfordshire men involved seem to have been middle-class businessmen who also owned land such as John George Fordham, maltster of Royston, Joseph Sharples, banker of Hitchin and William Wilshere, Hitchin attorney and landowner in Welwyn. In the event the Cambridge and Oxford project was a failure except in so far as a short stretch, described in Chapter One, between Royston and Hitchin was built in 1851 to connect the Great Northern eventually with Cambridge.

Otherwise the promotion of local lines seems to have been largely at the behest of businessmen rather than landowners. The Ware, Hadham and Buntingford Railway of 1856 was the brain child of Charles Adams, a surveyor of Barkway with much of the active backing coming from George Mickley, a tanner and currier of Buntingford and a committee of similar figures from the local building and farming community. Only Sir Henry Lushington, a retired judge of the Indian Judiciary and Charles Ellis of Wyddial Hall could be described as landowners.

On the other side of the county, the Hemel Hempstead and Harpenden railway of 1863, known for some reason as the 'Nicky line', was promoted by John Grover, John Barrow and Henry Balderston all merchants trading in corn, coal and manure in the immediate area. They seem to have coped without a gentry figurehead. Not so the Hatfield and St Albans line which managed to enrol Lord Ebury of Moor Park and Algernon Capel of Hadham Hall.

All things considered, the role of the landowning community was to provide an endless supply of impressive social figureheads to be wheeled out when required to provide social prestige and supportive investment. Although they undoubtedly played a part in the economic development of the county, it would be stretching credibility to call them all entrepreneurs.

The landowner and the environment

The landed gentry were the only members of rural society who had enough economic security to give them genuine freedom to decide how they spent their time. They were neither under other men's orders like the farm workers nor tied to an unrelenting pattern of the seasons' tasks in the manner of the farmers. This is not to say that they had no economic function – they took the long-term decisions about the fixed capital of the land and its buildings. The pattern of fields, woods, drains, water courses and roads was as the landlords decreed. They built cottages to rent and helped to establish village schools. They helped to maintain law and order in their capacity as magistrates and in some cases represented the county or its boroughs as Members of Parliament. Needless to say, they did all this very much on their own terms and to a large extent in their own interest. The structure of rural society makes it difficult to distinguish between altruism and long-term self-interest on the part of those at the top of the tree.

For the rest of their time, there can be no doubt that their favourite occupation was the pursuit of wild animals. Field bloodsports were considered the proper occupation of the country gentleman and to an extent of the country lady as well. Hunting, shooting and fishing filled much of the year. It influenced other aspects of country life from the landscape to the legal system and was the linchpin of social life.

Fox hunting was the most prestigious of the field sports of the gentry. Hertfordshire was the territory of several hunts – most of the county was covered by the Hertfordshire Hunt. In the east, however, the Puckeridge Hunt based at Brent Pelham held sway while the Enfield Chase Hunt worked the Middlesex border in the south and the Old Berkeley with kennels at Chipperfield worked the southern Chilterns in the south-west.

The Hertfordshire Hunt had been founded in the early years of the nineteenth century by the Marchioness of Salisbury as the Hatfield Hunt. When she relinquished control in 1828, the position of Master of the Hunt was taken over by Sir Thomas Sebright of Beechwood Hall, Flamstead and the hunt became the Hertfordshire Hunt. A succession of Hertfordshire gentlemen and nobility succeeded to the post including Frederick Delme-Radcliffe of Hitchin Priory, Lord Dacre of Kimpton Hoo and George Leigh of Luton Hoo.

In a lowland county, the only quarry of the hunter was the fox. Neither stag hunting nor otter hunting had any significant following in this county. Although active membership of the hunt conferred social prestige, as far as is known, fox hunting had little effect on either the social system or on the landscape of well-wooded Hertfordshire. Only in the extreme north, where the fields had been laid out geometrically by the process of enclosure, was it necessary to plant the special coverts for foxes that are so characteristic of the midland counties. There is one, named as such, between Cadwell and Wilbury Hill near modern Letchworth and there may be others.

The only feature of the countryside that can be traced back to the practice of fox hunting is the survival of the fox itself. Along with the secretive badger and the aquatic otter, the fox survived the nineteenth century in southern England. The other medium-sized predators, the pine marten, the polecat and the wild cat did not, although the polecat has returned in recent years with a little help from its friends. The larger predators, the wolf and the bear were, of course, long gone.

Where killed.	When.	Grouse.	Par-tridge.	Pheasant.	Wood-cock.	Snipe.	Wild Fowl.	Hare.	Rabbit.	Total each Day and.
		207	503	7	3	70	162	90	990
	15 Monday									
Hallonod & Sadler Springs	16 Tuesday	"	"	16	"	"	"	4	3	23
Furze Fields	17 Wednesd.	"	"	20	"	"	"	1	4	33
Furze Fields	18 Thursday			6	"					6
	19 Friday									
	20 Saturday									
	Total ...		207	553	7	3	10	167	105	1052
		Killing shots				Missing shots				

Memorandum of Game, to whom sent, &c. &c.

16 Sir Wm Gordon &c.

17 Sir Wm Gordon &c.

18 Three Scoundrels invaded the Furze Fields, which they would not quit for the notice, and expostulations of Bowra. I promise them their days shooting shall be an expensive amusement. and will spare nothing to bring them to punishment.

8.1 A page from the Game Book of the Gorhambury Estate, near St Albans, dating from 1816 and showing the day's bag of game. It indicates the range of game species shot on this mid-Hertfordshire estate. It also illustrates the wrath of the landowners when three poachers were apprehended on the estate. It is obvious that the three intruders were quite unrepentant and defied Bowra the keeper in his efforts to persuade them to desist. It is evident that not all poaching was either secret or nocturnal. The guests on this occasion included Sir Henry and Gerald Wellesley, members of the Duke of Wellington's family and Lord Cranbourne, eldest son of Lord Salisbury

The survival of the fox as the only highly mobile and terrestrial predator was almost certainly due to the protection offered to the species by the landowners' hunting interest and to the extreme adaptability of the fox itself, although here its success in penetrating the urban environment seems to have been a twentieth-century phenomenon. The larger predators that did not have status as a quarry for an upper-class sport were treated as vermin both by the farming community and the sporting interests. With every man's hand against them, they soon succumbed to the invention of the breech-loading shotgun. Hunting was viewed with indifference by the labourers and with general approval by the farmers as long as the hunters were reasonably generous about paying for any damage.

HERTFORDSHIRE.

IMPORTANT SALE.

THE TEMPLE DINSLEY ESTATE.

A very choice RESIDENTIAL PROPERTY in the County of Hertford, situate at Preston, about three miles from the capital

MARKET TOWN OF HITCHIN.

Where there is a first-class Station on the Great Northern Railway, with junctions to the Cambridge and Midland Railways, 33 miles from London.

THE ESTATE, which was formerly possessed by the Knights Templars and subsequently by Sir Ralph Sadlier, Secretary of State to King Henry VIII., comprises a FINE OLD MANSION, fit for a family of distinction, and on which a very considerable sum has been recently expended in substantial and decorative repairs, standing in a beautiful undulating Park of 25 acres, well timbered with stately oak, elm, lime, walnut and other trees; well-arranged pleasure grounds, kitchen garden, in which there are several newly-erected glass-houses, stabling for six horses, carriage houses and small homestead; together with several WELL-CULTIVATED FARMS, about 160 Acres of Woodland, superior Residence or Shooting Box, near to the Mansion, and about 40 COTTAGES in the village of Preston; the whole embracing an area of about

560 ACRES

of very fertile Land, the whole of which is Freehold and Tithe Free.

This exceedingly valuable Property, which is situate in one of the most delightful parts of the County of Hertford, is near to the estates of Lord Caithness, C. C. Hale, Esq., Lord Lytton, Lord Dacre, Lady Glamis, F. P. Delme Radcliffe, Esq., G. Oakley, Esq., and others. It is in a favourite hunting district, and within an easy distance of the kennels and principal meets of Mr. Leigh's hounds, and the sporting capabilities are of a high character, and afford excellent partridge and pheasant shooting.

Messrs. HARDING & EVE

Are instructed by the Proprietor to offer the above valuable property *by auction* (unless previously disposed of by contract),

AT THE AUCTION MART, LONDON,

On MONDAY, July 7th 1873.

Further particulars may be obtained of Messrs. Wade, solicitors, Hitchin and Shefford; and of Messrs. Harding & Eve, auctioneers, land and estate agents and surveyors, St. Alban's and Hitchin, Herts, and Silsoe, Beds.

8.2 A Hertfordshire estate for sale from the Herts Mercury *of 17 May 1873. Temple Dinsley at Preston near Hitchin was home to a Quaker family in the early nineteenth century. The social and sporting advantages of the county were emphasised as the main selling point of this landed estate rather than its agricultural profitability*

Shooting had a much more drastic effect on the county. The main game species were the pheasant and the common or grey partridge and perhaps right at the end of our period the red-legged or French partridge. Other game species included 'wild fowl', mainly ducks, woodcock, snipe, along with the rabbit and the hare. Shooting rather than hunting was a continuous activity throughout the winter months on landed estates. It affected the relationship between landlord and tenant and it created tension between the propertied classes and the proletariat. It became the dominant use for woodland taking precedence over all forms of forestry, including the production of both timber and coppice firewood. For many landowners, shooting was the primary motive for wanting to live in the country at all.

Field sports acted as a link between the county gentry and the national, or even the international, elite of the day. Lord Verulam entertained Princess Victoria and Count Esterhazy on the Gorhambury Estate in the 1830s and even the more intelligent and enterprising figures such as John Bennet Lawes were frequent guests at shooting occasions.

Partridges were the main quarry in the early part of the century when the usual method of shooting took the form of walking the fields accompanied by dogs. The pheasant gained in importance as the century wore on although five times as many pheasants as partridges were shot on the Gorhambury Estate in the 1820s. Pheasants are a woodland species although they feed in fields as well as woodlands. Their numbers can be built up by judicious protection and by the augmentation of specially bred birds. Pheasants were shot in a different way from the partridges. Instead of walking the fields and shooting birds as they rose, the pheasant shooters stood in line facing a woodland through which teams of beaters passed to force the birds into flight. The birds were shot down as they emerge in flight out of the woodland.

The existence of the partridge probably had little effect on the landscape unless it discouraged some landowners from grubbing up hedgerows, although this was a laborious business before the coming of modern machinery. Farm land was usually tenanted and if it was kept in hand by the estate it was for farming purposes rather than for shooting.

Pheasants, on the other hand, were a much more significant source of both landscape modification and social conflict. Woods originally planted or managed for forestry were kept in hand as pheasant preserves. Being semi-domesticated, pheasants were easier to catch and therefore to poach. Woodlands became jealously guarded monospecific sanctuaries for pheasants with members of the public rigorously excluded. Spring-guns and mantraps were in common use at the beginning of the century and had not entirely vanished at the end of it.

Where game was concerned, landlords claimed a monopoly of predation. All other predators both human and animal were rigorously suppressed. Poaching was, of course, a criminal offence but not one that was regarded with the same seriousness by all classes. Some estates kept a meticulous record of the season's shooting. The person who maintained the Gorhambury game book regarded conflict with the poachers as an undeclared war but with no great bitterness. Catching and punishing the poachers was almost an extension of the sport. In his evidence to the Select Committee on the Game Laws in 1848, the Marquess of Salisbury affected a nostalgic tolerance for the local poacher catching rabbits to feed his family but expressed abhorrence at what he claimed was a new type of poacher in the organised gangs emanating from the towns. Interestingly, similar comments from rural dwellers to the effect that organised rural crime emanating from the towns is a novel phenomenon is still to be heard today. It must be part of the 'golden age' myth of country life. Incidentally, any claimed tolerance of the local poacher as a loveable rogue to be treated with amused indulgence is not borne out by the sentences imposed when they were caught.

The impression that the lower classes did not see poaching in the same light was borne out by the evidence of the chaplain to Hertford gaol who related theological arguments with poachers in custody maintaining that God had put wild animals on earth for the benefit of all and not just the landlords.[7]

The strained relations between landlord and tenant over the game laws has already been mentioned in Chapter Seven. The tenant's problem was not so much concern about poaching as the damage that game itself could do to their crops and that they were powerless to prevent. Radicals in Parliament such as John Bright could produce tenants who were prepared to compromise their reputation with landowners in order to make their feelings known, but no doubt many other tenant farmers suffered in silence.

Apart from general damage, it is not clear how far the game laws were actually deleterious to progressive farming as opposed to just being a nuisance. James Nowlson of Harpfield Hall, St Albans told the commission that damage by game animals could be serious. He went so far as to say that hares, which the farmer was barred from shooting, made effective crop rotation impossible by depleting the stock of turnips. This, in its turn, meant that the farmer could not maintain the number of sheep necessary to fertilise the soil and so support an adequate crop of wheat. In his view 'high farming' and the strict preservation of game were incompatible.

Both the Marquess of Salisbury and Captain Robertson, the Chief Constable of Hertfordshire, advanced the argument that the presence of gamekeepers on an estate acted as a deterrent to other rural malefactors such as sheep stealers or rick burners. Both cited the example of William Baker, owner of the Bayford-bury estate, who had resumed game preservation partly at the request of his ten-antry because the presence of keepers helped to prevent damage and theft on the farms and on the estate.

Animal predators were dealt with even more ruthlessly than human preda-tors of game. at least two and possibly three species of carnivorous mammal were eliminated from Hertfordshire in the name of game preservation in the course of the nineteenth century. They were the pine marten, the polecat and, possibly, the true wildcat. All three seem to have been present in the 1820s. There is always the possibility that what are referred to as 'wild cats' refer only to feral domestic cats but this seems unlikely. Even today, populations of feral domestic cats do not establish themselves in either farmland or woodland although they are frequent enough in derelict urban areas. A polecat and a 'wild cat' were shot on the same day at Furzefield, Gorhambury on 29 October 1816.[8] According to the Zoological Society of London, the last reliable sighting of a pine marten in Hertfordshire was as late as December 1872 in the south of the county.[9]

The smaller and more agile weasel and stoat both survived in spite of perse-cution and the rigorous guardianship of woods and rivers may well have helped the secretive badger and the otter to survive. Badgers would have certainly been dug up for baiting purposes by marauding gangs if the woods had been less strictly policed.

The larger bird predators fared similarly. The larger raptors, buzzards, harri-ers and possibly the red kite, were all present in the county at the start of the century and gone by the end of it while the smaller and more agile spar-rowhawks and kestrels survived.

At times all species were at risk. On 16 January 1826, the bag at Gorhambury included a thrush, a starling, a sparrow, two chaffinches, a 'tomtit', a redwing, two water wagtails and a treecreeper, all shot by Lord Grimstone and Mr Paget.

In spite of the distortion caused to Hertfordshire's ecology by wiping out the major predators, it is just possible that on balance the landlord-dominated countryside was a benefit to wildlife. The landlords maintained a habitat where a rich variety of wildlife could survive. Without the landlords and their sporting interests, it is all too easy to imagine a land-hungry peasantry, if left to themselves, cutting down the woods and trying to cultivate every inch of the land. That of course has been a defence that the landlords themselves have advanced whenever the subject has been raised. They have all too often been taken at their own valuation as the stewards of the countryside but on the question of the survival of woodland in a crowded county, they may well have a point.

Finally, the present Hertfordshire fauna includes animals that were actually introduced by landlords either in or fairly near this county. These include some of the most familiar mammals in the present Hertfordshire countryside such as the muntjac deer and the grey squirrel. In addition, the nocturnal and elusive edible dormouse was also a nineteenth-century introduction, probably on the Rothschild estate at Tring, and its British population is still confined to that area of the Chilterns.

The dominance of the landowner

It is axiomatic of course that, in a landed society, ownership of land conferred both economic power and social status. No one would seriously doubt that nineteenth-century Hertfordshire was led by men like the Marquess of Salisbury, Lord Verulam and Lord Cowper. More locally, power was wielded by the lesser landowners such as Frederick Delme Radcliffe of Hitchin Priory, William Wilshere of Welwyn Frythe or William Baker of Bayfordbury. How far did this power extend? Were there any parts of Hertfordshire where the squire literally owned all he surveyed?

Outright ownership of an entire community could create a 'close' or 'closed' parish. This meant that one individual was in a position to say who could live in the parish at all. They could of course decide who managed to obtain the tenancy of a farm. Here the landowner, however absolute his ownership, still had to appreciate that the number of skilled farmers with proven experience of agricultural management, commercial shrewdness and, adequate working capital was limited. Although many tenants were legally only 'tenants at will' they could not be treated in an arbitrary fashion even by the most tyrannical of landlords.

The position of the labourer was different. In general, the labourer had little bargaining power and both farmers and landowners were in a position to pick and choose. The farmer hired and fired but, in a closed parish, it was the landlord who was in a position to exclude any who did not contribute in the form of regular, obedient work. The marginal, the indifferent and the shiftless could all be excluded and this could also include any person of independence and spirit among the lower orders. Good cottages, allotments and a village school did not necessarily make up for a life of circumspect deference.

The surplus population, whether ejected by the owners of close parishes or unwilling to accept a life of subservient restraint, tended to move to those parishes where no one was in a position to exclude them. This could of course be a town or even London itself but, even without leaving the land, it was still possible to live in an open parish. In these villages there was no single landowner and, while they were far from being egalitarian communities, property was more widely spread. There were still wealthy landowners, although they were not necessarily resident in the parish. As well as the farmers whose status was measured by their acres, and also to an extent by their status as freeholders or tenants, there was also an intermediate group of professionals, annuitants, shop keepers, innkeepers, craftsmen, petty traders of many kinds and finally the mass of farm workers and straw plaiting womenfolk. Life in an open village was rougher, more varied, but not necessarily more brutal. If there were more beerhouses there was also a choice of chapels. There was more choice of employment, religious denomination, shops, friends or marriage partners. An open parish was a step towards an urban society. The disadvantages were less security, less paternal care from a caring landlord and perhaps poorer cottages than on a well-run estate. Residents of an unregulated open parish might find themselves living in a rented rookery owned by an innkeeper or a blacksmith's widow who collected every penny of rent and never got around to mending a leaky roof.

Open parishes tended to be more varied mainly because they were usually larger. A person had to be very obnoxious to be excluded from an open parish although anecdotal evidence indicates that this could sometimes happen. The Midlands tradition of 'tin panning out' a notorious drunk or slut was probably not unknown in Hertfordshire, although hard evidence is not easy to come by. Even now it is not something people like to talk about. Further research needs to be done as to whether landlords permitted religious diversity but the advantage of an open village is that if a religious congregation could get enough assets together to build a chapel in an open parish, no one would stop them.

There is no definitive list of closed or open parishes in Hertfordshire. The majority of Hertfordshire parishes were open. Of the larger settlements only Hatfield appears to have been dominated by its local great house and even here the Cecils did not own all the town nor did they control all the farmland in this very large parish. Most villages were either open in the sense of being villages in the way Pirton was, with no overall owner and no resident grandee, or, closed, like St Paul's Walden with three major landowners resident and also at least three substantial owner-occupying farmers plus some cottage property owned by people of lesser status. In this county, parishes that were totally or almost totally owned by one individual, whether resident or not, were very much a minority.

In some counties, including parts of neighbouring Bedfordshire, a definite pattern can be ascertained by which open and closed parishes alternate – each proprietorial parish seems to have offloaded its surplus population on to a neighbouring open parish. This pattern can be seen in east Bedfordshire near Biggleswade where single-proprietor parishes Edworth, Eyeworth and Cockayne Hatley alternate with open Dunton, Wrestlingworth and Potton. Possibly this pattern can be extended southwards into Hertfordshire where open Hinxworth and open Ashwell pair with closed Radwell, Caldecote and Astwick, the latter in Bedfordshire. On the whole no obvious pattern emerges in the distribution of Hertfordshire closed parishes. All one can say is that some villages randomly scattered in the county were places where all the property was in the same hands.

Closed parishes tended to be small. It is difficult to see whether this was cause or effect. Until the passing of the Union Changeability Act 1863, landowners had an incentive to keep residents to a minimum in order to keep down the poor rates. Equally, it is far more likely that a parish that was already small would fall into the hands of a single proprietor. Some, like Knebworth or Hexton, were virtually extensions of the estate and all the cottages were situated at the gates of the park. This type of closed parish had perforce to adopt a very deferential life style even if it was sometimes the beneficiary of considerate treatment. By the nineteenth century no landowner who cared for his reputation wanted to have a slum at his front gate. The other type of closed parish was where a single landlord owned all the parish but did not live there himself. These places could become forgotten and neglected settlements and tended to become depopulated. In same cases a vicar or a leading tenant farmer acted as a squire and made some effort to look after the community, but in other instances the tiny settlement could degenerate to become a forlorn collection of tumbledown cottages for a forgotten and dwindling community that still happened to possess a church. Hertfordshire parishes with a single but non-resident proprietor included Radwell, Caldecote and Wallington (although Shaw Green in the south of this parish belonged to Adolphus Meetkerk, the virtual sole proprietor of neighbouring Rushden).

Some of the open parishes consisted of a small and select settlement near to the great house and often bearing the name of the parish while a larger and more 'open' community developed as what was technically a hamlet in that it did not possess the parish church. These overspill communities came to contain the bulk of the parish population. Examples are the Waldens where the small settlements of St Paul's and King's Walden consisted of cottages owned by the squires, the Bowes-Lyons at St Paul's Walden and the Hales at King's Walden while, in each case, the bulk of the population lived in larger settlements elsewhere in the parish – Whitwell and Breachwood Green respectively. These settlements had a multiplicity of land ownership, a full range of crafts and services and were strongholds of religious dissent. It was almost a case of a closed and an open community co-existing within the same parish.

Other parishes were open in the sense that no one landowner controlled the parish but the men who did own the property were men of the landowning class. At Sandon, for example, the land was divided among a number of proprietors but nearly all the land was owned by wealthy landowners living elsewhere. The largest owner was Edward King Fordham, an Ashwell maltster, who owned 1,226 acres (thirty-one per cent of Sandon), but the four next largest landowners were not local owner-occupiers but were John Alington of Letchworth Hall with 301 acres, Robert Baker of Bayfordbury with 703 acres, Robert Gregg of Hamels Park, Puckeridge who was also a cotton manufacturer from Wilmslow, Cheshire with 110 acres, and John Izzard Pryor of Walkern Hall, a Baldock maltster, with 415 acres. The Dean and Chapter of St Paul's Cathedral also owned 415 acres of the parish. This hardly adds up to a democratic community of yeoman proprietors.

Patrons of education?

The country landowners were in a strong position to sponsor and advance education in the villages. Some, but by no means all, carried out their responsibilites admirably. In Hertfordshire, two families from the gentry stand out: the Abel Smiths and the Giles-Pullers. The Abel Smiths set up in Hertfordshire when Samuel Smith, son of a Nottingham banker, bought Woodhall near Watton-at-Stone in 1801. His son, Abel Smith represented Hertfordshire in the House of Commons from 1854 to 1898. He had schools built at Bramfield, Bengeo, Stapleford, Sacombe and Watton-at-Stone, provided for their maintenance and even supplied some winter clothing for the children. Another family, the Giles-Pullers of Ware, built schools in Ware itself and at Standon as well as co-operating with the Smiths to built Hockerill Teachers' College at Bishop's Stortford which opened in 1853.

The titled aristocracy of Hertfordshire had a less impressive record than the local gentry. Lord Cowper of Panshanger was a major patron of schools in the neighbouring borough of Hertford but it has to be said that neither Lord Verulam at St Albans nor the Earl of Essex of Cassiobury near Watford had a particularly impressive record of providing schools in their respective districts. It was noted that, had as much money been spent on education as had in fact been spent on bribery and treating in the notoriously corrupt politics of St Albans, the schools would be been very well provided for indeed. [10]

The role of the landowner

It is a matter of political preference whether one regards the agricultural landowner as an essential component of the agricultural economy or merely a parasite. Criticism of the landowners was indeed more strident in the nineteenth century than it is today now that landed society plays a less obvious role in national life. In the nineteenth century, the landed gentry were criticised not only by a small fringe of socialists and land reformers but by substantial citizens such as the free-trading, laissez-faire radicals of the type of John Bright and Joseph Chamberlain who tended to see the landowner, particularly members of the peerage, as men who reap where they have not sown. In their eyes the aristocracy did not have the moral high ground.

Later, during the agricultural depression, landowners were seen by radical opinion as a burden on the land which hampered the British farmer in his attempts to compete against his North American rivals who could own their land outright and farm it as they liked. Attempts to split the farmer from the landowner over the game laws, tenants' rights or more technical matters such as the strict settlement of estates met with little success. Part of the harm that the landowner generated in rural society was a regrettable tendency to encourage the lower orders to ape the lifestyle of their social superiors. The gentry would probably have regarded this as no more than the more affluent and successful members of the farming community having a commendable desire to aspire to the manners and lifestyle of a gentleman. Nevertheless there were those who pointed out that some farmers in economic difficulties had hitherto indulged themselves and their families in all the trappings of a Victorian upper-class lifestyle. The incoming Scots or Welsh tenants who came to take up abandoned holdings in the Home Counties were by contrast believed to be men of a sturdy and frugal peasant background. The mere replacement of one set of tenants by another was, of course, not all that critics of the landowning classes had in mind. However, the prospects of land reform in the sense of getting rid of the landowner completely is not the present concern.

Perhaps the most enduring legacy of the landowners as far as Hertfordshire is concerned is the survival of the distinctive pattern of the landscape – in particular the woodlands and much rural housing. If this country had been an egalitarian land of independent yeoman farmers in the eighteenth and nineteenth centuries it is more than likely that the woodlands in an arable county such as Hertfordshire would simply have been cleared for agriculture. How far the survival of woodland serves as some kind of justification for a very unequal social structure is debatable.

Europe may not have had a vast stockpile of wheat but virtually all of eastern and northern Europe had abundant timber. Industrial Britain could have imported all it needed by seeking no further than the other side of the North Sea and the Baltic. It is very unlikely that woodlands would have survived at all in southern England if they had been left to market forces. It was the landowner, with his insistence on sporting rights, who preserved the woods for future generations even if other people got precious little chance to enjoy them. It is to the woods of Hertfordshire that we must now turn.

References

1. Return of Owners of Land. BPP 1874 LXXII.
2. Bateman, J., *The Great Landowners of Great Britain and Ireland*, 1876.
3. Thompson, F.M.L., *English Landed Society in the Nineteenth Century*, 1963.
4. Stone, L. and Fawtier Stone, J.C., *An Open Elite? England 1540–1880*, 1984.
5. Chauncy, Sir Henry, *The Historical Antiquities of Hertfordshire*, 1700.
6. Cockman, F.G., *Railways of Hertfordshire*, 1974.
7. SC on the Game Laws. BPP 1848. Questions 3740–3747.
8. HALS Gorhambury papers.
9. Alston, E R. in the *Proc. Zoo. Soc. London*, 1879, p. 468.
10. Hurt, J.S., *Bringing Literacy to Rural England*, 1972; Children's Employment Commission. BPP 1843 XIV QQs 287–9; Children's Employment Commission, second report. BPP 1864 XXII xli.

CHAPTER NINE

Forestry

J UDGING BY THE MAPS, neither the amount nor the general distribution of woodland in Hertfordshire was very different in the eighteenth and nineteenth centuries from the state of affairs today. At present woodland covers about six per cent of the county. This means that Hertfordshire is distinctly less well wooded than other southern counties such as Kent, Sussex, Surrey or Buckinghamshire. On the other hand it is more wooded than its northern neighbours, Bedfordshire and Cambridgeshire, and about the same as Essex to the east.

It was not always so. Domesday evidence indicates that in the early Middle Ages about half of the county south and west of a line from Tring to Ware was well wooded while the area north and east of this line was less wooded. Forest still amounted to about fifteen per cent of the total land surface.

Hertfordshire contained no medieval royal forests set aside by the king for hunting. The medieval forest was an area set aside by royal decree and not necessarily actually planted with trees. Given the climate and soils of lowland areas in most parts of England, however, if such a district were not already wooded, it would soon have reverted to forest as a result of the mere absence of cultivation. There is little harm, therefore, in regarding a medieval forest as being what the word conjures up today – an extensive area of more or less natural woodland interspersed with scrub, heath and swamp. The fact that only the king's rangers were allowed to enter the area (with the possible exception of a few local villagers allowed in on sufferance to cut coppice wood or to hunt vermin) did nothing to detract from the fearsome reputation of such places.[1]

The absence of such vast tracts of wild terrain makes for a striking contrast with Essex where there were several large royal forests. Two of them, Epping Forest and Hatfield Forest, were within a few miles of the Hertfordshire border. (The latter takes its name from Hatfield Broad Oak and has no connection with

Hatfield in Hertfordshire). Immediately to the south in Middlesex was Enfield Chase and some of the larger woods in the south-east of Hertfordshire could be regarded as outlying woodlands or 'purlieus' of the chase. These would include Broxbourne, Wormley and Northaw Great Woods in what is still a heavily wooded part of the county. A 'chase' as opposed to a 'forest', in the Middle Ages, was a hunting ground that belonged to a nobleman or a bishop and not to the king. They served the same purpose of being a personal hunting terrain.

If Hertfordshire was not provided with any official royal hunting forests, it was compensated, to some extent, by being well endowed with private hunting parks which were maintained to provide wood-pasture for deer and ground game in the vicinity of large private houses.[2] Private woodland on the estates existed partly as cover for game and partly to provide building timber and supplies of faggots from coppice, wood that was cut from a stump at intervals of from seven to about fifteen years. There is a record of coppice from a wood at Offley dating from 1393. The coppicing of deciduous woodland, particularly hornbeam but also hazel and occasionally other trees such as ash, oak or beech was a very important method of forestry management through to the early twentieth century. A variant of this practice was pollarding, which involved cutting the branches higher on the trunk of the tree and above human (or animal) height. This was a very frequent practice for willows but also carried out on hornbeam, a very common tree in Hertfordshire, where grazing animals could gain access in wood-pasture or on the edges of woodlands. The use of coppicing or pollarding meant that supplies of wood could be obtained without the trees themselves having to be felled.[3]

Nevertheless, a considerable amount of ancient woodland dating from the Middle Ages or before did survive in this county and continues to survive as woodland to this day. With practice, it is easy to tell ancient woodland from more recent plantations.

Ancient woodlands that survive today tend to be fairly large or, if not large, are scattered fragments of larger woods. They invariably belong to estates and are kept in hand by the estate owners. They tend to be of irregular outline, sometimes with large serrations where arable land has been cut out of them at some stage in the past. They are frequently bounded and sometimes subdivided by banks and ditches. In many cases they are situated on parish boundaries and different sections of the same wood may bear different names on either side of the parish boundary. Where a recent plantation has been added to ancient woodland, the new planting has usually been given a separate name. More recently,

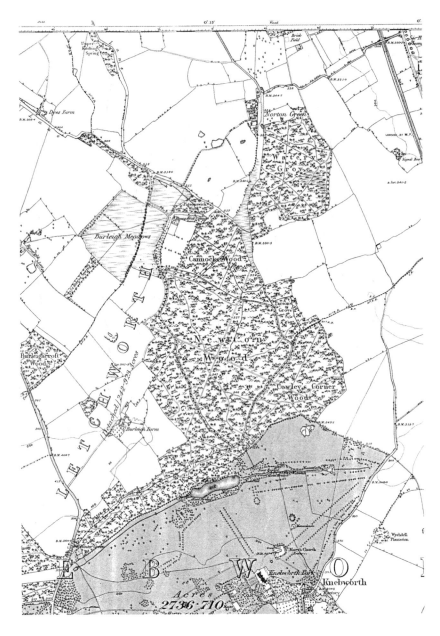

some ancient woodland has been clear felled and replaced by conifers with
sometimes a fringe of deciduous trees left around the edges.

According to a survey carried out in 1979,[4] eighteen different stand-types of
ancient semi-natural woodland were found in Hertfordshire. By far the commonest was a combination of standard oak and coppiced hornbeam. This type
of woodland consists typically of oak trees left as standards to grow to full height

9.1. (Opposite) Ancient woodlands on the Knebworth Estate. Ancient woodlands are those woods believed to have been in existence since at the least the seventeenth century. Typically they are deciduous. In Hertfordshire this usually means standard oak trees grown to full height and coppiced hornbeam cut at intervals of about twelve years from low-growing stumps or stools. They have survived mainly on the larger landed estates. Most of this area is in the parish of Knebworth but Burleigh Farm to the west of the ancient woodland was, in the nineteenth century, a detached portion of the parish of Letchworth some ten miles to the north. It was then a small village and now incorporated into the twentieth-century Garden City. The hamlet to the west is Langley, a dependency of Hitchin some five miles to the north. This pattern supports the theory that the settlements of this part of Hertfordshire arose from colonisation from the north in the form of medieval clearances cutting into the ancient woodland: a process called 'assarting'. The serrated edge of the woodland on its western boundary is typical of this process (OS map 1881 XX NE)

inter-planted with hornbeam cut at intervals at or near ground level. The other common stand-types were ash and sycamore woods in the north-east of the county and beech on the Chilterns in the west. As beech was not usually coppiced in this county and was frequently planted by landowners as a standing timber crop to be clear felled when ready, it is not easy to tell from appearances whether a beech wood is ancient and the historical record has to be consulted if available. Beech woods do not usually contain any underwood.

One other type of woodland that was common in the nineteenth century but is almost non-existent today was the elm-clone wood where a single suckering elm had, over the years, colonised an area of woodland or a stretch of hedgerow. These still exist as shrubs but Dutch-elm disease has made full-grown elm trees extremely rare. In the nineteenth century, oak, ash and elm in the hedgerows were an important marketable resource and one of great significance for the tenant farmer who was sometimes allowed to sell this timber.

Landowners have probably laid out new plantations throughout Hertfordshire's history but new plantations have been more common in times of agricultural recession. As far as is known virtually all the conifer woodland of the county results from deliberate plantation. Much of the present stock dates from the twentieth century but some is older. It has been suggested that roadside clumps of Scots pines were planted by or on behalf of Scottish cattle drovers to indicate the routes of drove roads or, on hilltops, to mark pasture fields where overnight grazing was permitted. It sounds romantic and perhaps unlikely but there are enough examples on the routes of known drove roads to make the idea plausible.

Where birch or hawthorn predominates, on the other hand, as on the commons on the Chilterns or on the gravelly heaths around Welwyn, the trees have usually self-sown on land once used for grazing. On some of the chalk slopes around Lilley and Offley, thorn scrub has turned once chalk grassland into scrubby woodland. Mazebeard Spring on the edge of Lilley Hoo is a case in point. Stands of holly have taken over where there was once heath as at Hertford Heath. It was probably originally planted as winter fodder where the grazing was poor and has now grown to replace the heather and gorse. Much open chalk grassland contains a large number of hawthorn seedlings that would quickly take over if grazing were to cease.

Planting by landowners also accounts for most of the sweet and horse chestnut woodland in the county. Some large areas of ancient oak woodland were planted with mixtures of sweet chestnut in the nineteenth century as at Hitch Wood and at Panshanger while in some parts largely treeless areas were heavily forested by oak and sweet chestnut planting. Ashridge, now one of Hertfordshire's most extensive areas of woodland, was largely common grazing before the nineteenth century. Similar methods were used on the Lautour estate on the north-eastern Chilterns around Ravensburgh Castle at Hexton.

Much of the new planting carried out by landowners consisted of amenity planting on their estates. Many of the exotic, or semi-exotic, species now present were planted during the nineteenth century and this includes most of the sweet chestnut, the walnut and the exotic conifers such as the Wellingtonias still to be seen. The Baker estates at Bayfordbury, for example, undertook extensive planting of exotics such as Lebanon cedar, Spanish chestnut and Turkey oak.[5] William Wilshere at Hitchin planted such exotics as the holm oak and poplar.[6] Although there is often extensive evidence of the planting of trees on the estates it is less easy to obtain knowledge of the distribution of tree species already present. Some idea of species present at various dates can be inferred from valuations but these do no more than offer rough estimates of numbers of trees on estates although sometimes, as at Beechwood Park, Flamstead in 1800, there appears to be an actual count.[7]

A map of 1778 survives of the Standon Green area on the Giles-Puller estates[8] that marks individual trees in the parishes of Standon and Thundridge and differentiates between oak, ash, elm and non-specific pollards. Oak was the commonest as a hedgerow tree. Ash was frequent as a hedgerow tree although no monospecific stands of this tree were marked. Elm was distinctly infrequent and was then confined to one small area at Standon Green and one stretch of roadside hedge. Unfortunately the extensive area of ancient woodland known as Standon Plashes is not included on this map, which covers the area on either side of Ermine Street (the present A10). Standon Plashes is largely an oak-horn-beam wood but contains a considerable area of ash probably cultivated as ash poles, which will be discussed below.

The marketing of forest products

The main forestry products were timber, wood and bark. 'Timber' meant the solid timber of the trunks and branches of full sized trees, while 'wood' usually referred to lighter branches or shoots from coppiced or pollarded stock. It was used mainly for firewood, the interwoven plashings used for sheep hurdles or for the infill of timber-frame buildings as a basis for wattle and daub and sometimes for small articles such as tool handles. Bark was cut for use in tanneries.

Before the coming of railways most of the products of Hertfordshire wood-lands were used locally. The standard oak trees were used for building construc-tion, ash for wagon wheels and tool handles, elm for coffins and beech for furniture. It is possible that some timber was sent out of the county if communi-cations were favourable. An annual timber sale was held each January on the Broxbourne estate to which naval contractors were invited. The proximity of the Lee Navigation, giving direct access to the Thames, would have made this an economic proposition.

It was the coppiced underwood that was of most importance for the local community. Coppiced woodlands were subdivided and small areas of coppice hazel or hornbeam were rented out to local people who could cut coppice wood either for their own use as firewood or for sale. A local man could make this a full-time activity over the winter season by taking on more than one woodland allotment from which he could then cut firewood and sell around the district.

Records of individual woodlands indicate that on the Sebright estate at Beechwood Park, Flamstead, faggots were cut by the estate workers and sold in lots of a hundred cut poles, or 'roods', to Dan Birdseye, Davy Jones and to the 'Breeches maker at Market Street' for sixteen shillings per hundred in 1760. Heavy timber went to Isaac Harvey of Hempstead for one shilling and four pence per foot or twenty-eight pounds and two shillings in all in August 1763.[9] At Wain Wood, St Ippolyts, between 1730 and 1735 about five acres of underwood was cut each year. About half was rented out by Thomas Merrick, the bailiff or wood-ward, to about five local people and the rest divided into twenty-rood lots (a

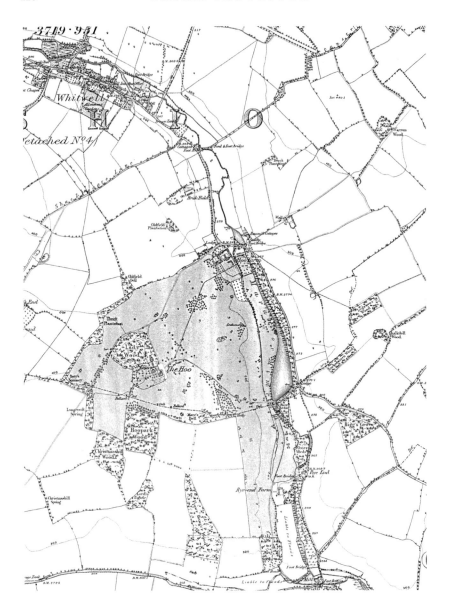

9.2 Ancient woodlands on the Kimpton Hoo Estate (OS map 1881 XX SW)

rood was twenty-two square yards) and let out to about thirty local people, presumably for their own use. The bark was sold separately.[10] On some estates, the
regular customers were invited to a wood feast in a local inn by the woodward. A
list of those invited to the Knebworth Wood Feast remains on record.

On some estates a whole complex of woodland was administered as a unit.

Range Woods Fell in the West Hall Wood 1846

Nº	Price		Price	£	s	d		Nº	Fells				Brought up	24	£	20	4	2
1	10	Sibley Thomas	18		15			23	10	Clark	Robert			24	1		0	0	
2	10	Do	12		10			24	10	Do	"			24	1		0	0	
3	12	Do	12		12			25	10	Woodward James				26	1		1	8	
4	13½	Hawkins	12		13	6		26	10	Seymour John				24	1				
5	10	Turner Thomas	18		15			27	10	Clark Robert				20			16	8	
6	10	Smith Edmund	24	1	0	0		28	10	Do	"			18			13	4	
7	10	Sibley Thomas	24	1	0	0		29	10	Munroe George				24	1				
8	10	Do	24	1				30	9½	Clark Robert				22			17	5	
9	10	Tomblin William	20		16	8		31	11½	Do	"			10			17	3	
10	10	South	18		15			32	10	Brown Thomas Junr				24	1				
11	16	Freluck	22	1	9	4		33	10	Clark Robert				24	1				
12	16	Clark Robert	24	1	12	0		34	10	Do	"			22			18	4	
13	10	Young Francis	24	1	0	0		35	10	Tomblin Thomas				24	1		0		
14	10	Tomblin Alex	24	1	0	0		36	10	Maquot Thomas				24	1				
15	10	Woodward James	24	1	0	0		37	10	Bentley William				20			18	4	
16	10	Clark Robert	20		16	8		38	10	Clark Robert				20			16	8	
17	10	Do	"	20		16	8		39	10	Catlin James				24	1				
18	10	Crew Prince	24	1	0	0		40	12	Clark Robert				20	1				
19	10	Crew Alex	24	1	0	0		41	11½	Do	"			20			3	4	
20	8	Clark Robert	20		13	4		42	10	Munroe C				24	1				
21	9½	Do	24		19			43	10	Clark Robert				24	1				
22	10	Do	24	1	0	0		44	10	Catlin William				24	1		1	8	
			Carried up £	20	4	2								Carried over £			41	8	10

9.3 A page from the wood-cutting book of Kimpton Hoo Estate, 1846.
This extract from the management of the Kimpton Hoo Estate illustrates the way in which estate woodland was leased out to woodmen on a rotation basis to cut coppice wood, usually hornbeam, and sell the firewood over a winter season. After mid-century the arrival of railways made coal available and the practice of coppicing for firewood died out

The Brand-Dacre Estate at Kimpton Hoo comprised a series of small woodlands, once no doubt parts of a large ancient woodland long since broken up. The woods were drawn up in sequences and each winter a wood or part of a wood, or in some cases two small woods, were designated in strict rotation and coppicing would be let out. Christmas Wood, Round Wood, Dovehouse Wood or the Lawn would each be cut in turn and the coppicing carried out by a number of locals. Some of these can be identified as villagers in either Kimpton or Whitwell. A well-wooded estate like the Hoo could afford to let out its under-wood to local people without regarding this as being any problem for the pro-duction of heavy timber. On a small estate the two could conflict. In 1803, a Mrs Chracherode owned two small and widely separated estates at Wymondley and Berkhamsted. At Wymondley, the valuer pointed out that the production of heavy timber, mostly oak, ash and elm, in Round Wood, Chanterey Wood and Bury Wood at Wymondley was high. However the extent of main timber had overshadowed coppice. In another wood, Simons Green Spring, it was the use of the wood for pasture that was adversely affecting the regrowth of coppice stools.[11] The Berkhamsted portion of the estate specialised in beech for the Chiltern furniture trade.

Beech woodland was most common on the Chilterns in the west of the region. During the agricultural depression of the last years of the nineteenth century landlords began planting beech all the way along the ridge. New plantations appeared on both the Bedfordshire and the Hertfordshire chalk hills, from Streatley through Hexton, the Weston Hills near Baldock to Therfield Heath, around Barkway and Cokenach and into Essex. Sometimes, beech plantations were added to existing woodlands. Tingley Plantation near Pirton, for example, was planted near to the ancient Tingley Wood. Sometimes new shelter belts to deflect the wind were planted out in the fields where no woodland had existed before, creating the characteristic open landscape of south Cambridgeshire and north Essex where the sweep of vast corn fields is bounded by lines of beeches.

In the north-east of the county, some woods were managed on a different regime. The tallest trees in, for example, Friars Wood at Sandon, are ashes. These are now as tall as if they were standard trees. Closer examination shows that the full-grown trees each arise from a coppice stool. At one time they must have been, in effect, coppiced to produce ash poles. The underwood here is a mixture of hazel and field-maple. Hazel was in demand for sheep hurdles and for the infill of timber-frame buildings but the purpose of the maple is not known, although it does also appear to have been coppiced. In this wood even the oak appears to have once been coppiced or, on the edge of the wood, pollarded. Possibly in this area it was the custom to coppice or pollard every tree. Further south, Rundells Wood at Kingswoodbury near Clothall is also ash and maple but is edged with alternate ash and hornbeam growing from massive ancient stools.

The coming of the popular weekly local newspapers changed the methods of marketing timber. Advertisements were put in the paper to attract purchasers to a sale of timber either already fallen or marked for felling. These timber sales were a regular feature of the advertisement columns of local newspapers and a statistical analysis of their contents would provide a comprehensive guide to timber production and its place in the agricultural economy would be more completely understood.

The practice of advertising timber sales predates the railway. The three-day sale at Broxbournebury in January 1845 had the benefit of both the Lee Navigation and the new Eastern Counties Railway. Fifteen hundred ash poles were on sale on the first day, with seventy poles of elm, fifty more of ash and three hundred poles of oak timber on the second. Range wood from the coppice was sold

TWO FREEHOLD TENEMENTS,
With Yards, Gardens, Workshop, and Barn,
SITUATE AT HARE STREET.
In the Parish of Layston, Herts.,
WILL BE SOLD BY AUCTION, BY
COCKETT & NASH,
On FRIDAY, the 27th day of February, 1846,
AT THE BELL Public-House, HARE STREET,
By order of the Proprietor.
Particulars, with conditions of Sale, may be had of Messrs. Nash and Thurnall, Solicitors; and of the Auctioneers, at Royston, Herts.

8 ACRES of valuable RANGE WOOD,
PAUL'S WALDEN, HERTS.
TO BE SOLD BY AUCTION, BY
Mr. MARKS,
UPON THE PREMISES,
On MONDAY, February 23, 1846, at 12 o'clock,
EIGHT ACRES of heavy WOOD, lying in Reynold's Wood, Dovehouse Close Wood, and Paul's Walden Plantation, in convenient lots.
A deposit of 20l. per cent. will be required of all purchasers above the amount of three pounds, and credit given for the remainder until Midsummer next, on approved security.
The Company is requested to meet the Auctioneer at the Bull Inn, Whitewell, at Twelve o'Clock, and proceed to the place of Sale.
Catalogues may be had at the usual Public Houses, and of the Auctioneer, Hitchin, Herts.

RANGE WOOD,
IN ROSEGROVE WOOD,
Near Bendish and Breachwood Green, Herts,
TO BE SOLD BY AUCTION, BY
Mr. MARKS,
UPON THE PREMISES,
On WEDNESDAY, February 25th, 1846,
At One o'Clock,
SEVEN ACRES of Capital UNDERWOOD, now lying in Rosegrove Wood, in convenient Lots, without reserve.
May be viewed by enquiry at the Red Lion, Bendish.
A deposit of 20l. per cent. will be required of all purchasers above the amount of two pounds, and six months' credit given for the remainder on approved security.
The company is requested to meet the Auctioneer at the Red Lion, Bendish, at Twelve o'Clock, and proceed thence to the place of Sale.
Catalogues may be had at the neighbouring Public-houses, and of the Auctioneer, Hitchin.

AN EXTENSIVE SALE OF VERY VALUABLE
TIMBER,
IN ALL 1,431 TREES,
On the MOOR PARK and CHORLEYWOOD ESTATES, RICKMERSWORTH, Herts; adjoining good Roads, and near to the Grand Junction Canal.
SEDGWICK & SON
Have been honoured with Instructions
TO SELL BY AUCTION,
AT THE SWAN INN, RICKMERSWORTH,
On FRIDAY, February 27, 1846, at Eleven o'Clock,
In convenient Lots,
634 OAK, 405, Elm, 194 Ash, 55 Beech, 10 Asp, 1 Birch, 7 Fir, 4 Chesnut, 6 Maple, 1 Lime, 3 Alder, and 3 Sycamore Timber Trees, chiefly of very large dimensions, and of prime growth and quality, with their lop, tops, and bark, standing in Moor Park, and on Scot's Hill, The Moor, Sandy Lodge, Aston's Lodge, Kewferry, The Moor Park, Stocker's and Maple Lodge Farms, near Rickmersworth; also on the Bury Lands, and Appletree, and Blacket's Farms, near Chorleywood. Also 108 oak, ask, elm, cherry, and other timber trees, felled and lying on the above Estates.
Each tree is marked with the number of its lot in white paint, and may be viewed by applying on the respective Premises 14 days prior to the Sale (Sundays excepted), where catalogues may be had; catalogues may also be had at the Essex Arms, Watford; the George, Chesham; at the Feathers Hotel, Waterloo Bridge, London; at Mr. Lake's, Printer, Uxbridge; at the place of Sale; of Mr. Elliot; and of Messrs. Sedgwick & Son, Land and Timber Surveyors, and Estate Agents, Rickmersworth, Herts.

ELIGIBLE INVESTMENTS,
In HERTS., BUCKS., and SURREY,
CONSISTING OF
FREEHOLD, COPYHOLD, & LEASEHOLD
ESTATES,
AT RICKMERSWORTH, CHESHAM, AND WALWORTH.

SEDGWICK & SON
Have been favoured with Instructions from the Trustees for Sale under the Will of the late Mr. WILLIAM HUNT,
TO SELL BY AUCTION,
AT THE MART, LONDON,
On FRIDAY, March 6th, at Twelve, in 5 lots,
The following very desirable Property, viz.:

9.4 The advertising of timber sales from the Herts Mercury *of 21 February 1846*

on the third. Good transport facilities were helpful but not actually essential for the woodland owner, because in the same month one hundred and sixty elm poles, with one hundred and seventy of ash and one hundred and twenty of oak, were offered for sale on the Fordham estates in Kelshall, far from either water or rail transport.

The coming of railways, and therefore cheap coal, served to tip the balance of the forest economy away from the production of coppiced firewood and at the same time facilitated the marketing of heavy hardwood timber. Beech for the furniture trade was in demand right through the century but as cheap railway bricks and imported Memel pine became available for timber buildings, the demand for oak for construction and hazel for wattle and daub fell away. Sales brochures for landed estates continued to mention the presence of heavy timber on an estate but by the 1890s, largely ignored the sales of coppiced products, although sales to local people prepared to carry out coppicing on site still continued. The emphasis was, however, on something quite different – the potential of estate woodlands for shooting. Woodland had ceased to be an essential component of a rural economy for the local community that had no other source of fuel and had become an appurtenance of a gentrified lifestyle.

References

1.   Rackham, O., *History of the Countryside*, 1986.
2.   HALS D/Ex 85.E1 Charter for Mortgrove Wood, Ardeley 1374.
3.   HALS Wood book, Wain Wood, St Ippolyts.
4.   Hinton, R., *Ancient Woodlands of Hertfordshire*, 1979.
5.   HALS Bayfordbury papers PC 369.
6.   HALS Wilshere papers 61182–6, 1817.
7.   HALS Sebright papers 18230 Beechwood Estate, Flamstead 1763–75.
8.   HALS Giles-Puller papers, Manor of Great Barwick 1778 A2832.
9.   HALS Sebright papers 18204 and ff.
10. HALS D/ERE 114 1–10.
11. HALS Wilshere papers: survey of Mrs Cracherode's manor and property 60953A + B.

CHAPTER TEN

The village community

A LTHOUGH THE MINUTIAE of property have been well documented over the centuries, the records of the people themselves have not. Prominent families apart, the written records of individuals have always been highly selective and usually scant. To a great extent, the nineteenth-century passion for social statistics began to put matters right. The British national census began in 1801 but it was not until 1841 that the first attempt was made to count the members of every household. In 1851 the census took the form of a detailed account of persons' ages, trades, civil condition and place of birth. When the data of the enumerators' returns were made public, it became possible for the first time to reconstruct an entire community from knowledge of every individual within it.

The parish as a social and political unit was very important in the nineteenth century. Country people were very conscious of which parish they belonged to. It mattered for the rates that they paid and for the relief that the poorer inhabitants were entitled to receive.

Today, the visible community of houses within immediate sight of each other tends to be regarded as the 'village community' and people are often vague about whether or not another settlement three miles away is in their parish or not. In the nineteenth century when the possession of 'settlement' was important, people knew exactly where parish boundaries were. Everyone knew which house was on which side of a parish border and who was entitled to claim settlement because he had been been born into the parish, or which woman could do the same because her husband, even if long gone, could do the same. Even the anti-social were keenly aware of the parish and its extent. Rioting farm workers might wreck a threshing machine the moment it was brought across a parish boundary but not a moment sooner. A prize fight might be held in a certain corner of a field because it was known that it was on the right side of a border where perhaps a parish constable known to be assiduous in such matters could not interfere while a colleague might turn a blind eye.

In one case, enshrined in local legend if not established in historical documentation, the people of a parish heaved an unknown corpse over a fence rather than have their own parish incur the cost of a pauper's funeral, only to discover to their chagrin than the body belonged not to some nameless vagabond but to a local man who had made good in London. He had collapsed and died whilst making his way back to the village of his birth. Embarrassment turned to fury when it turned out that he had left his fortune to endow a charity for the benefit of the parish where he had planned to end his days and now, thanks to their meanness, it was a neighbouring parish that stood to gain. This was the reputed origin of Rand's Educational Foundation of Holwell.

Totally nucleated parishes where the present village comprises the entire population of a parish with the exception of a few isolated farms are rather rare in Hertfordshire. There are some examples such as Ashwell and Pirton mostly on the clay vale north of the chalk. They were open-field parishes which were enclosed relatively late at a time when funds were not available to build new premises extensively away from the village. Even these villages may not have seemed as nucleated in the past as they are now. Pirton extends round a triangle of country roads with perceptible settlements within the overall enclosure at Great Green, Little Green and Burge End, implying the end of the 'borough'.

One fundamental distinction between parishes is that between an open parish where property belonged to a number of land owners or even individual house owners and close parishes where one landowner controlled the entire parish or a very large part of it. There is no definitive list of either type but it was usually fairly obvious which was which. A village like Pirton, for example, had a number of owners of property while nearby Hexton was almost, but not entirely, owned by the Lautour family of Hexton Manor or their successors. In other parishes, even when there was an obvious great house, there were other substantial properties within the parish that acted as centres of power and influence. Great Offley is an example.

Offley is a high-street village set at right angles to a main road. It contains the great house, Offley Place and the church. There are several farms loosely attached at either end of the high street causing the integral part of the village to extend north of the main Hitchin to Luton road. This was an area of nineteenth-century population expansion. The nineteenth-century National School is in this portion. However, the parish of Offley also includes two other manor houses

that were both centres of Domesday manors: Little Offley and Welbury were traditional manors and were both some two miles to the north of the main village.
Little Offley is a seventeenth-century farmstead while Welbury was owned in the
early part of the nineteenth century by a landowner, Radcliffe of Hitchin Priory,
with an estate on the edge of a nearby town. He sold to a newcomer, Francis
Gosling, a London banker who build the Victorian mansion of Welbury House
around 1870.

Finally, the parish of Offley included farm-labourer hamlets, without any
middle- or upper-class residents, clustered around village greens well away from
the main village of Cockernhoe and Tea Green.

In other parishes, the nominate settlement of the parish had dwindled to a
few cottages remaining in the immediate vicinity of the great house and the
parish church. Over the years, everyone else had decamped to a settlement elsewhere in the parish. This had happened in both the Waldens. At St Paul's
Walden, only a few cottages remained around the parish church while on the
other side of the manor house, St Paul's Waldenbury, most of the population
now lived along the Lilley Bottom Road in the settlement of Whitwell. Similarly
at King's Walden, the bulk of the population now lived in Breachwood Green.

Not all Hertfordshire parishes possessed any real geographical coherence or
unity at all. The township of Hitchin included a string of hamlets in Charlton,
Preston and Langley that stretch some seven miles to the south. The independent parishes of the Wymondleys and St Ippolyts lie between Hitchin and the last
of its far-flung settlements. Letchworth, a tiny but distinct parish that later gave
its name to the early twentieth-century garden city, included territory over ten
miles away to the south at Burleigh Farm, near Knebworth. Even the hamlet of
Norton Green, also on the edge of the Knebworth woods, may indicate population shift. It may well have been that, in the remote historical past, these small
settlements in the woodlands near Knebworth were settled by incomers from
the northern chalklands in search of new land.

Geographical mobility

To what extent did the nineteenth-century villager 'belong' to the parish?
Belonging to a parish community was of crucial importance for everyone until
the reform of the Poor Law and of considerable importance after it. The parish
was the only unit of government that had the obligation in law to sustain those
in want. In order to claim sustenance if one became indigent in any way, it was

necessary to establish 'settlement' within a specific parish. This could be acquired by birth, adoption, marriage or by being accepted as an apprentice. Neither employment by itself nor mere residence could confer settlement. Settlement gave a person the right to live in a parish, to be married or buried in the parish church and, until the change in the Poor Law in 1834, it conferred the right to basic sustenance from the parish vestry. An individual unable to claim settlement could be forcibly ejected from the parish if without visible means of support.

It may come as a surprise therefore to learn that a significant proportion of the Hertfordshire village community was not merely of origin outwith the parish but actually in many cases from outside the county altogether. Obviously a parish on the county boundary like Hexton or the hamlet of Cockernhoe in Offley is likely to contain a proportion of inhabitants coming from nearby Bedfordshire but, even so, we find that as many as ten to twenty per cent of the population of the parish in 1851 came from neither Bedfordshire nor Hertfordshire.

Communities varied considerably in this respect. At Graveley, well inside the county but on a main road, twenty per cent of its habitants were born outside the county, while Breachwood Green, an exclusively farming and straw plaiting community was entirely inhabited by the Hertfordshire-born, with the exception of a few from the Luton area of Bedfordshire.

One significant occupational group that were actually more likely than not to be born outside the district were the indoor servants in the great houses. Recruited by agencies or by personal recommendation, the servants might come from any part of the British Isles, and not infrequently from overseas. They were indeed the only rural occupational group where foreigners were at all common. There is no discernible pattern, except possibly a tendency for servants to come from the same general district as their masters. Thus Henry Rogers, a Lincolnshire man who lived at Stagenhoe House in 1851, employed several others from this county in his household.

Railway families

The other main group that were likely to be born outside the county were the railway families, who of course were only present in those villages that happened to have a station. As with the house servants, it was only the most junior and unskilled employees who were likely to be recruited locally. The 1851 census picked up some of the navvies who built the railway, as the GNR had just been constructed. Although the railway contractors were more in the habit than is usually realised of hiring local labour, a large number of the navvies were itinerants, including many Irish and Scots. The families of railway company employees were also likely to be born outside the county. There is a discernible tendency for railway people to come from the districts that the line passed through. This could be Yorkshire, in the case of the Great Northern, and the English Midlands in the case of the Midland Railway, but railway families could come from more or less anywhere in the country. They were as likely to come from Devon or Kent as from the obvious industrial counties. Sometimes the birth places of children in the family give a clue to where the parents had been employed. In some cases this was France, where a significant number of British railwaymen had been temporarily employed in the early days of railways. Some localities, such as the Victorian streets near Hitchin station, became virtual railway suburbs and almost duplicate townships with their own Anglican parish church, Baptist chapel and elementary school separate from the traditional market-town centre. Railway families were sometimes to be found in villages that do not seem particularly convenient for the railway.

The railwaymen, together with the policemen, the postmen, gas workers and the like, began to create a new working class even in rural areas who were more likely to send their children to school and to belong to friendly societies or even trade unions.

Policemen and school teachers in particular were invariably non-natives of the parish. Mobility at a local level was also a feature of the local community. In spite of strict settlement laws, the proportion of those born outside the parish could amount to at least thirty per cent and could be more than half the population. 'Out-parish' births as opposed to 'out-county' births were by no means confined largely to railway families and to domestic servants. Many ordinary working-class families contained a partner who was not native to the parish. It was still distinctly unusual for both partners in a working-class family to originate outside the parish but quite often it was the husband who was the incomer.

The farm workers

Farm workers were the largest single occupational group in nineteenth-century Hertfordshire. In the sample studied of north and central Hertfordshire parishes about sixty per cent of the adult male population worked on the land and about forty-five per cent were designated as agricultural labourers. The others working on the land included the farmers and their families, specialist farm workers such as shepherds, ploughmen, horsemen and cowmen, and those who worked outdoors on the estate as bailiffs, woodmen, groundsmen, gardeners and the like. In addition, grooms and gamekeepers also did some outdoor work. Finally there was the small but significant class of 'farm servants' – farm employees who lived in the farmer's household but were not members of his family.

To an extent, the live-in farm servant was a relic of the days when most farm employees lived in the farmer's own household and this was still the practice to some degree in the St Albans area. Most living-in farm servants were young men employed as horsemen or cowmen. Unfortunately we do not know what sort of families most of the live-in farm servants came from, except that they do tend to come from further afield than the ordinary day workers. This tends to strengthen the possibility that they were, in effect, apprentices and were possibly the sons of farmers who had some prospect of either inheriting farms of their own or at least of becoming bailiffs or farm managers.

There may well have been a certain amount of variation in the way different census enumerators interpreted their instructions. I think we may assume that a ploughman was in practice little different from any other farm worker but perhaps a haybinder might be an itinerant freelancer while, in some villages, a shepherd worked on his own account looking after the sheep of more than one master.

The trend in nineteenth-century Hertfordshire was for farm workers to be hired and paid by the day, living in their own households and not that of their employers. This is not to say that they were an undifferentiated mass. They were employed on an individual basis by an employer who was mindful of the skills and stamina of each employee. Farm accounts show a variety of employment practices in both day work and piece work. Sometimes piece work was organised by subcontracting to small groups or to temporary workgangs who undertook a task at an agreed rate. It was the nearest the farm worker came to collective bargaining before the onset of the union in the 1870s.

Farm workers paid by the day were usually, but not invariably, locally born. It was unusual for their households to contain anyone who did not work on the land, with the exception of women folk who were nearly always occupied as straw plaiters. Although female and child labour as such was not really a feature of Hertfordshire agriculture as it was in some parts of the country, there were some women who gave their main occupation as farm work. Although this was rare, most country women would undertake some farm work at times of heavy

10.1 Straw plaiters near Hitchin

labour demand. The same was largely true of village children. Although no branch of Hertfordshire agriculture was as dependent on child labour as was the onion picking trade of East Bedfordshire, children were expected to work on the land at times of crisis and full-time farm work could begin for a country boy at around the age of twelve. The main economic occupation of a Hertfordshire country woman or child, however, was likely to be not farm work but straw plaiting.

Straw plaiters in the community

Throughout the nineteenth century the most common female occupation in rural Hertfordshire was straw plaiting. Most of the wives and unmarried daughters of the farm workers seem to have been engaged in this trade. The origins and development of the straw plait trade have been described earlier. (see pp. 71–2)

Male straw plaiters were also to be found but in very small numbers. Many small boys were expected to do straw plait and the trade seems to have been almost universal for both sexes at an early age. Some boys, presumably those too puny for farm work, continued the trade into adolescence. In some communities such as the hamlets of Cockernhoe, Tea Green and Mangrove Green, all close to the hat-making trade of Luton, male straw plaiters were fairly common, and could amount to about twenty-five per cent of the total number of plaiters. All were locally born. The trade could have been an alternative occupation for the sickly or incapacitated males of the labouring class.

The overall numbers of female plaiters should be approached with caution. Not all enumerators bothered to record the paid employment of housewives. Practically all the working-class women of King's Walden and Kimpton were put down as straw plaiters in the census of 1851 while hardly any of the working-class wives in nearby St Paul's Walden are put down as craftswomen, although the main settlement of this parish, Whitwell, supported two male plait dealers. It is difficult to believe that the women of St Paul's Walden did not also work at straw plaiting. Hexton, in the heart of the plait district had only a few plaiters, possibly because there was demand for servants at the great house of this small close parish. Graveley, a village on a main road which contained a significant number of upper-middle-class families who also employed servants, had a simi-larly lower proportion of plaiters. In small communities of cottages such as Highbury on the edge of Hitchin or Ashbrook in St Ippolyts, where there was not any alternative occupation, almost all the female population were engaged in straw plaiting.

Like the farm workers, straw plaiters were almost always locally born. Only a few parts of the country possessed a plaiting tradition to the extent of Hertfordshire and Bedfordshire and it must have been a difficult skill for an outsider to learn. Nevertheless two Kimpton housewives. Sarah and Eliza Swain, both came from Framlingham in Suffolk while Harriet Claridge of Cockernhoe came from Bedford. More typically, all the plaiters in Cockernhoe were born either in Cockernhoe itself or one or other of the surrounding parishes.

The age range of plaiters was extremely wide. In the Offley hamlets, the female plaiters ranged from seven to seventy-five years of age while all the male plaiters were under twenty-nine. At Preston the plaiters were aged from nine to seventy-three while at Kimpton, where school attendance was more rigorously enforced, the age range was from twelve to eighty-eight. Some children went to plait schools that were little more than workshops for child labour with little more than a pretence at education.

Plait schools were to be found in most villages in north and central Hertfordshire in the years around mid-century. They were run by village women and served mainly as workshops employing child labour. Some of them claimed to provide what was probably very rudimentary education or perhaps a little reading of the scriptures. Children went to the plait school between the ages of about five, sometimes as early as three, and went on to farmwork or domestic service at about twelve. In 1819 a government factory inspector reported that the plait school was the main provider of education for the working-class child in Hertfordshire. There were at that date very few alternatives to the plait school which was Hertfordshire's variant on the nearly universal 'dame schools' to be found all over the country.

There can be be no doubt that many, probably most, working-class parents wanted their children to learn to plait and do little beyond plaiting. Even when a plait school teacher offered to provide education in a wider sense, the offer was not always taken up. On the contrary, elementary schools, when they came into being, had to put two or three hours of plaiting into the working day at paid plait work if they wanted to attract village children. Their parents needed them to earn the sixpence a day that child plaiters could bring to the family budget. The Rev J.W. Thirlwell of Ickleford reported in the *Journal of Education* in 1843[1] that too much teaching in the three Rs would cause parents to withdraw their children from the village elementary school and have them send their children

10.2 Straw plaiters in North Hertfordshire

to a plait school. John Allen, inspector of Anglican schools made the same point about Pirton School in 1845 and added that without plaiting schools simply would not attract any custom in a Hertfordshire village.

Plait schools escaped all inspection both from the school inspectors and the factory inspectors until the Workshops Regulation Act 1867. Even then it took the test case of *Beadon* v. *Parrott* to bring plait schools within the orbit of the inspector.[3] After that children under the age of eight could not be employed in a plait school and children under thirteen were limited to six and a half hours' work a day and had to attend school for ten hours a week. Even so illicit plait work went on and inspectors had great difficulty tracking down illegal plait schools still operating in Hertfordshire villages. An owner of a plait workshop only had to bundle the children out of the back door at the first hint that a government inspector was in the village.

The place of the straw plaiter in the family structure was surprisingly variable. Most were the wives or daughters of farm workers but some were heads of households. Some were widows and a number were lodgers or visitors. Straw plaiting could offer the working-class woman a measure of independence and this was sometimes resented by middle-class commentators – sometimes on moral grounds but more often because it made it more difficult to get servants and more expensive to retain them. No Hertfordshire community seems to have

Evidence of Charlotte Humphreys and Sarah Gilmore to Major Burns

Charlotte Humphreys (Rickmansworth): 'Been at the trade all my life. Children commence learning about seven years old. Parents pay 3d a week for each child and for this they are taught the trade and how to read. The mistress employs 15 to 20 at work in a room. The parents get the profits of the child's labour. A good worker will earn about 2s a week. I have four children at work and consider it as healthy as any other. Think it is healthy – la sir, more so than picking stones and working in the fields.' Signed X (Charlotte Humphreys' mark.)

Sarah Gilmore age 16 (Rickmansworth): 'Been at plaiting eight years. Did not go to school, my mother learned me. Work in a general way from 8 to 8. Can read, can't write, don't attend Sunday School. If I worked all the time could earn 4/6 a fortnight ... It ain't hard work, don't hurt my health. Work on my own account. Signed X (Sarah Gilmore's mark.)

(BPP 1843 XIV, p. 64)

incurred the reputation of Toddington in Bedfordshire, then a rumbustious open parish where it was said that men preferred to live on the legitimate earnings of the straw plaiting women who exhibited an independence quite out of keeping with Victorian attitudes and where the illegitimacy rates reflected a thoroughly deplorable attitude.

Straw plaiting could even offer a measure of opportunity for social advancement for the skilled or for the enterprising. A dexterous woman could become a bonnet sewer and earn quite reasonable money while some women became plait dealers. Most of the travelling dealers were men but some women combined plait dealing with shop keeping or running a beer house; others acted as intermediaries with the travelling men. A case in the St Albans petty sessions of 1845 where a woman was accused of stealing plait gives some insight into the working of the trade.[2] Here, a male wholesale dealer was in the habit of meeting female

Evidence of Mrs Norris, Mrs Hancock and Sarah Ann Meagher aged 7 re Plait School at Berkhamsted

Mrs Norris: 'My average number of children is 20 but I have had 30. Most of them plait, the youngest do nothing and are only sent to be kept quiet. They begin to plait about 5 years old. School is from 8.45 a.m. till 12 and from 2.00 p.m. till 4.00 p.m. The little one there is standing up to work because she is tired of sitting and will soon be going. 4.30 p.m. is quite the outside I reckon to keep any. The fever took off a good many about here a few months ago.'

Mrs Hancock: 'I keep only a night plait school viz from 5 p.m. till 8.00 p.m. Some of them go to other plait schools or to reading school in the day time before they come to me. If they have not done their work I keep them perhaps a quarter of an hour over their time. I have a big stick to frighten them but I do not like to use it'. One boy 10 years old is very quick. He does eight yards each evening. My girl can't do more than five yards of the same plait. It is worth about 7d a score. There are a number of plait schools in the town (Berkhamstead). I think about a dozen.'

Sarah Ann Meagher age 7: '... I go to Scott's plait school three times a day – 8 a.m. till 12 p.m., 1 p.m. till 4 p.m. and 5 p.m. till 8 p.m. Mother sets me five yards to do in each school, one at dinner and one at tea time. If I am a good girl and do five, she does not hit me but the mistress does sometimes'. (I met this girl with another plaiting along the street at tea time.– Inspector.)'

(Children's Employment Commission BPP 1864 XXII, p. 205)

retail dealers in the public houses of the city. The accused woman was a retail dealer who bought up the plait of her neighbours and negotiated with travelling dealers.

Crafts and tradespeople

Although Hertfordshire possessed very few factory industries and there was no vast industrial proletariat in this county, it may came as a surprise that as much as half the population in a rural village did not work as farm labourers. Among the males, the non-labouring population included the farmers themselves and their families – some of whom may have lived in a manner little different from the labourers. There were specialist workers on the land such as jobbing hedgers, ploughmen and shepherds, along with tradesmen, craftsmen, members of rural professions and an upper class of gentry and clergy of varying status and importance.

Villages in the nineteenth century were far more self-sufficient than they have since become. Most villages possessed blacksmiths, carpenters and wheelwrights. There were shoemakers and tailors among the men and dressmakers among the women. The straw plait trade could not have been carried on without a network of plait dealers and straw factors. In the villages around Luton a certain amount of finishing work such as bonnet sewing was carried on as out-work by village women. Agriculture demanded specialist work such as hurdle making while by mid-century the new occupations such as policemen, postmen and school teachers were in evidence. The new professionalism of these occupations was not as clear-cut as is sometimes thought. The new police force that started in 1841 did not immediately eliminate the part-time village constable. In 1845, a Standon man accused of killing his wife was arrested by the parish constable and handed over to the regular county police.

Village children were as likely to be taught by child minders in plait schools as by the school teachers appointed to the new schools of the British or National societies. The pastoral monopoly of the vicar was invaded by the ministers of a multiplicity of religious sects. In some villages, the village community included temporary gangs of navvies followed by more permanent residents employed on the railways as stationmasters, porters, platelayers and other personnel. Finally, even in the nineteenth century, Hertfordshire villages were beginning to attract a number of people of independent means or who had retired from a profession or a business and had settled down to village life after a career in the colonies, in trade or at sea. One such was Benjamin Hore of Whitwell in 1851, a retired sea captain who lived with his Devonport-born wife and a large and assorted household of children and adolescents of other families born in India and the Cape.

The geographical origins of the craftsmen were usually fairly local but not as local as those of the farm workers. The small close parish of Hexton with a population of 293 in 1851 contained ten craftsmen; four of them, a baker, a blacksmith, a shoemaker and a beehive maker, were locally born; a tailor, a carpenter and a blacksmith came from Clophill, Westoning and Pulloxhill respectively, while a miller and a man of unstated occupation came from Princethorp, Northamptonshire, and Market Street, Hertford respectively.

Larger villages such as Kimpton contained not only the expected bricklayers, carpenters, blacksmiths, grocers and innkeepers but also such oddities as a historical engraver from St Marylebone, Middlesex. More expectedly, Kimpton had as many as seven dealers in straw plait. Villages situated on a main road, such as Ickleford, Graveley or Little Wymondley, tended to have more people connected with travel and transport such as innkeepers, ostlers, horse-copers and the tollkeepers who worked for the turnpike trusts. Surprisingly, in view of the fact that none of these villages possessed a station, there were railway families present in 1851, although the omnibus driver residing at Whitwell is more to be expected. Possibly shortage of housing obliged some people with urban or railway employment to live in the villages.

A village of about 500 persons seems to have supported about five carpenters, perhaps three blacksmiths and one wheelwright or common carrier. Millers work out about the same in overall number but their numbers were very much determined by the geographical conditions needed for either a windmill or a water mill. Hertfordshire has a low rainfall and produced a large quantity of corn, which was not all milled locally. Mills seem to have been built wherever the conditions were right and water mills were in operation on all Hertfordshire streams of suitable size supplemented by windmills. Hitchin for example possessed at least six water mills and two windmills in the middle decades of the century.

Among the shopkeepers, grocers were the commonest with about three in a village of 500. Butchers and bakers were fewer. Meat was a luxury for the bulk of the farm-working population with the possible exception of pig meat. Bakers were commoner because home bread making was already going out of fashion and the baker had the ancillary social function of being the only tradesman with a regularly heated oven and able to keep puddings hot and to dry clothes in wet weather. There were several trades where an ancillary specialist function enabled craftsmen to survive. Carpenters, for example, often doubled as undertakers and carriers were unofficial postmen and acted as taxi drivers. Most towns possessed a specialist undertaker, an important role given the importance placed on funerals and mourning, but in the villages the local carpenter had to suffice. He became indispensable as soon as it became essential to be buried in a coffin not merely a shroud. The work of the monumental mason, on the other hand, was still a middle-class luxury.

Sometimes the distribution of tradesmen is difficult to account for. It is difficult to see why King's Walden should have supported nine shoemakers while Ickleford had three and Offley only one.

Women were very important as both shopkeepers and crafts people. The female straw plaiter was the skilled craftsperson underpinning the main domestic industry. Lace making was dominant in north Buckinghamshire and in Bedfordshire north of the Ouse but there were some lacemakers in the Hertfordshire villages. Most villages had female dressmakers, laundresses, charwomen and midwives. Many women, many of them widows, ran small businesses of all kinds, not only as shop keepers or beer sellers but also in trades usually associated with men such as builders, farmers or merchants. Widows had an important role as proprietors of cottages, since purchase of cottage property was a frequent way of providing for a widow or for old age for a married couple.

The plenitude of village craftsmen and craftswomen meant that the villagers had rarely to go outside their own community for any service or purpose at all except perhaps in dire emergency. A once-in-a-lifetime visit to a solicitor might be the only occasion a villager had to go outside his village.

The widespread provision of services within the village is of course a major difference between the nineteenth-century village and its modern counterpart. Towards the end of the nineteenth century the situation had begun to change. By and large, the railway had made little difference to the village retail community except perhaps to introduce a new figure in the coal merchant. The horse-drawn omnibuses also had made little difference as they ran mostly along the main roads and linked only the market towns and some larger villages. Towards the end of the century, horse-drawn vans had started to come out to the villages in competition with village shops but it was not until the era of the motor bus in the 1920s that the village really changed. For the first time, the villagers had a rapid and flexible, not to say congenial and friendly, means of travel to the nearest town. The village craftsman, and to an extent also the shopkeeper, was undermined at a stroke. The shops of Hitchin, St Albans, Watford or Bishops Stortford could supply anything that the villagers were likely either to want or be able to afford at far greater choice and at a more competitive price that the

10.3 Hitchin straw plait market

village tailors or shoemakers could not really hope to match. The internal combustion engine added one new tradesman to the village – the garage man – but
in the end it took away all the others.

Church and chapel in the village

Any account of the nineteenth-century village would be incomplete without a
look at the churches. The importance of religion in Victorian England is undeniable. Hertfordshire was of course an area of Christian belief and overwhelmingly
Protestant. Small Roman Catholic and Jewish congregations did exist in the
towns but their numbers were statistically insignificant, at least until the very
end of the century. Although the Roman Catholics possessed a college in St
Edmunds at Puckeridge and there is evidence of a Jewish community in Hertford
indicated by sales of a Jewish publication, the vast majority of Hertfordshire
people belonged either to the Church of England or to one or other of the Nonconformist Churches.

The comparative numbers of Anglicans and Nonconformists and the precise
nature of their relationship has long been a matter of controversy. Nationally,
there was only one attempt to ascertain the total number of practising Chris-

tians. This was the religious census of 1851. The result was inconclusive. The census was oddly organised. The Church of England was asked about the seating capacity of churches. The Nonconformists, by contrast, were asked how many had actually attended on Sunday 30 March 1851. No check was made to see if anyone had attended both morning or evening services or indeed had attended one chapel in the morning and another in the evening, thus boosting the numbers of both. Not surprisingly, both Anglicans and Dissenters claimed a numerical victory. The exercise was not repeated.

Nevertheless the 1851 religious census does represent the most important effort to discover the religious affiliations of Britain and throws much light on the state of religion in Hertfordshire.

The Church of England was of course well entrenched. Not being one of the counties where large industrial populations had outrun the resources of the Church, the towns and villages of the county had ample Church provision and were well provided with clergy. There was by definition a parish church in every parish but these were not always geographically well placed. In some parishes the main residential settlement was no longer situated around the parish church – if indeed it ever had been. This was the case in the two Waldens. The parish churches were in the nominate settlements of King's and St Paul's Walden but the bulk of the population in either case live in Whitwell and Breachwood Green. Even in the town of Stevenage, the main settlement seems to have migrated to settle along the Great North Road. There were many cases of hamlets growing up far from the parish church to which they officially belonged and in some, such as Preston near Hitchin, the church had begun to hold services in church rooms in order not to lose contact with such places. In the larger growing towns, new Victorian parish churches were built and in some towns, such as Hitchin, the new Victorian town brought into being by the railway virtually duplicated the resources of the traditional market town by the construction of large new churches, both Anglican (Holy Saviour) and Nonconformist (Walsworth Road, Baptist).

The distribution of Nonconformist churches reveals more details of Hertfordshire's religious sociology. Two groups were virtually confined to the towns. The Religious Society of Friends (Quakers) had meetings in Hitchin, Baldock, Berkhamsted, Hertford and Bishops Stortford. Their numbers included bankers, businessmen and professional men whose influence was considerable. The Unitarians, who had a comparable status in some parts of the country, had a congregation in Royston. A very different and much more recent group, the

Latter Day Saints (Mormons), had churches in St Albans and Flamstead.

The vast majority of the Nonconformist churches in the villages belonged to the theologically orthodox sects, often with a fundamentalist biblical approach to their creed.

Some chapels belonged to the tradition of 'old dissent' traceable to the Calvinist Puritanism of the seventeenth century. This might be only to be expected in a county that had been staunchly loyal to Parliament in the Civil War. Independent chapels were widespread and show no particular local pattern of distribution. The Baptists, both the General Baptists and the Particular Baptists, show a distinct concentration towards the western parishes in the Chiltern hills, long a centre of dissent going back to the Reformation itself, and even to the Lollards before that. Another Calvinist sect, Lady Huntingdon's Connexion, a Calvinist revival group founded in the eighteenth century, maintained a college at Cheshunt but this does not seem to have given it a foothold in the rest of the county. The other precursors of the Methodist revival, the Moravians, who were well supported in parts of Bedfordshire, and the Bible Christians, numerous in the west country, do not seem to have been significant in Hertfordshire.

The Methodists, newly founded in the eighteenth century as a revivalist adjunct to the established Church, were expanding in the county in 1851. They had long since ceased to be regarded as a handmaiden of the Anglican church and had become separate churches within the Nonconformist tradition. Very roughly, the divisions between the Wesleyans and the Primitive Methodists paralleled the difference between the General and Particular Baptists. The Wesleyans had established churches in all the market towns and were penetrating the villages. Some owners of close parishes who were otherwise hostile to Nonconformism were prepared to tolerate the presence of a Wesleyan chapel with their tradition of obedience to authority. The Primitive Methodists were very much a minority group and the distribution in 1851 shows an uneven coverage in the centre and east of the county. They seem to have had difficulty in penetrating the Baptist strongholds in the west. The Primitive Methodists were operating with small circuits based on market towns but evidently spreading into the villages among the farm labouring population. The growth of union branches of the National Agricultural Labourers' Union (NALU) in the 1870s was to spread in much the same way, moving out into the villages from the market towns. Judging by the vocabulary used by union activists who often addressed each other as 'loving Christian friends' there were strong affinities between rural trade unionism and sectarian Christianity. Nineteenth century trade unionism carried a strong flavour of dissenting Christianity, whose chapels had done so much to train and inspire union activists. The social role of the Nonconformist churches has been a matter of controversy for some time with debates between those who see the Nonconformists as essentially pillars of the establishment preaching conformity to the powers that be and those who saw Nonconformism as part of England's stubborn radical tradition in defiance of the establishment. In Hertfordshire both elements were present.

It is important to realise that the expression 'Nonconformist' in a religious context, refers to those who do not conform to the practices of the established Church of England. It does not imply that such people did not conform to social norms. It was quite the reverse, many Nonconformists set a high value on the strict observance of social mores and made every effort to be thought of as respectable citizens.

There is no doubt about the influence in Hertfordshire of middle-class Nonconformism. Quakers and Wesleyan Methodists were prominent among promoters of urban Boards of Health and elementary schools in the tradition of the British School Society. Village Nonconformity was, on the whole, too poor and too humble in status to play a similar role in rural areas. Virtually all schools in the villages were founded with the support of the National School Society of the Church of England, often with the containment of village Nonconformity as an explicit objective of these new schools for the poor.

The churches of the theological right wing made little impact on the county. There were no traditional centres of Roman Catholicism in the county apart from St Edmund's College at Puckeridge, and Catholic churches made their appearance only at the end of the century and then only in the towns. The Salvation Army appeared at the same time. Even in 1851, however, the minority High Church movement of the Catholic Apostolic Church maintained a tiny foothold and made some attempt to penetrate the villages. The High Church wing of the Church of England, on the other hand, made considerable headway in the new areas of Victorian urban growth with churches by celebrated High Church architects such as William Butterfield being built at Hitchin and Chipping Barnet and major restorations taking place at Anstey and Berkhamsted.

The churches and chapels of Hertfordshire's villages would not have been as well supported as they were in the nineteenth century if their doctrine had not been widely believed and their role in society generally accepted. What social effect they had is open to question. On the positive side, it is undeniable that extensive educational initiatives were taken by the religious bodies. Socially and politically, the evidence is that the churches certainly and the chapels probably inculcated widespread acceptance of the status quo. If the lack of interest in the National Charter is anything to go by, Hertfordshire's tradition of radical dissent had long gone by the nineteenth century. Whether that was a commendable outcome or an unfortunate stultification of the energies of an otherwise sturdily independent populace is very much a matter of personal outlook.

References

The census enumerators' returns for nineteenth-century Hertfordshire are recorded on microfilm in the Hertfordshire Local Studies Library at County Hall, Hertford.

The original returns of the Religious Census of 1851 are preserved at the Public Record Office.

1.   *Journal of Education*, 1843, p. 280, quoted in Hurt, J. S., *Bringing literacy to Rural England*, 1972, p. 10.
2.   HMI Rev J. Allen's report. BPP 1846 XXXII, p. 49.
3.   *Beadon* v. *Parrott* 1871. Law Report Queen's Bench VI Michaelmas 1870 to Trinity 1871. This test case was brought by the Home Office against John Parrott, a plait-school owner of Leighton Buzzard, to decide whether plait schools were schools or workshops. If the latter, then it would be decided whether the ban on children under eight applied. From that date plait schools were regarded as workshops and were inspected by factory inspectors. But, according to John Dony's *History of the Straw Hat Industry* (Luton 1942), the law was often flouted with the complicity of local parents.

CHAPTER ELEVEN

Housing in rural Hertfordshire

Building materials

BEFORE THE TWENTIETH CENTURY most of the houses in rural Hertfordshire were built of local materials and by traditional methods. They were within the vernacular rather than the industrial traditions of architecture. Hertfordshire is effectively without any good building stone. Neither flint, which is too angular and difficult to work, nor chalk, which is too soft, is really ideal for construction although both have been widely used. Field stones and chalk 'clunch' are familiar materials used for the village churches of Hertfordshire.[1]

Timber frame was by far the most popular method of constructing domestic houses in Hertfordshire until the industrial age and the mass transport of heavy materials. The vast majority of timber-frame buildings remaining today are box-frame in construction. That means that the building is constructed with a framework of oak fitted together in a rectangular pattern rather in the manner of a set of scaffolding. The alternative method, more common in the west of England, is the 'cruck frame', constructed around an oak trunk split into two and the two halves propped against one another to make the shape of a capital 'A' around which the rest of the frame was built. Very few examples of the cruck-frame tradition are now extant in the east of England. There are so few in fact that there is serious doubt as to whether the cruck tradition was ever practised to any great extent in this county. The box-frames were usually made of oak with the vertical 'studs' placed in an intermediate position between the narrow spacing of East Anglia and the wide square appearance common in the western Chilterns. The box-frames were infrequently decorated on the surface with moulded plasterwork known as 'pargeting'. In Hertfordshire this was usually fairly simple in design. There is little of the exuberance of some Essex or Suffolk pargeting.

Not surprisingly, Hertfordshire's pargeted housing is usually to be seen in the north and east of the county. Hertford, Ashwell, Braughing and Bishops Stortford have some of the best examples. An alternative surface, clapboard is also a tradition of the eastern parishes. In the Chiltern parishes of the west, a brick infill is far more common for timber-frame buildings. The roofs of vernacular buildings in all parts of the county are either thatched or covered with sometimes highly variegated flat tiles in reds, browns and blacks. The curved 'pan-tiles', common in East Anglia, did not usually occur in Hertfordshire.

Brick was also a common building material used on its own, and most of the brick used in Hertfordshire was the warm red brick of the Hertfordshire brick earths. The rather austere white bricks of the Cambridgeshire gault are sometimes seen in the extreme north around Ashwell and Hinxworth while the drab grey of the London stock bricks are to be found in the south of the county and in many towns. Most bricks were made locally and small brickworks existed in most towns and in some villages.

Although most building materials were local in origin before the coming of the railways, timber and bricks could be brought by wagon from some distance. The materials for the Home Farm on the Kimpton Hoo estate were brought in from as much as ten miles away. Chalk came from Maidencroft near Hitchin, bricks and tiles from Rabley Heath near Welwyn and foreign timber was presumably imported through London.[2]

Farm outbuildings, as opposed to farmhouses or labourers' cottages, were often built entirely of timber. This was usually imported Memel pine from the Baltic. Brick gradually took over from the timber-frame in the course of the nineteenth century for houses. The bricks continued to be of local manufacture until the development of mass production of bricks by the Hoffman kiln process in the early twentieth century when production became concentrated on the deposits of Oxford clay with massive brick works in operation near Bedford and Peterborough. New roofing materials on the other hand were quickly made available in the middle of the nineteenth century by the coming of the railway, bringing cheap and uniform slates from the mines around Blaenau Ffestiniog in North Wales.

Housing standards and sanitation

The insanitary state of working-class housing was a matter of more investigation particularly in the second half of the century. It was of course the state of housing in the towns that gave rise to most anxiety from the point of view of public

PUBLIC HEALTH ACT.
(11 & 12 Vict., Cap. 63.)

REPORT

TO THE

GENERAL BOARD OF HEALTH,

ON A

PRELIMINARY INQUIRY

INTO THE SEWERAGE, DRAINAGE, AND SUPPLY OF
WATER, AND THE SANITARY CONDITION
OF THE INHABITANTS

OF THE TOWN OF

HITCHIN.

BY WILLIAM RANGER, Esq., C.E.
SUPERINTENDING INSPECTOR.

LONDON:
PRINTED BY W. CLOWES & SONS, STAMFORD STREET,
FOR HER MAJESTY'S STATIONERY OFFICE
1849.

11.1 Title page of the Ranger Report into the health of Hitchin, 1849.
The concerns about public health engendered by the onset of cholera and by the intractable
nature of poverty that was blamed on poor health gave rise to the Public Health Act 1848.
Most Hertfordshire towns did not have so high a death rate as to make action under the Act
mandatory but any town could commission a survey if enough of its residents wanted one

health. Rural areas were regarded as more healthy, and if housing problems existed, they were seen as the responsibility of the local landlords rather than as the business of any public authority. Before the Public Health Act of 1875 with its provision for rural sanitary authorities, local government in rural areas was even less geared for positive social action than the borough corporations and local boards of health that came into being in the towns in the 1830s and 1840s.

Nevertheless the great appetite for better information about society during the Victorian age that began with the Poor Law reform of 1834 continued with the investigations into public health that were to bring about the Health of Towns Report of 1842 and eventually led to an investigation into rural housing. Houses were of course private property and there was considerable hesitation about prying into what were seen as the private arrangements between landlord and tenant unless the dangers to public health justified such intrusions.

The Public Health Act of 1848 was primarily aimed at overcrowded industrial towns and only called for mandatory action when the death rate exceeded twenty-three per thousand per year. Nevertheless towns where the death rate was less than that could, if enough local demand was forthcoming, call for an investigation into public health and, again if sufficient public demand was expressed, establish a local board of health to carry out sanitary reforms. The public health aspects of this are the concern of the next chapter. For the present it is sufficient to state that the report on Hitchin carried out by William Ranger in 1849[3] identified considerable overcrowding and lack of sanitation in the alleys and courts of Hitchin. What was not explored at this stage was the possibility that overcrowding in the small market towns was not so much due to the 'pull' of labour demand in expanding industries but rather due to the 'push' factor resulting from restricted housing in many villages. Agricultural landowners were unwilling to support a larger population than they judged necessary to work on the land. This issue was touched upon in a later investigation. Dr H.J. Hunter, a medical officer employed by the Public Health Committee of the Privy Council, carried out the earliest comprehensive survey of rural housing in England in 1863–4.[4]

The Hunter Report considered samples of parishes from each county. In Hertfordshire Dr Hunter reported on rural parishes in the north east including Royston and Therfield and examined the housing of agricultural workers who had been obliged to live in the less salubrious parts of towns such as Baldock, Hitchin, Watford and Rickmansworth. He cited Berean Court at Rickmansworth as an example of small town slum conditions for rural workers but the sordid

EXTRACT FROM THE HUNTER REPORT

Eight parishes of Hertfordshire containing 13,250 acres would not appear to be overstocked with people when in 1851 they contained 2,448; nor were people over-accommodated with 535 houses. But those who had the power thought otherwise and, although the number of people rose in 1861 to 2,562 there were 32 more houses destroyed than were built. They now exceed five to a house.

Kelshall had some very small old thatched cottages. The floors are often good and the walls often of flint or plaster. There are none of the worst class here... About half the cots had only one bedroom. In these the largest families were four adults and seven children.

Sandon has some pretty good cots, none of which were observed to be crowded. They are generally old, detached, with gardens and let for £2 or £3 a year.

On the Green was a singularly filthy and dangerous well. There is, in Hertfordshire, a carelessness about the ease of access to wells and cleanliness about the well-mouth not so commonly seen elsewhere.

Near Dane End were some poor broken down cots, formally squattings; five in one bedroom and nine in two, were the largest families.

At Pirton near Hitchin, the growth of straw plaiting has lately crowded the village, houses not having been built in proportion. The people were said to be willing to pay for cots if they might, cheapness not being with them as with the farming men the first necessity. Pirton was not visited, but a gentleman living there said that fever is prevalent there.

The houses in Pirton were in 1851, 171, in 1861, 189. The inhabitants in 1851, 897 and in 1861, 1,023, about 5.4 to a house, a high but not extraordinary number.

Expulsion from the surrounding villages has probably something to do with the growth of people in Pirton. In nine cases out of ten, when the census reports a decrease in population in a parish, eviction rather than emigration is the first cause of the decrease.

(BPP 1865 XXVI, pp. 205–7)

state of housing crammed into the courts and yards of Baldock, Hitchin and, no doubt, most small country towns was little better. The temporary boards of health that had existed at Hitchin and Ware had resulted in improved water supply and sewerage but done little for either the fabric of housing or the problems of overcrowding.

In view of the efforts that landlords were putting into cottage building, it is surprising that Hunter seems to have noticed no great improvement in rural housing. Another investigation in the later 1860s throws more light on the situation. This was carried out by George Culley who reported to the Royal Commission on Children, Young Persons and Women in Agriculture of 1867. This had been set up primarily to investigate child and female labour in agriculture, not a major issue in this county but the commissioners interpreted their brief widely and reported extensively on conditions of housing and employment.[5]

By this date there was no doubt that some landlords had effected very considerable improvements. Abel Smith's estates at Watton-at-Stone came out of the investigation with great credit. A high standard of housing was reported at Watton itself and at Stapleford and Bramfield. The Cowper estates at Panshanger had carried out improvements at Tewin and Hertingfordbury. Cottages on the Baker estate of Bayfordbury were good at Bayford itself but there were some very bad cottages at nearby Little Berkhamsted. The housing on Hertfordshire's largest estate, that of the Cecils at Hatfield, had only a modest level of improvement. The Marquess of Salisbury does not seem to have taken the same lead in building housing on his estate that the Russells of Woburn had done in Bedfordshire. The Hatfield estate, although the largest estate in Hertfordshire, was nowhere near the size of Bedfordshire's largest estate at Woburn nor did the Cecils possess the amount of urban property or the mining interests that the Russells possessed in the west country.

Some landowners such as Mr Gaussen of North Mymms and, even more, the abrasive Charles Lattimore of Wheathampstead were open in their admission that housing conditions were not all they might be in rural Hertfordshire. Central Hertfordshire – Harpenden, Redbourn, Wheathampstead and the environs of St Albans – seems to have had more than its share of poor housing. This may well explain why the survival of the custom by which farm servants lived in at the farmhouse survived longer in this district than in most parts of Hertfordshire.

In the north of the county, the entire reconstruction of Willian by Charles Hancock after his purchase of it in 1868 was noted but other villages without

EXTRACT FROM THE ROYAL COMMISSION ON CHILDREN, YOUNG PERSONS AND WOMEN IN AGRICULTURE 1867

Tewin. *Population 547, acreage 2,615, cultivation chiefly arable*

The Rev. H.C. Daubeney: Boys are employed from 8 years of age chiefly during spring and autumn. Girls are not employed. Labourers' wives are generally employed in hay time and harvest, sometimes in stone picking and weeding in spring. A free school for all is provided by endowment from Earl Cowper's family and is taken advantage of with few exceptions.

Some old cottages have been taken down and others are rebuilding. We have sufficient and are fairly supplied with water. No evil results of overcrowding have come to my knowledge. All cottages have gardens and many have allotments also.

Harpenden area. *Wages: Shepherds 15/-, carters 13/-, day labourers 12/-**

Mr J.B. Lawes: Boys from 8 to 12 years are employed at crow keeping after wheat sowing for about six weeks. No girls are employed. Women are hardly employed at all – straw plait is more profitable. There is a National School and a British School but the plait takes away the girls.

The cottages are bad and insufficient for the labourers. A good many cottages have gardens and there is about 20 acres devoted to allotments divided into 160 gardens with clubhouses in the centre where the labourers can have their beer.

(BPP 1868–9 XIII)

*shillings per week – a shilling was divided into 12 pennies.

benevolent landowners had some very bad cottages. There were worse houses in the open parishes and the very worst were to be found in the rookeries of the small towns like Baldock, Hitchin and Stevenage.

Who owned the cottages?

The whole question of rural housing is fraught with misunderstandings. It is commonly assumed that the average farm worker lived in a tied cottage owned by the farmer. As we shall see he did not. Although some farmers owned cottages that they rented to their employees most did not and very few farmers possessed enough cottages for all their workers.

Another common view is that it was the larger agricultural landowners who were the pacemakers of rural housing. This was certainly a common assumption at the time and there is a grain of truth in it. Benevolent landowners did exist and even those who only considered their own interests were alive to the need to retain some workers on the land by providing a counter-incentive to the temptations of higher wages and better prospects in the towns. Rural wages always lagged behind urban wages, and decent houses, along with village schools and allotments, were seen as a counter-attraction to stem the persistent drift to the towns, particularly in the boom years of the 1850s and 1860s.

Model villages and extensive building programmes on the part of estate owners received wide publicity. Many of the houses still stand in country districts with the insignias of the estates still to be seen. The role of the agricultural landowner has seemed to be crucial to the rural scene. Some commentators did notice this at the time but others were ready to point out that the landowners often chose to spend money on cottages at or near to their country seats, sometimes to the extent of creating a model village. They were less concerned about the condition of their tenants living further from their doorsteps. Houses owned by agricultural landowners away from the seat of the estate were more likely to be below standard. Furthermore, much rural housing was owned not by agricultural landowners at all but by a multiplicity of small cottage proprietors whose only interest was as an investment. The small proprietor was not likely to be amenable to well meaning exhortation, but nor was he (or she, as many cottage proprietors were women, often widows) able to afford to spend much money on maintaining their properties. The small proprietor nevertheless provided essential housing for people who could not otherwise afford houses of their own at a time when there was no public provision. The extent and the quality of this housing is the subject of the next chapter.

Our evidence for the state of housing in the third quarter of the century is provided by the surveys carried out by sanitary officers employed by the Rural Sanitary Authorities set up under the Public Health Act of 1875. Not all the records have survived but one surely was carried out for the Hitchin RSA by an inspector, Robert Vincent in 1877, covering the villages of North Hertfordshire.[6] The survey showed that the difference in quality between the cottages belonging to the great agricultural landowners and those belonging to lesser folk was not as great as contemporary commentators tended to assume. At Offley for example with a population of 1,346 in 1871 and 259 houses, 142 houses or fifty-four per cent belonged to agricultural landowners. Sixty-six of them were owned by Mrs Hughes of Offley Place who owned cottages in Offley itself and a number of small developments outside the village such as a group called Flint Cottages on the main road to Luton. Other major landowners owned groups of cottages in the various hamlets that made up the rest of the parish. Apart from these, the cottages of Offley included twenty-five cottages owned by the school trustees and seventy-four owned by individual small proprietors. These included a local butcher, a grocer, a horse dealer, and a dealer in straw plait who seems to have accumulated an empire of cottage property throughout the district in the course of his travels.

It has been suggested that the smaller proprietors tended to demand higher rents and might even encourage overcrowding particularly of persons engaged in domestic industry. The levels of rents in this case are not known but the evidence of overcrowding does not seem conclusive in this case. If anything it was the cottages belonging to the agricultural landowners that were more likely to be crowded. The average number in the households in Offley works out at 4.7 in houses belonging to great landowners, 4.3 in houses belonging to small proprietors and 4.4 in houses belonging to the school trustees. Most of the cottages possessed two bedrooms or more. One-room cottages still existed but had become rare.

The other features of the cottages showed no great disparity among the various types of owner. Almost all the cottages had gardens but virtually none had any form of drainage. Only John Foster, a grocer, possessed a water closet. All the others had earth closets, which were often shared. The seven Clay Pit cottages belonging to the school trustees shared two privies between them.

Water supply seems to have been the most variable amenity. This was bound to be a problem in a village situated high on a chalk ridge but much depended on the actual situation of the cottages. At Mangrove Green, for example, where the squire, Sowerby of Putteridge Bury, and a Mr Common, whose cottages were administered by a Luton auctioneer, owned the cottages there was a good system of tanks. Nearby Cockernhoe, where Mr Sowerby also owned most of the houses, there was no proper water supply for seven houses and at Tea Green, the authority had to provide a well and charge the expense to a landlord, Mr Hale of King's Waldenbury. At the time of the survey, the inhabitants of Tea Green had to get their drinking water from a pond.

One may conclude that although the agricultural landowners did invest in cottage property and may well have set a standard by the houses actually on their estates, the cottages that they owned in the villages were little different from the cottages owned by the general run of property owners. One myth that can be safely nailed is the belief that the farmers provided 'tied' cottages for their employees as a means of gaining further control over their workforce. They did not. The farmers' control over their workers was complete enough in their capacity as employers without any need to achieve power through the threat of eviction. Nor did farmers generally want to tie up working capital in house property. It is true that some farmers were also cottage proprietors but then so were some shopkeepers, innkeepers or millers. By and large, the Hertfordshire farm worker did not live in a house provided by his boss, although he may well have lived in a cottage owned by his employer's landlord – a very different proposition.

References

1. Brunskill, R.W., *An Illustrated Handbook of Vernacular Architecture*, 1971.
2. HALS Dacre papers.
3. Hitchin museum. Ranger Report on *The Health of Hitchin*, 1849.
4. BPP 1865 XXVI, p. 265.
5. BPP 1868–9 XIII, pp. 734–60. Hertfordshire returns.
6. RSA Report for Hitchin, Robert Vincent, 1877. (HALS 10/6/1).

CHAPTER TWELVE

The labourer's diet and health

Diet

DIET IS AN IMPORTANT determinant of health for any community and nineteenth-century Hertfordshire was no exception. Unfortunately although some specimen diets were given to investigating commissions from time to time there is little direct evidence gathered from the poor themselves. One attempt to collect data was made in 1864 by Dr Edward Smith, a medical officer in the service of the Public Health Committee of the Privy Council.[1]

Dr Smith examined a series of household diets from all over the British Isles, including fourteen from rural Hertfordshire. He found that, apart from years of exceptional famine or economic depression, it was the rural population of southern England that suffered the most meagre diet of any country people in the British Isles. Wages tended to be higher in the northern counties of England and in lowland Scotland. The Scottish Highlands and the hill country of Wales, together with much of Ireland, were largely inhabited by an impoverished peasantry. Their lives may have been limited in the extreme but even subsistence peasants who had some access to cultivatable land could provide themselves with oatmeal, potatoes and other vegetables, and possibly possessed chickens and pigs. The rural population of the southern counties of England, on the other hand, were overwhelmingly an employed population entirely dependent on a low cash wage, sometimes with the addition of the proceeds of domestic industry. Some labourers had gardens or allotments but many did not and landlords frowned upon pigs or chickens. All food had to be bought. The farm workers' choice of shops was extremely limited. There was often only one tiny shop selling bread, sugar, tea, rice, perhaps some household goods and simple remedies, all of them at prices in excess of those that the urban housewife was accustomed to by the sheer economics of distribution. Fresh meat, fish and even milk could be virtually unobtainable in a small rural village.

To some extent the situation improved as the century wore on. Prices of several foodstuffs fell in the course of the century. Tea, coffee, cocoa and rice were upper-class luxuries in 1800 but commonplace items of the working-class diet towards the end of the century. Some basic processed foods were available towards the end of the century as, for example, jam, marmalade and treacle became available. In the 1820s the typical Hertfordshire working man must have lived like Thomas Smart of Eversholt, Bedfordshire[2] who told a Parliamentary commission of 1824 that he lived on bread, potatoes and a little salt. He drank only water and had only applied for parish relief to pay for funerals when six of his thirteen children had died, presumably of malnutrition. This reluctance to avail himself of the public funds was considered most commendable by the commissioners, who do not seem to have considered the bare poverty of Mr Smart's life as anything out of the ordinary.

Dr Smith's evidence was collected a generation later and he concentrated on a group of parishes in the west of the county, Flamstead, Harpenden, Wheathampstead, Nomansland Common and Sandridge. All are contiguous settlements in the valley of the Ver above St Albans and by no means the poorest part of the county. The farming environment in this part of the Chiltern fringe was probably little different from Thomas Smart's Eversholt some ten miles to the north. It is not clear to what degree they were typical of the county but it may be guessed that the results were not atypical of most districts but were probably in advance of the poorest areas of the north-east around Buntingford or Royston.

The Hertfordshire families that Smith investigated had incomes of from nine to ten shillings a week from the male head of household supplemented by perhaps five shillings from family earnings at straw plait. They lived on bread, potatoes, meat, a little butter or dripping, sometimes some rice and, occasionally, a herring.

Fruit is not recorded and green vegetables, which featured in the diets of some rural counties such as Oxfordshire and Hampshire, are not mentioned. Bacon, which featured in the Cambridgeshire diet was not included here. Possibly there were better facilities for keeping a pig in the fenland communities.

The report says nothing of tea, coffee or even beer which may cause an element of doubt as we know that beer was drunk in some quantities, and without tea or even coffee it is difficult to account for the consumption of sugar.

The diet was monotonous and probably lacking in vitamins but certainly represents an advance on the meagre subsistence of Thomas Smart in 1824. Whether it was adequate for the needs of people doing heavy work or domestic chores is open to question. A twentieth-century study by Barker, Oddy and Yudkin in 1970[3] has translated Smith's findings into more modern terms and it would seem that the farm labourer's daily intake of food worked out at about 2,760 kcals per person with seventy grams of protein, fifty-four grams of fat, four hundred and eighty milligrams of calcium and fifteen milligrams of iron. An adult male carrying out heavy farm work might require between 3,000 and 4,000 kcals per day while an adolescent may require 2,700 to 3,000 kcals. A women doing light work might require about 2,700 kcals and more when she was pregnant.

The conclusion must be therefore that, although the Hertfordshire workers' diet was not the least adequate, it was superior to that found in Somerset or Wiltshire, but it was still not really adequate for needs of a working population. Furthermore, the Chiltern valleys were a relatively prosperous part of the county. Had Smith looked at the east Hertfordshire parishes along the Essex border the situation would have probably been found to be worse.

Health

The effect that the combination of poor diet and housing had on the Hertford-shire population can be assessed from mortality rates. The amount of morbidity – the rates of disease as opposed to death – are less available. The Hertfordshire death rates for the nineteenth century remained persistently below those for the better paid populations of the more insanitary towns of the period, but were higher than the death rates in the better paid and more healthy rural north of England and in the south of Scotland. The Greenhow Report on the health of the England in 1864 found that the healthiest area was the Glendale district of Northumberland while the least healthy was industrial Liverpool.[4]

The actual pattern of fatal diseases in Hertfordshire was not significantly different from that in England and Wales as a whole. Respiratory diseases were the most frequent cause of death followed by typhus, a disease always associated with poverty. Diarrhoea, measles and smallpox were also prevalent while cholera, which caused more terror than any other single disease, was still dangerous but feared out of all proportion to its actual incidence.

Public health measures under the first Public Health Act of 1848 had made some impact on those towns such as Hitchin and Ware that had decided to implement the Act, but had little effect on the country villages. In the towns there was some evidence that diseases such as dysentery, which is caused by a bacillus, or typhus, caused by a rickettsia, were losing ground to virus-generated diseases like influenza which is what one would expect to be the consequence of an improved water supply and better sanitation. The effect was noticed at the time even if the explanation was not yet understood. At the time the knowledge of bacterial causes of disease was just beginning to be appreciated while any notion of the existence of viruses was yet far into the future.

Perhaps the best guide we have to the overall health of the population is contained in the reports made by medical officers of health to the rural sanitary authorities in the 1880s and 1890s. Even so, apart from some special surveys such as one that was made of bargees on the Grand Junction Canal who turned out to be a surprisingly healthy lot, there were no general surveys. The medical officers concerned themselves with notifiable diseases and with coping with emergencies. The evidence of disease tends to be scattered among the monthly reports to meeting of sanitary committees.

Occasionally, the medical officer did publish a general report on the health of his district. One such was written by Dr George Turner, Medical Officer of Health for the RSA of Bishops Stortford.[5] This covered a series of parishes based on the Poor Law Union of Bishops Stortford and comprised parishes on both sides of the Hertfordshire and Essex border. It had been a deliberate policy of Edwin Chadwick and the early Poor Law commissioners to ignore county boundaries in a move to outflank the opposition of the county magistrates.[6]

The population of the Bishops Stortford district in 1891 had been 14,902. There had been 246 births and 229 deaths in that year which gave a birth rate of 16.5 and a death rate of 15.3 which indicates a healthy district by the standards of the time. What doctors at the time called the 'zymotic' diseases – broadly speaking the diseases that were thought to be infectious – accounted for sixteen deaths in the Bishops Stortford area. Measles had accounted for five, diarrhoea for four, diphtheria and whooping cough for two each and scarlet fever, puerperal fever and enteric fever for one each.

Cases of notifiable diseases in Bishops Storford in 1891

| Scarlet fever | 44 | Diphtheria | 34 |
| Enteric fever | 23 | Erysipelas | 16 |

The great nineteenth-century scourges of cholera and smallpox seem to have disappeared. In fact smallpox had not long gone as there had been cases in the Essex villages of Thorley, Elsenham and the Hallingburys at this time. It must also be remembered that tuberculosis, which in its various forms was the biggest single killer in rural England at this time, does not enter the list because it was not considered to be a 'zymotic' or infectious disease but rather some form of hereditary condition. Tuberculosis was thought to be a congenital condition possessed by unfortunate people afflicted with a 'weak chest'.

Medical officers were instructed to report any outbreaks of serious infectious disease and to try to trace the origins of any infections. Dr Turner cited the progress of three epidemics in 1891. It is not known how typical either the year or the district was but his report gives some idea of the degree of risk of disease that country people had to face in the nineteenth century. In that year there were three major epidemics. Scarlet fever broke out in a cottage at Much Hadham and spread to Thorley, Stansted Mountfichet, Sawbridgeworth, Furneaux Pelham and Little Hallingbury – some forty-five cases in all. An outbreak of diphtheria occurred in the remote and insanitary hamlet of Patmore Heath. It was thought have been introduced by a stray cat, which seems unlikely, but it spread to the rest of the Albury parish as well as to Thorley, Ugley, Furneaux Pelham and Much Hadham. Finally, an outbreak of typhoid occurred in Ugley with five cases in Henham and Thorley on the Essex side of the Stort. At this time Bishops Stortford itself had a purified water supply but this was not available in the villages which still relied on wells or even ponds and ditches. A harvest worker out in the hot fields might have the choice between drinking polluted ditch water and risking typhoid or suffering from heat exhaustion.

Any conclusion about the Hertfordshire worker must be something of a paradox. His diet was inadequate, his water supply dangerous and his work hard and exposed to the elements and his housing indifferent and yet by the standards of the day his health was good and his prospects of longevity were reasonable. To a great extent this was a comment on the towns rather than the country. As contemporary commentators realised, the industrial towns were killers. Poor housing, water supply and sanitation contributed to the spread of infectious diseases. We now know that tuberculosis was a product of poor diet and bad housing. There was no absolute standard of health. Rural health was only good when compared with contemporary towns. It was not satisfactory by modern standards.

This does not solve the problem of how the rural workers coped with heavy agricultural work on what was theoretically an inadequate diet. The answer is that, like his counterpart in the developing countries today, the nineteenth century worker found his work onerous and tiring but did not exert as much effort as he would if his diet had been better. Many must have plodded through a weary day. His recreations were largely passive. There was none of the hunting, shooting or active social life enjoyed by the rural upper classes and the reason may well not have been entirely due to social repression. Many farm workers must have had little energy left over for sports, poaching or even serious trouble-making. The well-known docility and patience of the nineteenth-century farm worker may well have been basically no more than extreme weariness due to undernourishment.

References

1. BPP 1864 XXVIII, p. 246: 6th Annual Report of the Medical Officer of Health of the Privy Council by Dr E. Smith.
2. BPP 1824 VI.
3. Barker I.C., Oddy, D.J. and Yudkin, J., *The Dietary Surveys of Dr Edward Smith 1862–3*, Staples, London, 1970, p. 43.
4. Greenhow Report. *Papers relating to the Sanitary State of England 1864.*
5. PRO MOH. RSA Bishops Stortford.
6. Finer, S.E., *The Life and Times of Edwin Chadwick*, 1952.

CHAPTER THIRTEEN

Trade unions and pressure groups

The National Agricultural Labourers' Union

WHATEVER THE EFFECT OF improved housing and other amenities such as village schools and allotments, there was no doubt that the farm worker was still badly paid. Wages had risen from about eight to nine shillings a week in the 1820s and 1830s to ten to eleven shillings in the 1860s but farm workers were still at the bottom of the economic heap even within a rural society, let alone by the standards of urban areas. It was true that the standards of living of the farm worker had risen to some extent because the prices of ordinary commodities had come down. The reasons for this were partly because of advances in technology and partly as a result of cheap overseas imports. In some cases, the fall in prices had been dramatic. Tea, for example, had been an upper-class luxury in the eighteenth century and had become a household commonplace by the second half of the nineteenth century. By this time, rice was now part of the working-class diet because of cheap foreign imports and sea fish was now available, at least in the towns, as a result of refrigeration on the railways. Ultimately the availability of cheap overseas imports was to prove a very mixed blessing if not a direct threat to the rural way of life when cheap grain, meat and straw plait also became available.[1]

In the 1860s, farm workers were still the basis on which rested a thriving industry. Depression in agriculture was yet to come. The reasons for this unenviable position have already been explored and amount to a combination of the farm workers' undoubted skills being too widely diffused in a farming society taken together with the lack of bargaining power of employees who had no organised union.

In 1872, a farm workers' trade union made a sudden, if belated, appearance. It is possible that the suddenness was more apparent than real and that farm workers were accustomed to degree of collective bargaining over harvest wages but a formally organised trade union had been hitherto unknown. The famous Tolpuddle case in 1830s Dorset was far more significant as a poignant legend of trade union history than a milestone in the development of labour relations on the land. It had no known counterpart in Hertfordshire and the experience was certainly not an encouragement to any farm workers to even try to emulate their West Country brethren given the brutal over-reaction of the Dorset gentry and judiciary to the six bold men of Tolpuddle.

In 1872, a Warwickshire farm worker, Joseph Arch of Barford, called a meeting at Wellesbourne Mountford and set up a union that came to be known as the National Agricultural Labourers' Union (NALU). In the course of 1872 and 1873 branches of NALU were set up in many parts of the country and in some counties separate farm workers' unions on similar lines were established to represent local men.[2]

It has never been entirely clear why the farm workers should have suddenly turned to trade unionism, but it is certainly significant that they were conscious of missing out on a long period of prosperity and were aware of the growing disparity between urban and rural wages. Some of the influences on the farm workers may also have come from outside agriculture altogether. Some farm workers had acquired a degree of administrative experience by serving as elders or deacons in Nonconformist chapels. Arch himself was a lay preacher and had connections with the Midland radicalism of Joseph Chamberlain whose career as a leader of municipal radicalism had included an element of land reform. One of the leading figures of Midland radicalism at this time was Jesse Collings who had coined the phrase, 'Three acres and a cow', as an objective of popular land reform.

By the 1870s trade unions were breaking the bounds of being exclusively trade associations or friendly societies for skilled workers who had served formal apprenticeships and the movement was looking to pastures new. Miners, railwaymen, dock workers and women workers were all becoming targets for union activity with varying degrees of success. The farm workers were seen as virgin territory by an expanding and newly confident trade union movement.

This is not to say that the new unionism was solely the product of outside influence. Opponents of trade unions tended to blame agitators from the towns for making the farm workers discontented with their lot. Employers tended to see the workforce as contented and naturally quiescent until their habitual contentment was disturbed by outside agitators. The truth may often be that the

GRAVELEY.

AGRICULTURAL LABOURERS' MEETING.

A meeting of labourers was held at Graveley on Monday evening, when Mr. T. H. Haines, the district secretary, and others, addressed the gathering on the advisability of joining the Union. The arguments used were the same as at similar meetings, but as the wages received by the labourers at Graveley are rather higher than the surrounding districts, the speakers did not receive the encouragement usually accorded them. Mr. Mr. James Wright, resident farmer, addressed the meeting, and was listened to with attention. He pointed out that, by joining the Union, the men were squandering part of the money which they pleaded they worked so hard for, whereas, by placing the same amount in a properly organized benefit society, they would be making a provision for the day of sickness and trouble. Replying to the charge that farmers were hard masters, Mr. Wright pointed out that when labourers took the contract for harvest work they were harder on each other than the masters were. Mr. Wright also pointed out that it would be impossible for farmers to arrange that the day's work should consist of 9½ hours five days in the week, and six on Saturdays. Moreover, an account must be taken of the time-lost by the men during wet weather, and then, taking the year through, the men would find that they could not possibly make up for lost time. In concluding Mr. Wright told the men he had no feeling in the matter, the men might join the Union if they liked, it would not in any way alter his feeling towards them, but he would add, it was impossible to carry out the proposals made by the agitators on the part of the Union. They say "give a man what he is worth, if he is worth 6s. give him 6s., if 16s. give him 16s." The farmers hold this opinion and would act up to it, but men who were not worth so much, would object to another man on the same farm receiving more money than they did.

Mr. Culpin addressed the meeting and it then separated.

13.1 *A meeting of the Agricultural Labourers' Union at Graveley, 1873, from the* Herts Mercury *of 31 May 1873. Note the guarded but not entirely hostile attitude of the local employer. It may also be significant that the local newspaper saw fit to report the views of an employer – not perhaps the course of action it would have taken if reporting on a powerful industrial trade union* social elite, who rarely, if ever, heard a disrespectful voice spoken to their faces, too easily mistook patient resignation in a deferential society for contentment. A workforce unaccustomed to seeking any form of redress may not know how to organise itself with any effect without some example from outside.

There is evidence that the Hertfordshire workers did try to emulate the men of Warwickshire and a locally organised strike was attempted in the Watton-at-Stone area of Hertfordshire in 1872. It was quickly suppressed when the leaders were summoned before Stevenage magistrates at the instigation of Abel Smith MP. This seems to have been independent of the national union but in February 1873 a district office of the NALU was set up in Luton. This established the Hertfordshire and South Bedfordshire District of the NALU with the object of setting up branches in the villages.[3]

In the spring of 1873 meetings were held in Hertford, Stevenage, Watton-at-Stone, Sandridge, Baldock, Graveley and Weston. The meetings were sometimes chaired by men who were not themselves farm workers. John Stallybrass, a local butcher, chaired a meeting held in Hertford on 29 March 1873. The Sandridge branch was led by a village carpenter called William Paul who sent a circular to local farmers on 22 March demanding an extra two shillings a week for the farm workers. A meeting was held on Nomansland Common to determine strike action. According to the *Hertfordshire Mercury* about eighty men of Sandridge went on strike for at least three weeks. This was, it seems well supported enough to cause consternation among the employers who called an emergency meeting at the Hertford Chamber of Agriculture on 7 June to discuss their reaction to the union.

Opinions among the farmers were divided. The well-known Charles Lattimore, outspoken defender of tenants' rights against the landlords, was adamantly opposed to a workers' union and called for unified action against it in the form of lockouts and blacklisting. As a Wheathampstead farmer his farm was near the centre of the Sandridge strike.

Other employers such as Alfred Ransom of Hitchin took a more conciliatory line with trade unions and even spoke in their defence at public meetings.[4]

In some places, attempts to organise a union were undermined by local men opposed to the union who were able to exploit all too successfully the inexperience of the farm workers. At Weston, for example, a meeting was to be addressed by T.H. Haines, the district secretary of NALU from Luton on 12 July 1873. Heckling and disruption was organised by a baker named Garrett and, to cause more diversion, free beer was provided by a farmer named Wensman with the apparent object of turning the meeting into a noisy but ineffective boozing session. This seems to have been all too successful and Haines' efforts to hold a meeting were shouted down. This experience must, however, be set against a meeting of farmers at Barton-le-Clay, just outside the county, at which a plan that members of the union should be blacklisted was abandoned when it was pointed out that all the local farm workers had already joined it. The lists of branches that were recorded as contributing to union funds in the course of 1873–4 and the occasional reports of the union's social events at that time show that many of the farm workers' meetings were soberly attended and resulted in village branches being set up. For a time at least many village branches in many parts of the county were well subscribed to by what must have been a significant number of farm workers. As any trade union organiser knows, however, what action, if any, the members were prepared to take to further the objectives of the union was quite a different matter.

The big moment of the NALU in Hertfordshire came on the 23 June 1873 when Joseph Arch himself came to the county to address the farm workers on Butts Close, Hitchin. Henry Taylor, the general secretary of the NALU, accompanied him. A Mr Culpin, chairman of the Stevenage branch, chaired the meeting. Alfred Ransom, a leading Hitchin businessman and a Quaker with liberal sympathies, also attended.[5]

In his speech, Joseph Arch called for better wages, changes in the land laws and he also demanded the vote for the working man who was still without the franchise if he lived outside a borough. Although there was some opposition from a group of farmers on the edge of the crowd, the meeting had been well attended and Arch's speech was cheered by an enthusiastic crowd. There can have been no doubt that the farm workers had found a leader at last.

It was of course one thing to cheer a charismatic leader and quite another to undertake the patient, administrative work necessary to build up a union. It was still more difficult to persuade powerless people in a strictly hierarchical and ultra-deferential society to stand up and be counted.

As it happened, the Hitchin meeting was not only the peak of the Union's influence in the county but was also the beginning of a long decline. In the following year the farmers counter-attacked with a widespread lockout. This began in Suffolk and seems to have been most effective in East Anglia. It is not very clear how far the example of the East Anglian farmers was followed in Hertfordshire but the Union seems to have gone into steep decline in much the same way in this county.

NALU had always followed a conventional trade union policy of trying to obtain better wages by negotiating with employers using the threat of strike action as a sanction. The only technique that was perhaps unique to the farm workers was a parallel policy of encouraging emigration to the colonies in an attempt to thin out the numbers of farm workers and create a shortage of skilled labour.

This policy had not been entirely without success. Farm workers' wages reached a nineteenth-century peak in the mid 1870s. Nevertheless farm wages were still a long way from catching up with industrial wages and some rural workers still hankered for an older form of redress – land reform. One of the NALU leaders, Henry Vincent, editor of the well-produced and successful farm workers' newspaper the *Labourers Union Chronicle*, left NALU in 1874 to form a rival union. This was National Farm Workers' Association whose object to obtain land for its members thus reviving the old dream of the Diggers and the Chartists. It is not known how much support this received in Hertfordshire but it was sufficient to warrant calling a meeting of both unions on Nomansland Common to try to effect reconciliation. Whether this was achieved or not is difficult to say because little more was heard of either organisation in this county.

The surprising thing is not that the union lacked staying power but that it got off the ground in the first place. Hertfordshire lacked almost any tradition of organised labour. Nor was the experience of this county in any way unique.[6]

Farm workers' unions spread widely in the early seventies in many counties and collapsed just as completely in most of them. Apart from anything else, the farm workers were unlucky in their timing. The union had come into being just in time for the great agricultural depression of the 1870s. It is difficult to believe that the influence of the union had been anything other than minimal. The only permanent impact had been to put the enfranchisement of the farm worker firmly on the political agenda but it was to be over a decade before even that was to come about.

Looked at more closely, Hertfordshire should certainly be included as a county where farm workers' unions took a hold, albeit briefly. Trade unionism flourished among rural workers, but only where certain conditions were present. Union branches were set up where farms were large, where arable farming prevailed and where farm workers lived in their own cottages, not with the farmer's family in the farmhouses.[7] All of these applied in Hertfordshire. One might add that the farm workers were most likely to be successfully organised where there was some proximity to a town with a radical tradition. The original organisers of NALU in the Midlands were in close touch with the Birmingham radicals. Even a genteel town like Leamington Spa could provide the base for a group of radicals able to provide some encouragement and practical support for rural unionists.

In Bedfordshire and Hertfordshire it was the straw-hat-making town of Luton with its close contacts with the surrounding countryside that, by the nature of its industry, provided a focus for union activity. It was in the deepest countryside far away from the influence of the towns that unionism was least successful. Few of the villages of east Hertfordshire for example managed to organise union branches and the disastrous experience at Weston showed how difficult it was for a stranger from Luton to obtain a hearing.

Very often the success of the union depended upon a sympathiser from outside the ranks of the farm workers. Nonetheless the union did get off the ground in some areas. It was, however, unlucky in its timing. Depression was about to strike. The union foundered mainly because the agricultural depression created a genuine inability on the part of many employers to pay any better wages, creating yet more disillusion in the ranks of the workers and their families. Coping with the depression, everyone involved with agriculture was in much the same position. Faced with economic ruin the farmers too made some attempt to organise in order to protect their interests. It is to that we must now turn.

The Farmers' Alliance

Farmers had infinitely more opportunity to organise themselves. They had infinitely more freedom to meet and associate with whomsoever they pleased. They had capital, they may have had little leisure but were masters of their own time, they had the vote and to an extent were listened to by men of influence in the locality. Many other people of influence in a rural area – lawyers, merchants, land agents, ultimately even the landlords themselves, were dependent on the farmers' well-being and would support their cause in their own interests.

However the farmers had lacked a pressure group of their own – although the officially neutral organisations such as county agricultural associations, chambers of agriculture and the Royal Agricultural Society of England itself sometimes took up the cudgels on behalf of the agricultural interest when the occasion arose. The Hertfordshire farmers had not been entirely unorganised in that respect. Following the lead of the national Royal Agricultural Society of England, formed in 1838, some local associations of farmers had been set up primarily to meet and discuss new developments in agricultural practice. The first of these in the county seems to have been the Tring Agricultural Society established in 1841 with Lord Brownlow as its president. The West Hertfordshire Agricultural Society at Watford followed this in 1865 under the patronage of the Earl of Essex. The Hertfordshire Chamber of Agriculture was formed in 1868 with Baron Dimsdale as its president and C.H. Lattimore as secretary. As we have seen there had been times when the farmers had formed organisations to defend their interests in times of crisis. The agricultural protection association brought into being at the time of the Corn Law crisis had been a case in point. It had of course been defeated but since the repeal of the Corn Laws in 1846 the farmers had continued to prosper. The fact was that the vast stockpile of corn that some had feared would pour into the country did not then exist. By the 1870s, with the opening up of North America, it did exist and overseas competition became a problem. The economics of the depression will be considered later but one of the effects of the depression was to bring forward a tendency among farmers to band together not only to combat the recession but also to press for the redress for some older grievances.

In July 1879 a meeting was held at Exeter Hall in London, a popular venue for gatherings with a radical tinge, with the object of forming a Farmers' Alliance to protect the interests of tenant farmers. It called for the reform of the game laws, obtaining the representation of farmers in the local administration of counties and, hopefully, getting some tenant farmers into Parliament.[8] Officially it was not party-political but, in contrast to the Tory-aligned protectionist associations at the time of the Corn Law crisis, the Farmers' Alliance was distinctly radical in tone. It owed more to the campaign organised by those opposed to the protectionists of the forties and who wanted to campaign for tenants' rights and against the game laws: Richard Cobden, John Bright and, in Hertfordshire, Charles Lattimore.

The new alliance attracted local men from the outset. The initial list of supporters included James Odams of the Grange, Bishops Stortford, who acted as treasurer; John Allen of Cole Green near Hertford; and James Long of Henlow, Bedfordshire who wrote an introductory article about the Alliance in the *Farmers' Magazine*.[9] James Howard MP of the Bedford Agricultural Machine Company became a leader of the Alliance and Henry Evershed, who had written the prize essay on the Agriculture of Hertfordshire in the *Journal of the Royal Agricultural Society of England* was on the inaugural committee.

As might be expected of a movement that had come into being as a result of a collapse of corn prices, the Alliance was strongest in the arable counties. However, there were also foci of activity in some pastoral farming areas where there was a strong Liberal tradition such as Cornwall and parts of Scotland and Wales.

On the 11 November 1879 a meeting was held in the Town Hall at Hitchin to set up a Hertfordshire branch. It was chaired by Edward King Fordham of Ashwell and addressed by James Howard MP.[10] The chairman spoke of the many burdens that had been placed on the farmer – the poor rates, the highway rates, church rates, rural sanitary authorities and, in some parishes, the school boards. James Howard told the meeting that farmers could no longer look to the landlords to act as their champions. The game laws and the struggle over tenant rights had showed that landlord and tenant interests were far from identical and that landlords could no longed be relied upon to defend the agricultural interest. He called for more tenant farmers in Parliament but was careful to distance the farmers' movement from the more militant peasant unrest led by Parnell in Ireland.

By no means all the objectives of the Farmers' Alliance received equal approval from the Hertfordshire audience. The desirability of compensation for un-exhausted improvements was well supported although there was doubt as to whether the landlords should be put under a legal obligation to compensate an out-going tenant for any residual value arising from improvements he had made to his holding. Landowners usually claimed that they did compensate tenants who had invested in their holdings and there was no need to make the payments mandatory. The claim that farmers had to bear an unfair burden of local rates was enthusiastically applauded but, apart from the malt tax, which was universally disliked in a corn-producing region, there was little agreement about what should be done. There was a whole range of local impositions such as poor, highway and school rates for which there was little practical alternative. Wider questions such as the reform of the land laws and the abolition of strict settlement, dear to the hearts of liberal lawyers critical of the landed aristocracy, met with general indifference on the part of the Hitchin audience. It was not an easy point for a lay audience to grasp.

The meeting at Hitchin does not seem to have given rise to an organised branch of the Alliance. When a Royal Commission came to Hitchin three years later to gather information about the state of agriculture, there was no reference to any organised representative opinion but plenty of individual comment.[11]

Nationally, the Farmers' Alliance achieved some of its objectives. The Ground Game Act (1880) allowed tenant farmers to shoot hares on their land.

The Agricultural Holdings Act (1883) provided some security for tenant farmers although landlords seem to have had no difficulty in evading its provisions by putting exclusion clauses in new leases when they came up for renewal. As far as its membership was concerned it seems that the Hertfordshire experience was fairly typical. It is obvious enough why the farm labourers found it difficult to organise a union – it is less clear why the farmers' attempts at organising should have proved such a damp squib. The fact was that in the intensely hierarchical society of nineteenth-century rural England any kind of political activity was suspect if the landed elite did not endorse it. Even the more respectable members of the community were expected to know their place. Attending a meeting or a dinner was acceptable, but organised action was not. Furthermore it was far from clear what effective action the farmers could take. The farm workers could, when greatly daring, go on strike. Farmers as small independent businessmen could not. The skilled lobbying and publicity methods used by the farm lobby today were not available in the nineteenth century. The farmers were at an awkward stage when the landowners were ceasing to champion their cause effectively and yet modern methods of political persuasion had not yet arrived.

At a more modest social level, the reluctance to stand up and be counted undermined the efforts of most would-be reformers. The facility of the nineteenth-century countryman to applaud an opinion at a meeting but to exhibit reluctance to get personally involved was amply illustrated in 1885. On 11 March, Jesse Collings MP, the leader of the Liberal land reformers, addressed a packed and enthusiastic audience at Biggleswade where he called for redistribution of the land, allotments for the poor and the abolition of the great estates.[12]

Very shortly afterwards, one of the few unenclosed parishes, Clothall near Baldock, was enclosed at the instigation of just such a landlord, the Marquess of Salisbury, the largest landowner in the county. Under current legislation, a portion of this land, which was largely common land, had to be set aside both for public recreation and as allotments for the poor if demand was established. This somewhat marginal provision was very far from the thoroughgoing land reform that Collings had called for but, none the less, land for the poor was there for the taking. The Assistant Land Commissioner, Henry Milman, called the statutory meeting at the Rose and Crown, Baldock on 11 February 1885 to ascertain such demand. No claimants for public land appeared. Perhaps it is unreasonable to expect Hertfordshire villagers to stand up in public in front of the Cecils but there is no reason to believe that they would not have received a fair hearing if any of them had done so.

Land reform in the sense of the redistribution of land away from the major landowners and in favour of a revived small peasantry was widely discussed and had some following in both political parties. It received more support in political meetings than it did among working farmers.

The Agricultural Union

One solution that did have some appeal to the working farmers was a revival of the old agricultural tariff. The Liberal Party with its affiliation to free trade was not interested in this approach and the Conservative Party, which had painful memories of the split caused by the Corn Law crisis of the 1840s, had no wish to repeat the experience. It was significant that the group who wished to bring back an agricultural tariff consisted mainly of those Liberals led by Joseph Chamberlain who had broken with the Liberal Party over the Irish Home Rule issue and were in process of gravitating towards the Conservatives. Among the agricultural community, a landowner, Lord Winchilsea, tried to unite the whole 'agricultural interest' – landlords, farmers and even labourers – in a single body to be known as the Agricultural Union. Winchilsea was invited to address the farmers of Hertfordshire at the County Show held at Hatfield on 29 July 1893. The location suggests that the current Conservative Prime minister, Lord Salisbury, was at least tolerant of the idea of protection. In fact Winchilsea refused to come out unequivocally in favour of a revived agricultural tariff for corn although he expressed support for an embargo on imported live animals. The issue was debated at the Hertford Farmers' Club and while there was some support for the embargo on the grounds that it might prevent cattle disease it would be ineffective without a tariff on the import of meat, which would be politically disastrous. The new union had a differentiated subscription of ten shillings and sixpence for farmers and one shilling for labourers but in either case the appeal in this county was limited.

The Land and Labour League

A very different approach, this time aimed only at the labourer, was derived from the economic theories of an American writer, Henry 'Single Tax' George whose book *Progress and Poverty* had been received with a degree of interest on both sides of the Atlantic. He called for a single land tax, which in Britain would be a means to expropriate and ultimately eliminate all landlords. In Britain, the

English Land Restoration League led by Henry Verinder promulgated the ideas of Henry George. A Mr W.H. Boon set up a local branch, the Hertfordshire Land and Labour League, at Potters Bar. The chosen method of the League was to tour the countryside in red horse-drawn vans, holding meetings on village greens. It was the dream of peasant land reform all over again.

In May 1893, the red vans of the League set out to tour Hertfordshire from Shenley and Park Street in the south to Offley, Lilley and Hexton in the north. There were thirty-one meetings in all. Sometimes the League was well received with a brass band, as on Nomansland Common, or a procession of farm workers, as at Goffs Oak. On other occasions they were hounded off village greens and threatened with prosecution and even violence. Although the political alignment of the League was not always explicit, it received support and some assistance from embryonic socialist and labour groups and was prepared to provide assistance to farm workers trying to claim allotments. In Hertfordshire their activities may have contributed to the otherwise surprising local success of the new labour representation groups in the first Rural District elections at, for example, Welwyn in 1894.[13]

It should not pass notice that Ebenezer Howard included land reform in his conception of a new town in his book *Garden Cities of Tomorrow*. His idea was duly put into effect with a landed estate included in the plan for the first garden city at Letchworth in 1903. The Letchworth Garden City farms together with the Hertfordshire County Council's own rural estate of smallholdings were to be the lasting memorials to the long held dream of land reform in this county.[14]

The one thing that all the attempts to organise rural opinion into some form of collective action had in common is that they all failed. This was just as true of those movements inclined towards the Tories as it was of those that were associated with the radicals. The protectionists at the time of the Corn Laws and the pro-tariff lobby at the end of the century fizzled out, as did those movements associated with the radical wing of the Liberals, such as the anti-game-law lobby and the campaign for tenant rights. It was certainly the experience of the labour movement, which at that date had no associated political party. Trade unions on the land arose only to disappear soon afterwards and semi-socialist campaigns such as the Henry George movement's Land and Labour League in the 1890s met with little success. As this and previous chapters have indicated, efforts to mobilise rural opinion did not fail for want of trying nor even for lack of leadership. Sometimes it was a case of an outside element trying to introduce ideas that simply failed to take root. In other instances there certainly was considerable local interest and support but the tide of events outside the county brought about ultimate failure. This was certainly the case in the two contrasting movements – the farmers' protectionist movement of the Corn Law period in the 1840s and the farm workers' trade union of the 1870s. Neither group would have relished the comparison, but both were victims of the growing urban interests of this country overriding a rural pressure group however strongly supported it might be in an essentially agricultural county.

The protectionists did not succeed in either keeping or reviving the Corn Laws and the farm workers' union was fatally damaged, not by the opposition of the employers which was often overcome, but by the economic depression that had brought an end to agricultural prosperity. In both cases the urban free trade lobby, not in Hertfordshire but in the country as a whole, had proved to be too strong.

References

1. Armstrong, W.A., *The English Farm Labourer*, 1988.
2. Horn, P., *Joseph Arch*, 1971.
3. *Hertfordshire Express*, 8 March 1873.
4. *Hertfordshire Mercury*, 8 May 1873.
5. *Hitchin Gazette*, 22 July 1873.
6. *Labourers Union Chronicle* 1872–4 *passim*.
7. Dunbabin, J.P.D., 'The Incidence and Organisation of the Agricultural Trade Unions of the 1870s' in *Agricultural History Review*, 1968.
8. Bear, W., 'The Revolt of the Counties' in *Fortnightly Review* XXVII, 1880, pp. 720–5.
9. *Farmers' Magazine*, Dec 1879.
10. *Hitchin Gazette*, 22 July 1880.
11. BPP 1881 XVII. Evidence of J.B. Lawes p. 948–95.
12. *Hitchin Gazette*, 22 July 1893.
13. *The Church Reformer*, Aug–Sept 1893.
14. Howard, E., *Garden Cities of Tomorrow*, 1902.

CHAPTER FOURTEEN

Depression in agriculture

T HE LATER DECADES of the nineteenth century saw a prolonged depression in British agriculture. A series of poor summers in the middle of the 1870s coincided with a number of developments in overseas trade that were almost invariably detrimental to the British farmer. Following the end of the American Civil War in 1865, the transcontinental railroads had encouraged new settlements across the prairies. New strains of wheat suitable to the harsh conditions of the North American interior had enabled both the USA and Canada to become exporters of grain on a vast scale. As if this was not enough, new imports were beginning to come in from Australia and Argentina. The fears of the protectionists that a vast stockpile of grain was about to be deposited on to the British market, unrealistic in the 1840s when only the Baltic had been a serious competitor, were now being abundantly realised.

On previous occasions when the price of grain had fallen, the response of the British farmer had been to turn to beef production. Not, however, on this occasion. By an unlucky chance for the British farmer, the development of chilling and freezing techniques plus the growing reliability of steamships had made cheap meat available from the new lands in the United States, Argentina, Australia and New Zealand.

Finally, even Hertfordshire's cottage industry of straw plaiting, hitherto a lifeline for the working classes in their cottages, was undermined by imports of cheap straw plait first from China and then Japan.

As an arable county used to burgeoning prosperity, Hertfordshire was particularly badly hit. The farmers suddenly found themselves to be politically isolated. Great landowners that had provided political clout for the agricultural interest at the time of the Corn Law crisis were now not quite so heavily dependent on farm rents. The larger landlords such as the Cecils of Hatfield were cushioned by urban property and sought to develop highly rented estates of house property in London together with the ground rents of hotels and offices. This may have made it possible for some of the farm landlords to assist farmers by remitting rents but also served to take the edge off their political championship of the farmers' cause. The lesser landlords in a county like Hertfordshire were often prosperous townsmen, bankers or businessmen who had bought estates with a view to hunting or shooting and were not primarily concerned with agricultural management. Land agents who put up agricultural estates for sale in the latter years of the century emphasised the sporting facilities of the estate rather than its agricultural potential. They might also mention the distinguished nature of neighbouring landowners, the general gentility of the district, possibly the salubrious health of Hertfordshire or the ease with which one could get into London from nearby village stations. They tended to avoid any mention of the financial return that a landowner could hope to get from the rents of his farming tenants. Agricultural estates were seen more as the key to a gentlemanly lifestyle than as viable business propositions.

Nor did the farmers find much to comfort them in the attitudes of the major political parties of the day. The Liberal Party was traditionally in favour of free trade. Some radical elements within it had animosity against the landlords who 'wove not neither did they spin,' in sharp contrast to the industrious urban entrepreneur that the Liberals tended to prefer. The Liberals had little sympathy for the farmer whose case was seen as special pleading. If conceded it would restrict the import of cheap food. The Conservatives, more traditionally the farmers' party, were also, at this date, the party of Empire and would not wish to injure links with the expanding colonies. In any case, they too were now dependent on the votes of urban consumers and had no intention of going against a cheap food policy.

This is not to say that there was no concern in government circles about the prolonged depression in British agriculture. Even though Britain was by now a heavily industrialised nation, most of its industry was still coal-based and confined to the now traditional industrial areas of the Midlands and north, parts of Scotland and Wales and of course London, the greatest centre of population in the South. The economic problems of rural England could not, however, simply be ignored even by the most urban-minded of governments. Hertfordshire was not alone in being a largely agricultural county. Even from the special point of view of parliamentary representation there was no question of simply ignoring the voice of rural England.

Two royal commissions were established to look into the agricultural depression: the Richmond Commission of 1879–82[1] and the Shaw-Lefevre commission of 1894–7.[2] The first was heavily representative of the great landowners with estates in the corn-growing south of England, although not actually in Hertfordshire. The Shaw-Lefevre Commission involved more industrial and administrative interests. Both commissions collected evidence from Hertfordshire, including a statement by John Bennet Lawes of Rothamsted, the developer of superphosphate, which was the first widespread artificial fertiliser.[3] He was inclined to put the depression down to a series of wet summers accompanied by low corn prices. There were also written reports from investigators such as S.L.B. Druce, secretary of the Farmers' Club, and Aubrey Spencer an agricultural writer. There were also meetings held in Hertfordshire market towns where farmers and others involved in agriculture could make their views known directly to members of the Commission.

In addition, another royal commission was appointed to investigate the condition of the working classes in both town and country, the Royal Commission on Labour 1893.[4] An investigator from this Commission, Cecil Chapman reported on conditions in the Poor Law Union of Buntingford, an arable district of East Hertfordshire very badly hit by the depression in farming. It was part of Hertfordshire where the growth of residential towns, already characteristic of much of the rest of the county, was least noticeable.

There seems to have been a certain amount of uncertainty about the amount of land that had actually fallen out of use as a result of the depression. According to the Board of Trade returns 2,876 acres of farmland remained impossible to let in Hertfordshire in 1881 after six years of depression. According to the Hertfordshire Board of Agriculture, this only represented land that the landlords had put on the market for a prospective tenant and took no account of land that the landlords had despaired of ever persuading a worthwhile tenant to accept.

A number of solutions were canvassed as ways out of the recession. There were individual agriculturalists who claimed to have found a way to produce the traditional cereal crop at very low cost and still make a profit. Gilbert and Lawes at Rothamsted investigated a system used at Lois Weedon in Northamptonshire by which alternating strips of land were planted with wheat using only organic fertilisers. They pronounced it as unsuitable for Hertfordshire. Victorian industrialists tended to suspect that farmers did not use sufficiently rigorous scientific methods and occasionally successful businessmen with ample capital would enter farming to show the traditionalist farmers how it was done. One of the

ROYAL COMMISSION ON AGRICULTURE 1880, EXTRACTS FROM MR DRUCE'S REPORT ON HERTFORDSHIRE

'I visited Bishop's Stortford and its neighbourhood on the 22nd, 23rd, 24th and again on the 30th and 31st of December 1879 and held meetings there at which 15 to 20 farmers were present. I attended meetings of the Hertfordshire Chamber of Agriculture on the 7th and 28th of February 1880 to explain the objects of the enquiry. I also attended meetings in Hitchin on the 24th February and in Watford on 16th March.

In Herts the depression has been more severely felt by farmers on the heavy clay lands rather than the lighter soils.

The depression was attributed to the following causes:

A *The bad season and in particular the last season:* The rot among the sheep had produced fearful havoc and cased great stagnation in the trade. There had been bad farming occasioned by want of security for the tenant's capital. The malt tax and the game laws.

B *That which had depreciated the prices:* Foreign competition and the importation of fat stock and meat from abroad.

C *That which had increased the costs of production:* The high rent and rail charges were felt to be very oppressive, the increase in taxation and the high cost of labour. The principal local rates which were felt to be burdensome were the education rate and the highway rate partly due to the abolition of the turnpikes. The compulsory clauses of the Education Acts had told hardly on the farmers and they were unable to get the boy labour at as early an age as was once the case. When the boys came to work, they wanted higher wages and, even then, in many instances, left the farm for London or the railways.

In reply to my question whether any farmers had recently become bankrupt, the Hertfordshire Chamber of Agriculture stated that several had become bankrupt and the number had increased of late. Remissions of rent had been general usually by the large landowners not the small ones. In Bishops Stortford, one farmer told me that he had been asked by a landowner to recommend him a bailiff to take charge of 1,000 acres that he could not let. In Hitchin I was told that one landlord had 2,000 acres that he could not let and was cultivating himself.'

(*BPP 1881 XVI, p. 367*)

best known was J. J. Mechi of Tiptree in Essex who both published his accounts and wrote a popular textbook which was well received in Hertfordshire where conditions were similar. A Hertfordshire farmer, John Prout of Sawbridgeworth, adopted some of Mechi's methods. He produced traditional cereal crops with full use of steam power and large quantities of London manures, which Sawbridgeworth, being on the direct rail and river links between the Stort valley and the East End of London, was well placed to use.

Some landowners came to the conclusion that there was something in the argument that many Hertfordshire farmers had grown complacent and were too much given to trying to emulate the life of the country gentleman. There was a tendency to advertise lettings in those parts of the country where farmers had no such aspirations and were tough, frugal operators willing to work alongside their men and grow labour-consuming crops such as potatoes. Scots, Welsh and Cornish farmers were encouraged to take up tenancies. There were not many of them – although on some estates they constituted a majority of the tenants as at Knebworth where six out of nine tenants were Scottish in origin in the 1890s.

Other commentators thought that arable farming was no longer viable in Hertfordshire at all and greater attention should be paid to dairy farming and to market gardening. Dairy farming was indeed expanding at the time and appeared to be immune from overseas competition. Public health regulations had discouraged urban cow keeping and the great retail dairies were becoming established in London and other cities. The Express Dairy dates from 1864, the Aylesbury Dairy Company from 1866 and the Dairy Reform Company was founded in 1871.[5] There would appear to have been no problem for a Hertfordshire farmer who wished to market liquid milk.

Production of milk was a different matter. There was no problem in the river valleys. Some landowners, such as the Cowpers of Panshanger, with holdings in the well-watered valley of the Mimram, were willing to build milking parlours, which they did at Tewin and at Panshanger itself, but most parts of Hertfordshire were too dry. Dairy farming prospered in the lush water meadows of Hampshire and Wiltshire but not on the dry chalks and clays of arable Hertfordshire. The county is of course close to London but fast milk trains on main lines made it possible for counties up to a hundred miles away from London to compete without difficulty.[6]

Market gardening was another option, although in this case the problem of foreign competition was not to be entirely avoided. Fruit and vegetables could be imported into London from Holland, Belgium and northern France. Denmark too was making the switch from being a marginal corn-growing nation to being an efficient producer of dairy produce and making a better success at co-operative farming than was achieved in Britain. Even Ireland, long despised for agricultural backwardness, was in the process of becoming a formidable producer of butter and cheese also making use of co-operative creameries.

Even so, it is slightly surprising that market gardening did not make a greater contribution to Hertfordshire's economic recovery than it fact it did. In some districts, market gardening did indeed make much progress using the railways to import London manure and to take advantage of rapid developments in the markets. In the lower Lea Valley of Hertfordshire around Hoddesdon, Broxbourne and Cheshunt and in the Ivel Valley of East Bedfordshire around Sandy and Biggleswade, market gardening became a very important agricultural industry. Brussels sprouts replaced pickled onions as the most important gardening crops as a response to a change in popular taste. The urban housewife was becoming more willing to buy fresh vegetables in greengrocers and town markets. Hertfordshire developed something of a speciality in watercress grown in clear chalk streams. Scares about the purity of cress gathered on the polluted ditches nearer to London served to boost the demand for Hertfordshire's product.

By the time of the second royal commission it was becoming clear that none of these expedients was going to revive farming in Hertfordshire. In 1894 a series of meetings were held in Hertfordshire to decide what further could be done. In August, meetings were held in Bishops Stortford, St Albans, Hitchin and Tring. The general conclusion was that heavy arable farms were worst affected. There were some complaints about rail charges. It was said to be cheaper to send cattle and meat from New York to London than it was from Cheshire to London and cheaper to send onions from Antwerp to London than from Arlesey or Biggleswade. It was even alleged that it was cheaper to send market garden produce from Calais to Covent Garden than it was to send the same produce from Hitchin. One Hertfordshire landowner, Baron Dimsdale, suggested setting up a special tribunal to fix railway rates more fairly.

It was in the parishes either high and dry on the Chilterns or on the rolling clay of east Hertfordshire watered only by puny streams like the Rib, Beane or Quin that dairy farming was least rewarding. Potato growing was a possibility and a few farmers, often incomers, first from Devon and Cornwall then increasingly from Scotland were prepared to do this. They were willing to hire and fire casual labour from the villages as necessary. The report by Cecil Chapman on

ROYAL COMMISSION ON AGRICULTURE 1895
EXTRACT FROM AUBREY SPENCER'S REPORT ON
THE AGRICULTURE OF HERTFORDSHIRE AND THE
VALE OF AYLESBURY

'In the Vale of Aylesbury there are no farmers who have migrated from other parts* of the county and the same applies to the more western parts of Hertfordshire around Tring.

In other parts of Hertfordshire there has been a remarkable immigration of Scotch and Cornish farmers. This is particularly the case in the country around St Albans, Hatfield, Hertford and Hitchin and appears to have taken place since 1880. On some estates, as for instance, the Knebworth estate, the Scotchmen (*sic*) outnumber the Englishmen, the numbers being nine and against five or six. On another neighbouring estate, out of 30 tenants there are three Scotchmen and seven Cornishmen.

There is no doubt a certain amount of prejudice felt and expressed by the native Hertfordshire farmer against the Scotchmen. It is said that they work the farms out and were constantly changing from one farm to another. This opinion is not held by some of those most competent to judge. I visited several farms occupied by Scotchmen and was favourably impressed. If it had not been for their immigration, more land would have dropped out of cultivation.

The system adopted by Scotchmen includes, if the farm is near the railway, the growth of potatoes. Stock is little kept unless the farmer is going in for milk selling, which some do.'

(BPP 1895 XVI, IUC Edition, vol. 31, pp. 447–71)

*Farmers from Scotland, Wales and Cornwall settle in Hertfordshire.

EXTRACT FROM ROYAL COMMISSION ON LABOUR

A description of Buckland Village and its Co-operative Store

A parish, purely agricultural, consisting of 97 houses with a population of 486. There are no resident gentry. The houses may be classified as one rectory, five farmhouses, four public houses, three shops and 84 labourers' cottages. Twenty years ago when times were good and wages higher, labourers' families presented a poverty-stricken appearance. Shabbiness and rags abounded even on Sundays. Nearly everybody was in debt to the shops and the shops hopelessly in debt to the wholesale dealers. The chief result of the credit system was to make customers and shopkeepers reckless. Recklessness led to habits of intemperance. The money, which ought to have gone to the shops, went to the public houses, where there was no credit.

The working capital of the co-operative store is only £60 and all the farmers are shareholders. There are 50 shareholders. The plan is to buy all the groceries at Harrods stores on a month's credit and the drapery from a wholesale shop in Colchester. We have given up selling port. This co-operative store was started on the advice of Mr Albert Pell in 1876, 17 years ago, by Mr Burnaby. Shabbiness and rags are rarely seen now and drink and debt are the exception not the rule. Buckland Co-operative Store pays 5% to shareholders and divides profits.

(BPP 1893–4 XXXV, p. 160, Appendix IV)

the parishes around Buntingford[7] describes a countryside sunk in economic stagnation. Only the few Cornish and Scots who were prepared to work alongside their men claimed to be able to make the land pay and that was probably only by comparison with the even more harsh conditions that they had left behind them in their native lands. The prospect of being able to farm a fertile soil in a moderate climate was reward enough for these families long used to hardship. Chapman instances a Mr Gubbins of Wyddial as an example of a farmer from the West Country working in a better environment than he had been used to.

In Buckland, a local vicar, the Rev. Burnaby, (see p. 179) had organised a local co-operative among the villagers to buy goods wholesale from a store in Colchester, and even from Harrods of Knightsbridge, and selling on to members of the co-operative drawn from villagers in the surrounding district. The commissioners found that members of the co-operative were well provided with clothes and boots and claimed to have a higher standard of living during the depression than they had managed to enjoy in the days when farming was still prosperous.

The fact that it was possible to make meagre wages go a little bit further and as far as the farmers were concerned to scrape along hoping that landlords might remit the rents if little or no profits were being made, enabled agriculture to survive but not to flourish. Estates in widely scattered parts of the county remitted rents from farming tenants. On the Barclay estates at Brent Pelham[8] only between a quarter and a third of the normal rents were collected in 1895. The farms on the Gorhambury estate[9] paid only token rents, in some cases from as early as 1871.

Whether this is an argument in favour of agricultural landlords who were merely giving back what they had taken was a matter of intense political debate between the traditionalists and the land reformers whose division by no means reflected the normal lines of political debate. However pernicious the landlord system was thought to be in some circles, there was no sustained challenge to the position of landlords in England as there was in contemporary Ireland. Virtually all of Hertfordshire's landed proprietors remained firmly in place throughout our period unless they chose to sell out. Members of the lower orders who could not live with the system might move away to London, to America or even, after 1903, to Letchworth Garden City; but they did not break out into open rebellion.

References

1.   Richmond Commission BPP 1881 XVI.
2.   Shaw-Lefevre Commission BPP 1895 XVI.
3.   ibid. Evidence of J.B. Lawes pp. 948–59.

4. RC on Labour. BPP 1893 XXXV, p. 209.
5. Atkin, P.J., 'The Retail Milk Trade in London 1790–1914' in *EcHR*, Nov 1980, pp. 522–37.
6. Coppock, J.T., 'Agricultural Change in the Nineteenth Century' in Perry, P.J., *British Agriculture 1875–1914*, 1970.
7. RC on Labour. BPP 1893–4 XXXV Rep by Cecil M. Chapman on the Poor Law Union of Buntingford, pp. 299–316.
8. HALS Barclay papers. D/E Bc AA.
9. HALS Gorhambury papers. 1 A 90.

CHAPTER FIFTEEN

Conclusion

THE STORY OF HERTFORDSHIRE agriculture in the nineteenth century reveals a society that was enterprising but conservative. It was quick to take advantage of economic opportunity but only if change did not mean any radical transformation of the social order. Such changes as enclosure or the reform of the Poor Laws may have brought hardship to families at the lower end of the social hierarchy to a degree that is still debated but did not threaten the precedence of the hierarchy itself. The Corn Law crisis certainly did create anxiety among the tenant farmers, who were the middle tier of the social structure, but the landowning classes rode out the storm. The gentry first put themselves at the head of the farmers' defensive movement, although in Hertfordshire at least, it was actually run by the farmers themselves. The landowners later changed to persuading the farmers to accept the changes to free trade once it had become apparent that the bogey of overseas competition was not a real threat. It was to become so later in the century.

When overseas competition did in fact become a serious threat, the well-entrenched economic and social leadership of the countryside did not cope particularly well. Even so it was not overturned, partly because the solution canvassed by the radicals did not offer a very convincing alternative to the traditional state of affairs. If the traditional landlord, tenant and worker could not cope with change there was little evidence that either the tenants on their own, still less a new class of peasant proprietors would have coped any better. Even if the traditional landowners and their tenants could somehow have been supplanted it is not clear from where the new, enterprising, skilled peasant farmers would be recruited. The occasional incoming Scotsman or ambitious local farm worker who had managed to scrape together enough capital to take on a small-holding could be accommodated in the system as it stood.

How far Hertfordshire was unique among the farming counties of the south and east of England is difficult to say. Malting was obviously important in this county, which possibly meant that farmers took less interest in the Corn Laws than in some other counties, but they took a correspondingly lively interest in the Malt Tax. At the labourer level it was certainly true that straw plaiting enabled many farm-working families to survive. It goes a long way towards explaining why Hertfordshire and Bedfordshire had less social unrest than almost any comparable area. Hertfordshire was far less disturbed than Norfolk, Essex or Kent. The new Poor Law of 1834 was accepted with hardly a murmur. Chartism hardly made an appearance unless we count the accident that Feargus O'Connor's first land scheme was set up in 1848 on Hertfordshire soil at Herons-gate near Rickmansworth. It is most probable that the choice of a Hertfordshire location for new settlements thereafter owed more to the fact that it was a fertile county within easy reach of London than anything to do with local radicalism.

The relative tranquillity of Hertfordshire during the agrarian troubles early in the nineteenth century was, and sometimes still is, explained solely by the proximity of London. There may be something in the idea that London was close enough to be a social safety valve and a haven for the discontented, but this should be approached with caution. Other counties in the south-east, such as Kent and Sussex, were not particularly peaceful during the period of the Swing Riots. It is more likely that the existence of an alternative source of family income served to take the edge off rural poverty. It was certainly not the case that the presence of London had served to boost wages. With the possibly exception of the lower Lea Valley, Hertfordshire farm wages made for an East Anglian level of poverty.

The opportunity to develop a viable cottage industry in straw plaiting derives from a readily available supply of straw that farmers were prepared to allow labouring families to use. The reason why conditions should be different in Hertfordshire lies in nineteenth-century leasehold practice. Most landowners were adamant that tenant farmers were not allowed to sell the straw off the farm because they feared a long-term decline in the fertility of the soil. What seems to have happened in corn-growing Hertfordshire was that, being so close to the capital, large quantities of manure were readily available from the thousands of horses stabled in Victorian London. As a result, landowners who normally stipulated in leases, and most strictly enforced, a proviso that farmers must on no account diminish the fertility of the land by selling the straw were less concerned about this in Hertfordshire with its abundant alternative source of manure. The farmers therefore were at liberty to sell the straw to the working families in the villages with the acquiescence of the landowners. This provided the raw material for an important domestic industry that enabled many working families to survive. For those labourers that were still discontented, London was not far away.

The three-tier hierarchy of landlord, tenant and labourer proved to be as adaptable in Hertfordshire as in any other county. It was flexible enough to absorb the incomers from Scotland and the West Country as tenants, and occasionally provided the opportunity for local men to set up as smallholders, market gardeners or cultivators of watercress without radically disturbing the established social order.

Even when agriculture was not doing particularly well, Hertfordshire was still near enough to London to attract wealthy men prepared to set up as country landowners. These included wealthy Londoners such as the banker, Francis Gosling at Welbury and a Bond Street shopkeeper, Charles Hancock at Willian. There were also aristocrats with more assured social position who wanted to have a country estate within easy reach of London when their main estates were more remote – perhaps in Scotland or Ireland as in the case of the Earls of Strathmore and Caledon.

In spite of the collapse of agriculture the rural social structure of nineteenth-century England survived more or less intact into the twentieth century. It was the labourers that fled from the land, whether into local towns, London or even the colonies. The social elite remained largely in place. Attempts at land reform – even the attempt to link the reform of land ownership with the establishment of new urban communities as in the successful Garden City projects, first at Letchworth and then at Welwyn, did not disturb the stability of the traditional social pyramid.

Farming itself not only survived in the county but prospered. This, however, was the result of events in the twentieth century that would have been impossible to foresee before 1900. With Britain's vast empire and secure command of the seas, it would have seemed inconceivable that, by the second decade of the twentieth century, Britain would be a beleaguered nation once more dependent on its own food producers. Nor would free trade Britain have believed that agriculture, almost alone of industries, would receive permanent support from the taxpayer.

The trend towards mechanisation, which itself was a combination of the tradition of agricultural improvement with the mechanical revolution of the Industrial Revolution, continued after the turn of the century when the central problem of farm mechanisation was solved. This was the vexed question of how to design a source of primary motive power that could traverse the fields. The steam engine, centrepiece of the first Industrial Revolution, never proved entirely satisfactory as a versatile provider of motive power for agriculture. It was the internal combustion engine that really extended mechanical methodology to agriculture just as it did to other important fields of activity such as aviation, automobility and warfare, thus defining the principal distinction between the nineteenth and twentieth centuries. Appropriately the farm tractor first made its appearance in the arable south-east of England with the Ivel tractor of Dan Albone of Biggleswade, a few miles north of the Hertfordshire border.

The late nineteenth century was the last time when, in a rapidly industrialising world, the land was still being cultivated by renewable solar energy of the previous season's grass and corn transmitted by the muscle power of horse and labourer. Already the imported nitrates used as fertiliser were using up a finite mineral resource. In a few decades, agriculture like industry would become dependent on fossil resources both for fuel and for the manufacture and transport of fertiliser. In one sense, Hertfordshire agriculture with its early dependence on manure delivered from London in coal-powered steam trains was a forerunner of agriculture in the rest of country in being the product of mechanical power and fossil fuel.

In spite of, indeed partly because of, this remarkable technical progress, the flight from the land has continued unabated. This has not meant flight from the village. Villages which were once colonies of farm workers together with the crafts people and traders are now residential communities of people who for purely personal reasons choose to reside in a relatively small community living along with local residents who are survivors of the farm-labouring population. These people differing in background, accent and economic status may well feel like a relict population, deprived of social facilities and exiles in their own villages. The coming of the country bus in the twenties and thirties brought about the demise of the village tailors, dressmakers and shoemakers. The combination of the private car and the supermarket did the same for the village shop. Shops and schools can only survive in the larger commuter villages. Village churches too frequently flourish only in well-heeled commuter villages. Nonconformist chapels in the villages have a tendency to turn into rather strange cottage conversions.

There has probably been no other county, with the possible exception of extinct Middlesex, where the transformation of a prosperous nineteenth-century farming county into a residential and industrial county has been as complete as in Hertfordshire. In some ways the contrast has been more apparent that real. Hertfordshire began to acquire a commuter population almost as soon as the railways arrived. The process gathered speed with the creation of totally new towns in the Garden City movement at Letchworth and Welwyn and the suburban development around all the towns.

The coming of the post-1945 New Towns such as Stevenage and Hemel Hempstead needs no further mention here but the existence of considerable London overspill housing affecting several Hertfordshire towns including Hatfield, Hitchin, Letchworth and Royston should also be mentioned.

Some urbanising developments fell foul of the middle of the twentieth-century planning controls. 'Plot-land' developments by which townspeople bought plots of land in the country and built do-it-yourself habitations, made their appearance in the county in the 1920s at widely separated locations near Braughing in the east and Studham in the west but further developments were nipped in the bud by planning regulations. Speculative building by commercial builders was another matter. Much of the south of the county was affected by much the same type of semi-detached development that covered much of Middlesex to the south. A more distinctive Hertfordshire variant was for a builder to buy a farm or even a large wood and carve out plots for substantial residences standing in their own grounds. Thus, much of Hertfordshire near to railway stations became centres of leafy housing development that are neither town nor village. Examples can be found at Tewin Wood, Harmer Green and many other settlements in the Chilterns and in the environs of Welwyn and Hatfield. On this occasion the proximity of London did affect a change in legislation as most of the centre and south of the county became included in the metropolitan Green Belt with its strong presumption against further building. Needless to say, restrictions on further development were as much supported by recent incomers determined to pull up the ladder behind them as they were by fearful local inhabitants of the original communities.

The Green Belt, which was soon to be extended not merely to contain the spread of London but to be a means of preserving the separate identity of Hertfordshire's own towns, has helped to preserve the distinction between town and country. Of all the concepts of the town and country planner, it has been the sanctity of the Green Belt that has achieved almost iconic status in the public mind.

The long depression in agriculture, which lasted up to the Second World War, opened the way for progressive suburbanisation of much of the county as landowners were prepared to sell to speculative builders. The process continued even after the recovery of agriculture following the Second World War. The price of land for which planning permission was forthcoming almost always exceeded agricultural values.

Outside the zoned building land, agriculture since the Second World War has, on the whole, thrived – although with a degree of state support unthinkable in the nineteenth century.

The farm and land-owning lobby is still a force to be reckoned with but, if farming has survived, village life in the traditional sense has not. Villages are no longer communities of farm workers. They have become colonies of often prosperous residents dependent on urban employment and on urban facilities but who, for reasons of their own choice, prefer to live in a smaller community and have the independent transport to enable them to do so. They live alongside a relict population of the elderly and the 'left behind' descended from Hertfordshire's farm labouring population. Hertfordshire is no longer primarily an agricultural society.

If Hertfordshire's farming society had adapted better to the new conditions in the way that farmers did in much of the rest of Europe, the history of Hertfordshire and much else of rural England would have been a different story. Elsewhere in Europe: in Denmark, Holland, Belgium, even in once backward Ireland, farmers started from a much lower baseline of prosperity but, by forming co-operatives, raised their standards of both production and marketing, specialised in dairy produce, horticulture or market gardening and remained a viable farming society. In Hertfordshire they did not. They either weathered the depression as best they could and waited for conditions to improve or they sold out to developers.

The influx of newcomers to the villages had little to do with Hertfordshire's agricultural past. The Green Belt policy may have protected the appearance of the countryside by preventing urban sprawl but it did little to conserve the essential fabric of rural life. Modern residential villages are essentially detached portions of suburbia. Their present inhabitants have little or no organic connection with the land.

Attempts to change society through land reform – from the Chartists at Heronsgate to the 'Lloyd George' land settlement of the early twentieth century – all failed. It was the agricultural self-sufficiency aspect of Ebenezer Howard's Garden Cities that proved to be the least viable part of his grand plan. The Letchworth Garden City farms are managed much like any other farming property with perhaps a more generous provision of public access although, at the time of writing, countryside access reforms are set to change the situation in the rest of the country. There is no suggestion that the modern inhabitants of Letchworth or Welwyn Garden City are required to work on the land that belongs to their two communities, still less to live on its produce.

This reluctance to change was, of course, not untypical of British society as a whole. It was not only farming that refused to countenance any change that threatened to upset the social order. Change only occurred when it was imposed from without and when it was financially profitable to those who were already in possession of the land. In this sense the experience of the Garden Cities and the new towns merely repeated the experience of the enclosures a century before. The social problems of the poor – the paupers in one age and the socially deprived in another – had to wait until a solution appeared that was acceptable to those already in possession before any change could occur. British farming adapted to modern progress by accepting new technologies and by shedding labour. Arguably, the absence of a strong trade union that was able to perpetuate differentials and demarcations made rapid mechanical progress far more straightforward in farming than has been the case in some industries.

Agriculture itself has had its up and downs in Hertfordshire as it has in most counties. Specially protected since the Second World War it has arguably been well favoured by the state as a special case in an era when so many other industries have gone to the wall. Even the argument that the farmers provided half the nation's food during the war itself wears a little thin when one considers that the British merchant navy that supplied the other half at far greater risk has been allowed to dwindle to a remnant. In a globalised economy it is becoming less clear why farming should be treated as a special case. It is not even clear why British farming should be at a disadvantage in the first place. To the general public it is far from obvious why farming in a county with fertile soils, a good climate and with the largest market for food just down the road in London should be permanently unprofitable.

The farm worker has faced a contracting market for his skills but it is less clear why the farmer himself should face an insuperable obstacle. It has to be admitted of course that in a small crowded country where living space is at a premium land is likely to be very expensive. That is a tendency that we can see beginning in the nineteenth century when commuting by rail first became possible. Efficient transport made all of Hertfordshire into a potential residential area with the consequent pressure on land prices. The existence of planning controls has retained some rural land as farmland but it is fair to say that all land in the county has some 'hope value' that makes the purchase of farmland more expensive. This does not impose a disadvantage on farmers who already own their land. Indeed it provides a profitable escape route should farming cease to be viable. As long as land is kept available there seems no reason why Hertfordshire farming should be unprofitable.

Agriculture as a source of employment might be another matter. The trend towards less and less employment on the land has continued. Even in mainly agricultural counties, farm work now accounts for only a small proportion of the work force. In Hertfordshire it has become a very minor source of employment. What new forms of employment will prove to be on hand as industry itself moves away from the era of mass employment only time will tell. As heavy industry steadily reduces its capacity to employ workers on a vast scale, the industrial employee will be treading a path that the farm worker has trodden before. The experience of the farm worker is unlikely to be unique in the story of social change. In that sense, the history of Hertfordshire's agricultural society is firmly in the mainstream of English history.

Index